UNCOVERING THE SECRETS OF MAGAZINE WRITING

A Step-by-Step Guide to Writing Creative Nonfiction for Print and Internet Publication

NANCY M. HAMILTON

PEARSON

Boston ■ New York ■ San Francisco
Mexico City ■ Montreal ■ Toronto ■ London ■ Madrid ■ Munich ■ Paris
Hong Kong ■ Singapore ■ Tokyo ■ Cape Town ■ Sydney

Series Editor: *Molly Taylor*
Editorial Assistant: *Michael Kish*
Senior Marketing Manager: *Mandee Eckersley*
Editorial-Production Service: *Omegatype Typography, Inc.*
Manufacturing Buyer: *JoAnne Sweeney*
Composition and Prepress Buyer: *Linda Cox*
Cover Administrator: *Kristina Mose-Libon*
Electronic Composition: *Omegatype Typography, Inc.*

For related titles and support materials, visit our online catalog at www.ablongman.com.

Between the time Website information is gathered and then published, it is not unusual for some sites to have closed. Also, the transcription of URLs can result in typographical errors. The publisher would appreciate notification where these errors occur so that they may be corrected in subsequent editions.

Many of the designations used by manufacturers and sellers to distinguish their products are claimed as trademarks. Where those designations appear in this book, and Allyn and Bacon was aware of a trademark claim, the designations have been printed in initial or all caps.

Library of Congress Cataloging-in-Publication Data

Hamilton, Nancy M.
    Uncovering the secrets of magazine writing : a step-by-step guide to writing creative nonfiction for print and Internet publication / Nancy M. Hamilton.
        p.   cm.
    Includes index.
    ISBN 0-205-37631-2
    1. Journalism—Authorship.   I. Title.

PN4775.H236   2005
808'.06607—dc22

2004057263

Printed in the United States of America

10 9 8 7 6 5 4 3 2 1   09 08 07 06 05 04

Credits appear on page 240, which constitutes an extension of this copyright page.

To my editorial staffers at **The Palette** *who worked so well as a team;*
To Hugh Cunningham, who in teaching me to write let me find my own voice,
and to young Gracie and Ryan who will soon find theirs;
to Tom O'Toole, Jr., who inherited and honed the gift, and to
my father Ken, an inspired writer, and my mother Sophie, an accomplished pianist;
to Max Gunther, whose early book on magazine writing taught me so much,
and to Deborah Upshaw, Jimmy Stewart, Marilyn Johnson, Michelle Slatalla and
others for adding their
professional viewpoint to this book;
to Barbara Strauss Reed and Mary S. Nichols for their support and encouragement,
and to my former students
at the University of Florida, Bowling Green State University,
The University of Toledo, The Pennsylvania State University
and Humboldt State University;
to my doctor, Jill Gerard, for making the completion of this book possible;
and to Marcie Dail, for exposing me to possibilities beyond my limited vision.

CONTENTS

CHAPTER EIGHT
Branching Out 114

CHAPTER NINE
Step by Step 129

PREFACE

The 16 chapters of *Uncovering the Secrets of Magazine Writing* are designed to be user-friendly. Checklists and end-of-chapter assignments actually help you build your article step by step. You'll learn enough about today's magazine market and the magazine business to be able to brainstorm an idea and road test it, research it, find a suitable matching magazine, query the article, structure it, edit and revise it, format it, know which rates and rights are operable and turn it into a saleable piece.

Chapters are amplified with case histories, comments and anecdotes from writers and editors as well as from the author. Published articles and excerpts from them illustrate a variety of techniques such as transitions, dialogue and voice. Chapter 16 on editing and revision refers you to a helpful page of copyediting symbols and an example of their use.

Highlighting a few chapters are some novel, and I hope helpful, illustrations and exercises. For example, Chapter 2 on writing to readership contains a relationship grid and instructions for building a real or hypothetical family tree. In a later chapter, the grid will be used to match story ideas to magazine readership. From it, you'll be guided to select three magazines appropriate to your article. The family tree assignment illustrates the critical differences in magazine readers and the importance of paying close attention to readership profiles when selecting a magazine to query. The same chapter includes instructions on how to analyze magazine content to see if your article is a fit.

As you read this book and complete the exercises, try to approach your writing with the artist's eye, the journalist's ear and the craftsman's passionate devotion to the requirements of structure, style, detail and readership. You'll be in good company, your work appearing with the best. Said Norman Podhoretz, former editor of *Commentary:* "The discursive writing of people who think of themselves primarily as novelists turns out to be more interesting, more lively, more penetrating, more intelligent, more forceful, more original—in short, *better*—than their fiction. . . ." ("The Article as Art" in *The Reporter As Artist*, pp. 125–36, Communication Arts Books. Ronald Weber ed. New York: Hastings House. 1974.)

Before you get started with Chapter 1, make sure to orient yourself by reading the Introduction. In it you'll find encouragement, a discussion of the tools you'll need for writing and researching and some pitfalls you'll learn to avoid.

ACKNOWLEDGMENTS

Special thanks to W. Riley Nutt for his help in creating the Family Tree and Relationship Grid. My thanks to key editors at *National Fisherman* for their persistence in locating my archived article. I would also like to thank the following reviewers for their comments on the manuscript: Peter Gross, University of Oklahoma; Joe Mirando, Southeastern Louisiana University; Douglas Perret Starr, Texas A & M University; and Michael Streissguth, Le Moyne College.

ABOUT THE AUTHOR

Nancy M. Hamilton has been a freelance writer, magazine editor and photographer for several decades, selling to magazines and books worldwide. A graduate of the University of Florida with a master's degree in journalism and a specialization in crosscultural communication, she began her journalism career as a reporter and feature writer for the *Daytona Beach News-Journal.* In later years, she became an editor at *Audubon* magazine in New York City and took courses in creative writing at the New School in lower Manhattan. Her editorial career includes stints as a book editor and as contributing editor for such magazines as *Photographic Business and Product News* and *Today's Viewpoint.* At one time the managing editor and advertising manager of an arts-and-heritage magazine in northern California, she also has developed and edited several newsletters in the computer software and healthcare fields. In her secondary field of applied anthropology, she is believed to be the first working journalist in the nation to use the terms *ethnojournalism* and *ethno-photojournalism* for her work as writer-photographer in Europe and North America.

An accredited member of the Public Relations Society of America, she has been a communications consultant to Fortune 50 and Fortune 100 clients as well as to not-for-profit organizations. As a university faculty member in magazines and public relations, she was named Outstanding Faculty Member in Communications by Women In Communications, Inc. She is listed in several *Who's Who* books.

IF YOU WANT
TO BE A WRITER. . . .

Uncovering the Secrets of Magazine Writing is basically a conversational how-to—a journalist's bread-and-butter approach from a market-reality perspective. In it you'll find published examples from current magazines, editors' and writers' comments and step-by-step instructions. The book is written to be enjoyed, written to be employed by college students and others who have one goal in common—to sell and sell again to the mass and specialized magazine markets both in print and online.

My experience has taught me what sells, what doesn't and why. As a managing editor, writer/reporter, marketing and public relations director, photographer and university professor, I have spent many years developing a working relationship with the printed word. A self-disciplined exposure to the craft has taught me how to write lean, how to pare down words to the essential of an idea and how to edit and revise with a sometimes ruthless pen my own work and that of others.

Ideas are only as good as your ability, as the writer, to discover a story and shape, structure and style it into something that leaves the magazine reader with more than he or she had before. It is your unique way of revealing an old, or universal, truth. It is the "you" filtered through the editor's seasoned take on what his or her readers want to know.

Personally, I like stories that make me soar, that take me beyond myself and within myself—in short, stories that inspire me to be more, seemingly, than I am. Most articles don't do this. And most writers, frankly, don't conceive this as part of their mission. You might. The 20th century produced writers and book authors who were technically proficient: They could find the words, structure the thoughts, develop an organizational framework and deliver a message. Only a handful wrote *in spirit*. With the exception of a few New Journalists of the 50s and 60s, a few book authors, and a few writers who showcased in the more intellectual and thought-provoking magazines such as *Harper's*, *Atlantic Monthly*, *Esquire* and *The New Yorker*, most writers' styles and perspectives were imitative. Only a handful of them produced those wonderful passages that continue to breathe *in-spiration* and insight into a reader's life and activities.

Unfortunately, inspiration can't be taught and can't be learned. Still, it may be triggered momentarily by an incident, an individual, a situation, a work of art—and for a moment, you're allowed to see within. Mine is a case in point. In the 1970s, I wrote "on spec" (on speculation) the article "A Spiritual Guide to Nature Photography" for *Modern Maturity*, a magazine to which I contributed both articles and photographs over the years. Initially, I'd added photography to my writer's skillpack as a way to increase my income. To my surprise, I discovered that photography not only complemented my writing but defined it. In choosing camera angles, situations, lighting, composition and color or shades of gray, I was developing a new way of looking at people and things. This is particularly true when I photograph items in nature— landscapes, birds and animals, flowers, trees, rushing streams, sunlight refracted by a raindrop on a leaf. The concentration, camera angle and new perspective so absorb me that at times I feel at one with the process of growth. I cannot explain the feeling, or my literary results. As I wrote "A Spiritual Guide," the words seemed to roll off my pen. The article was purchased *without query*—without even a phone call—and paid for in record time. However, I do believe that true inspiration is divinely influenced—a gift that invokes the lasting feeling or emotion of a Pieta.

It is essential that you discipline yourself to sit with the published works of others. Don't confine yourself just to magazines; include novels, nonfiction books and poetry. Make a list of your favorites. My life favorites, for example, are writers such as Peter Mathiessen, Amy Tan, Maxine Hong Kingston, Annie Dillard, Louisa May Alcott, Joan Didion, JoAn Criddle, James Michener, poet Mark Van Dorn, Alice Walker, James Agee and the American Winston Churchill. I like certain magazines—I like the way their feature material flows; among my favorites are *Florida International* and *Fortune*.

Now examine your own choices. Reread the articles, the poems; read excerpts from the books. Listen to the music and cadence of the words and phrases. Roll them off your mental tongue. Do they fit the content? Does the material speak to you? What feeling does it invoke? What draws you to this writer or to that material? Why do you continue to come back to it? Can you identify easily with what's going on in the story? Can you find yourself in it? Is the material relevant and an easy read? Does the writer offer a new perspective on an existing situation? Note that different writers approach the same material in different ways. One writes a well-researched survey article about Alzheimer's disease; another writes a first-person narrative about being a caregiver for her Alzheimer's-afflicted mother. Examining published material exposes you to the distinctive flavors of different writing styles, slants and storylines. It also exposes you to rhythm and pacing, story organization and transitions, variety in word and sentence length, ways to begin and end articles, voice and point of view, figures of speech, and use of such literary techniques as dialogue, narrative and flashbacks that nonfiction writers borrow from the fiction vocabulary to make a story come alive.

In time, you'll develop your own style—a style sufficiently distinctive to be recognizable even without your byline or author's credit. Style development, however, is a process of maturing in the profession; it can't be pushed. It's said that poet Robert Frost developed his lean, sparse, waste-no-words style only after hard work and laborious red-penciling. My own style was ponderous and heavy in the early years: I had a romance with arcane and multisyllabic words (*antipodes* for exact opposites). The results were comprehensible to no one but me, and I had to teach myself to write simply.

The ability to write simple but effective articles—we refer to them as *stories* in the trade but I prefer *creative nonfiction*—comes only through editorial self-discipline. We write because we *must* write, we must have a voice. But none of us writes perfectly on the first go-around. Most of us write numerous drafts. In the process we're editing our thoughts, paring down words and sentences and throwing out a favorite line or expression because it isn't a fit. We'll probably need to correct grammar and punctuation, move paragraphs around to alter story organization and convert a declarative sentence to a question or a limp, state-of-being verb such as *is* to its more graphic component. Simultaneously we're writing and rewriting the opening paragraph—known as a *lead* or sometimes *lede* in the profession—and adding material from our notes while deleting others.

Writing is a highly personal craft. The muse to write or rewrite can strike at inconvenient times—at 2 a.m. when you're groggy with sleep, during lunchtime, even during a break at work. You grab a pad and start writing or rush to your computer and start typing before the muse flits away. You produce an article on spec or you're a magazine staffer driving an assignment on deadline. In both cases, you answer to an editor. Ultimately, one fact is indisputable: From short, crisp briefs to first-person narratives and lengthy, multisource stories for Internet or print publication, creating nonfiction is a step-by-step *process*. And what makes a magazine article publishable or saleable is as much perspiration as it might be inspiration.

Is writing fun? Yes. Can it be frustrating? Sure. Can anyone learn to do it? I think so. My most successful student was a C-average type—not particularly literary, not particularly fired up. But he had an interest in home aquariums, read the right magazines in that field, targeted what he wrote to the right readership—and sold the perfect how-to piece the first time out. So can you. Whether or not you have the creative spark, hold fast to this belief: Over time, through trial and error, through the mounting disappointment of rejection slips, your persistence will pay off.

Let's get started. First, make an educated guess of your writing weaknesses. If you generally falter in the areas of grammar, punctuation and sentence construction, I suggest your purchase the handy, spiral-bound *When Words Collide* by Lauren Kessler and Duncan McDonald or Strunk and White's classic *The Elements of Style* (see Additional Resources section). The latter is available in an online edition at Bartleby.com. One of these should nest beside your keyboard and be consulted regularly.

You will need a computer, of course—monitor, CPU, printer and peripherals as well as Internet access by external or internal modem. Either a Macintosh or a PC is acceptable. The printer should be inkjet (sometimes called deskjet) or laser—one capable of producing sharp, high-quality images. Your computer should be loaded with a fairly current version of Microsoft Word (included in Microsoft Office Suite) or MacWrite (a component of AppleWorks), software programs that are standard in the industry. Publishers may ask that you mail them both disk and hard copy (a printout) although the industry trend is toward accepting e-mail attachments.

You also need the following reference books: a current, full-size dictionary (for example, the *American Heritage Dictionary of the English Language* or *Webster's New World Dictionary*), a thesaurus, a fairly current *Associated Press Stylebook and Libel Manual* and a current *Writer's Market* (see Additional Resources). Although your software will include spelling and grammar checkers and sometimes a thesaurus, for absolute accuracy *in context*, I counsel you to rely on a printed dictionary, grammar guide and thesaurus rather than a software version. Remember: *You* can think, machines and microchips cannot. Note that dictionaries are also available on CD-ROM. Both the AP stylebook and *Writer's Market* are bibles of the profession; the stylebook provides editorial consistency for writers, editors and readers; *Writer's Market* is a thick, paperback compendium of about 8,000 book and magazine publishers, their editorial requirements, payment and other details. Although many publications use their own style sheet or a guide such as *The New York Times Manual of Style and Usage,* the AP stylebook is a safe bet for the newcomer because it's used more often; *do* purchase it. Consider also purchasing *Writer's Market:* Libraries often don't own current versions. Since magazine start-ups depart from the publishing landscape as frequently as editors change jobs, it makes good sense to use the latest edition of *Writer's Market.*

You also will need access to a good library and its Lexis-Nexis database system. The *New York Times* Article Archive and the *Wall Street Journal* index will help you research issues of consequence; to keep informed, put the parent publications of both on your daily or weekly must-read list, and add others. A list of periodicals' indexes can be found in Chapter 4 on fact finding and research.

HELPFUL EXERCISE

What do you like to read? Your choice of reading material often indicates something of your own writing style and the topics you'll choose to write about. Make a list of your favorite writers; match each to a few published examples of their work or excerpts from each. Since you'll probably refer to this material in the future, indicate pertinent publishing data: article or book title, author, title of the periodical or book, publisher and copyright date, page number(s) if appropriate and date of publication. Accompany the examples with a paragraph or two explaining what appeals to you about each writer.

CHAPTER ONE

MAGAZINES UNDER THE MICROSCOPE

The impressive number of magazines published in the United States and Canada—17,321 consumer and trade titles alone in 2002, according to the *National Directory of Magazines 2003*—reflects an average of 350 bold start-ups yearly. Alert to changing demographics and buying habits, the aging of baby boomers and the buying power of Gen Xers and Gen Yers, publishers and ambitious wanna-be's have scrambled to find and fill niche markets with start-ups, spin-offs, or ancillaries (*Martha Stewart Kids,* National Geographic's *Healthy Traveler*).

Heading the list of new consumer start-ups in 2002 were the city and regionals with 32 new titles. Slick and sophisticated with attention-getting graphics, these magazines promise taste-whetting editorial content that is often provocative. Some of them carry investigative stories that outshine those in big-city dailies. You'll find the tightly targeted city magazines waging a niche-and-turf tug of war against each other, each title battling for the lion's share of local advertising dollars. Typical among them in 2001 were newcomers *San Francisco Gourmet* and *San Francisco Socialite.* By segmenting the market into neighborhood niches, the pair aggressively carved into a terrain long held by established *San Francisco* magazine. The fact is, however, that the city and regionals are financially healthier than national magazines and provide a growth area for freelance writers. The Publishers Information Bureau reported that in the dwindling market economy of 2001, for example, city and regional titles lost only 0.3 percent of their ad dollars; at the same time, advertising in national magazines was down 11.7 percent. To write for these magazines, you'll need an intimate knowledge of the geographic area and a strong familiarity with the interests and concerns of readers living there.

MAGAZINES GET YOUNGER, TOO

Over the years, magazines have tooled and often retooled their look and content—known as *format* and *formula,* in trade terms—to cater to those niche markets and to the advertisers that reach them.

An aging *McCall's*, for example, reconstituted itself as the slick, younger-appealing *Rosie*, which has since ceased publication. *Ladies Home Journal* has trashed its trademark in-depth articles that hallmarked most of the 20th century in favor of crisp, informative, short "takes" that appeal to a busy readership with a shorter attention span. *Natural Health*, a slick, graphically pleasing magazine, provides a "News & Notes" section that helps make it one of the top-paying freelance venues in the nation ($75 for shorts, up to $2,000 for longer pieces). *O, The Oprah Magazine*, reflects the I/me era of a self-absorbed, media-jaded audience looking for solutions to loneliness, abuse and unhappiness. *In Style* takes its cue from *Entertainment Tonight*. *Young Senior*, catering to baby boomers' affluence and preretirement, debuted online in 2002.

Also debuting that year were more than 60 magazines notable for their infrequency. Among them were *Catalina*, a quarterly bilingual title for Hispanic women; *Adam*, a bimonthly men's magazine; *Cruiser Quarterly*, aimed at PT Cruiser owners; the bimonthly *Elite Traveler; eDesign* magazine and its Internet companion *ePregnancy*—both monthlies; *Go*, a quarterly for business travelers; Primedia's bimonthly *Simple Scrapbooks* targeted at the home hobbyist; *YM Jump*, a monthly that merged two magazines for teenage girls; and a revived *Life*, scheduled for eight issues in 2002.

Pop culture magazines such as *Raygun, Bikini* and *HuH* have been added to the niche market. Slick, hip, with haphazard editorial that defies being corralled, these magazines in content and design reflect a young adult culture that refuses to be mainstreamed. The biggest surprise to industry analysts, however, is the growing success of another niche market: men's lifestyles. The genre owes its origin to *Maxim*, the British lifestyle magazine for men founded in 1997.

ACCEPT THE CHALLENGE

Magazines today present the writer with both opportunities and challenges. Filled with informative short takes or "info-briefs" but short on the longer, in-depth stories that characterized previous years, 21st century publications offer their readers eye appeal, fewer pages and an efflorescence of information on more subjects than ever before. This means more topics for the writer to explore and cover—yet a greater need to make editorial content immediately relevant to an on-the-go readership that is increasingly segmented.

Titles do share readership, of course—young male readers of the style-and-fashion magazine *Details*, for example, may also read *Fortune, Newsweek* and *Wired* or even a trade magazine like *The American Salesman*. But you'll find that advertisers segment their markets by psychographics and demographics—in particular by age, gender and ethnic affiliation and breakdowns within each of these categories, as well as by lifestyles and buying habits. Note the differing readerships for *Rolling Stone* and *Vibe*, for *Budget Living* and *Cabin*

Life, and for the preretirement *Young Seniors* (for ages 50 and up) and, until recently, the more traditional *Modern Maturity* published by the American Association of Retired Persons (AARP). Until March 2003, AARP also published the preretirement title *My Generation* for roughly the same age group. On that date, AARP merged *Modern Maturity* with *My Generation* into *AARP The Magazine* and began publishing in three editions—one for ages 50 to 59, the second for ages 60 to 69 and the third for ages 70 and up. Now compare AARP's earlier and current magazines with *Reader's Digest's New Choices for the Best Years,* targeted to ages 55 to 65. Such market segmentation produces not only tightly targeted editorial products carrying articles and ads that speak to the needs and interests of those readers, but regional editions as well, usually with some changes in editorial content (for the Hispanic and Asian markets, for example).

Far ahead of its time, *Reader's Digest* is a case in point. With a combined total circulation in 2001 of more than 12.5 million, *Reader's Digest* for years has published 48 regional editions in 19 languages.

SOME MAKE IT, SOME DON'T

In the economics of magazine publishing, subscription and single-copy sales generally are marginal to profits. Fueled by ad revenue but drained by downturn economies, higher paper and printing costs, postal rate increases, media competition and weak advertiser spending, most consumer magazines operate on an average 46.5:53.5 ad/ed (advertising to editorial) ratio. The loss of even one advertiser in a downturn economy may mean a reduction in editorial pages. This constitutes a major loss of revenue for the publisher whose ad rates are tied to circulation (usually expressed as cost per thousand readers or CPM). A magazine that can't deliver to advertisers on its number of readers—or to readers on its promises—may not recover from its economic downslide.

The publishing landscape is littered with magazine casualties. Industry figures show it takes an average of more than four years to break even; the majority of magazine launches don't make it past the first year. Even the veterans are in trouble. *Mademoiselle* and *Working Woman,* for example, shut down business in 2001. A relative newcomer, its editorial focus vague and readership doubtful, editor Tina Brown's highly touted *Talk* folded in January 2002 after only a three-year run. Disappointing an affluent, up-and-coming black readership, Vanguarde Media announced bankruptcy in 2003, forcing closure of *Honey, Savoy* and *Heart & Soul.*

Web-based titles are particularly vulnerable to failure: Web advertising simply can't sustain them, and other than counting the number of hits or page views on a web site, there is no way to audit actual readership. According to a 2002 issue of the *CyberAtlas Newsletter,* an Insight Express survey reveals that most Americans prefer their magazine content bound and on paper rather than the equivalent online. The Internet offered 200 online magazines in 1996; the number escalated to a reported 2,000 in 2001 but has since dropped dramatically to 40 in 2002. While 85 percent of consumer magazines maintain some type of publishing presence on the Web, only Microsoft's *Slate,* an online magazine of news, opinion and political commentary, and *Salon,* a magazine offering daily news and commentary that was voted Best Online Magazine of 2001 by Yahoo Internet Life, remain significant players in the online publishing community. They do so by offering advertisers innovative ways to reach the target consumer on the Web.

HOW TO PLAY THE GAME

To become a player in the writing game, it's essential that you understand the difference in readership and editorial mission among the various categories of magazines. *Consumer magazines* can be either *general interest*—everyone is a potential reader (*Time, People, TV Guide, Reader's Digest*), or *special interest*—sometimes called *common interest* and a much larger category. The special interests are calved into categories such as women's, automotive, men's, health, fashion/beauty/grooming, computers, business and finance, home service/home and metro/regional/state. Among these are *Discover, Argosy, TWA Ambassador, Vermont Life, Orlando, Family Circle, Go, Essence, Boy's Life, Yoga Journal, Christianity Today, House Beautiful, Metropolitan Life, Sport Fishing, Backpacker, Men's Health* and alternative magazines such as *Mother Earth* and *Mother Jones.* Each title must satisfy a cadre of faithful readers to be successful, and all of these carry advertising targeted to that readership.

    Association magazines also target consumers but only those who are members of, say, the American Association of Retired Persons (AARP), The National Geographic Society, the American Automobile Association (AAA, publishers of different regional editions for membership), the National Audubon Society (and Audubon Societies in various states). Readers, who receive the publication as part of their membership fee, are those who have a vested interest in the success of an association that represents them. News stories and feature articles address those interests. Most association magazines carry both in-house and at-large advertising.

VERTICALS AND HORIZONTALS

Business magazines, not to be confused with corporate magazines, comprise a vast field of more than 4,000 titles. Known variously as trade magazines and specialized consumer magazines, business magazines fall into two categories: vertical, top-down publications, carrying news of specific industries, businesses or professions (glass manufacturing, commercial fishing, nursing or real estate, for example) to decision makers who work in them; and horizontal titles, reaching readers in specialized fields or occupations that cut across industries (accounting, purchasing) who have a built-in need to know.

Take the field of wines. *Wine Spectator,* for example, is a special-interest consumer title sold on newsstands and by subscription. *Vineyard & Winery Management* and *Wine Business Monthly,* on the other hand, are two titles targeted to people *in the industry* concerned with viticulture, wine making and wine marketing. Driving this industry are the people who work in a variety of professions and trades such as truck drivers and accountants. A truck driver or trucking executive would likely read *Overdrive;* the accountant, *Accounting Today.* All of these people—the reader of *Argosy* and *Essence,* the reader of *Wine Spectator* and *Wine Business Monthly*—may also read *PC Week.* Or *Time.* Or *Fortune.* Or *Business Week.* (Don't confuse trade titles with national and regional business magazines that are *not* industry or trade specific. Magazines such as *Fortune, Entrepreneur, Inc., Money* and *Florida Trend* fall into this category.)

Like some consumer magazines, business publications may sell thousands of ad pages per year—that's more than 2 million ad pages yearly, according to *Folio* magazine—and serve a special readership. Although the largest percentage has controlled rather than paid circulation, the yearly revenue of all is derived primarily from ad sales. (The controlled-circulation magazine is distributed free to qualified readers—to those who work in that field.)

The business-magazine field is so diversified and specialized that according to Standard Rate and Date Service, there are 65 such publications in health and nursing, 100 in the electronic engineering field and 58 in insurance. These numbers will vary as more niche specialty titles are launched. Outpacing all others, the fastest-growing business-magazine segments are medicine and computer/automation. Numerous magazines are published just for those segments alone; most make excellent venues for the freelance writer.

ALL PROFESSIONS COVERED

Health care or hair care, there is hardly a trade or profession that magazines don't cover. You should become knowledgeable, even expert, in a few of those areas. Remember that one body of information can provide you with several articles, each of them reworked to the specific interests and needs of a particular target audience. To write regularly for the publications that serve this segment is to earn a satisfying and steady freelance income.

Here are two cases in point: As I became a professional photographer, I also became intimate with the electronics and equipment of the trade and the needs and problems of the profession. I took this knowledge to a selection of business and consumer magazines whose readers were professionals in photography or just experienced photo-hobbyists. I began to write regularly for both categories of publications. In time, one of the business magazines tapped me to be an editorial consultant and writer-at-large, known in the trade as a *contributing editor*. Later, I also became a contributing editor for another title.

Now consider the case of California freelance writer Deborah Upshaw. For more than 15 years, she has been contributing articles on woods and woodworking, as well as on gardening and foods, to at least 36 different consumer and trade magazines. Here's what she has to say:

I had no formal training in writing. One day, I read a library book called *Magazine Writing Today* by Jerome P. Kelly. It inspired me to write for magazines and maybe earn a little money while still being a stay-at-home mother with two little children. I decided I had good English skills—I always earned A's in high school and college—and knew that I was never at a loss for words. So I got out a manual typewriter and began my journey into the world of freelance writing.

My first published piece was a fiction story written for children. It sold to a religious, Sunday school-type publication. I earned $35 for it. My next sale was a nonfiction piece—a profile of my husband that told about his wood sculptures. I earned $90 for that one. Later, as I began getting feature and cover stories in *Woodwork* magazine, I was making as much as $1,200 for an article.

I began writing for woodworking magazines right from the start. It was easy to develop a writing specialty about woodworking because it was a personal love of mine. I lived in Humboldt County in northern California, where there are lots of redwoods and other trees. This made it conducive to meeting woodworkers, most of a very high caliber. Slowly, I became a woods expert just by watching them create beautiful objects and furniture of wood and writing about the subject. In time, I became closely associated with the Humboldt Woodworking Society and the Woodworkers Guild. From that point, I was asked to judge woodworking exhibits. This allowed me to draw from an extensive source of professionals who would tell me "their story" and become the subject of a personality profile. I always do my own photography when it's necessary to illustrate the article.

In time, I became a contributing editor for *Woodwork* magazine. Even though they say, "write about something you know," I haven't limited myself to one category of material or to one magazine. Like woodworking, gardening and foods are also personal interests. I once had a call from an editor at *Veggie Life* who wanted something on citrus growing in the backyard garden. It wasn't something I would ever have suggested, but I ended up writing a nice, full-length article on the subject and having it published as a feature story. The editor did that a couple of other times, and I always said, "Yes, I can do that"—and somehow kept my promise. I've used *Writer's Market* like a bible. With it, I've gotten writing jobs for other national publications [such] as *Sunset* magazine and *Family Circle,* for *Miniature Collector* and *Horse Illustrated*—even for a couple of teacher's magazines. I usually pick a magazine with subject matter I personally would read. Even though I'm not one of these writers who feels a deep spiritual urge to write, there's something special about knowing that I thought of the idea, I developed and created it and I completed it, seeing it through to print. Getting a check is wonderful, of course. But writing the article is something I do all on my own, with nobody's help. Writing is like that. It's a very solitary experience. And it's very satisfying when you succeed in having an article published. No amount of money can equal that sense of satisfaction.

DON'T FORGET THE CORPORATES

The final magazine category—*company,* or *corporate, publications*—defies easy definition. In public relations terms, a for-profit or not-for-profit corporation may publish one or more specific titles that are geared either for external or internal audiences whose support is crucial to the success of organization goals. It serves the organization's corporate objectives to respond to the needs and interests of those publics. By communicating regularly with them through publications and via other means, the company keeps these audiences unified and faithful to organization goals. In years past, during favorable economies, large corporations such as Mobil (now Exxon Mobil), Owens-Illinois, Inc., and Marathon Oil—just to name a few of the major conglomerates—spent many thousands of dollars annually producing slick, glossy external magazines that paid top dollar to top freelancers. Those spendthrift days have largely disappeared, but there remain several company externals that continue to include freelance material.

A growing category of corporate titles can be labeled *custom publications.* These are designed to build brand loyalty among consumers. A corporation will see an unfulfilled niche it would like to target and develops, or "sponsors," a magazine to fill it. Thus, Sony Corporation publishes *Sony Style;* Bloomingdale's publishes *B;* and Pillsbury publishes *Fast and Healthy.* Custom publications often are produced *for* corporations by independent publishers who contract to write, edit, print and sometimes distribute. Although most of those corporate magazines are staff-written, some custom publishers do buy a small percentage of freelance material. Some of the titles even accept outside advertising, a slow-moving trend that began in the 1990s. IBM's controlled-circulation magazine *Beyond Computing* is an example.

HELPFUL EXERCISE

Alone or in a team, visit a local library not connected to your school. In the periodicals section where current magazines and daily newspapers are displayed on racks or shelved, compile a list of current magazine reading fare *by category.* Categorize each magazine you see; don't leave any out. Which are association titles? Business/trade titles? Which are consumer magazines? Within the consumer category, list the general-interest magazines and place the others by title under their common-interest subdivisions. (If you're not sure which is which, read the table of contents and the information below the magazine's masthead.) Now total up the magazines in each category. Does the library offer something for every reader? Does it cater instead to certain categories of readership? Why do you think this might be so? Now interview the librarian in charge of ordering these periodicals. On which basis or bases is the decision to order made? Does this agree with your assessment?

CHAPTER TWO

THE FAMILY TREE

As a former public relations and marketing consultant, I know the critical importance of building and maintaining reader loyalty by writing to readership. I know that marketing research plays a pivotal role in positioning a magazine, targeting and profiling its readership and periodically reassessing reader needs, wants, interests, attitudes, habits and belief structure. This is *relationship marketing* at its classic best. An editor, his or her staffers and stable of freelance writers are skilled at servicing, satisfying and maintaining that relationship.

As a magazine freelancer, I learned this the hard way. My article "Tiger of the Province," for example, saw the dawn in a 25 percent kill fee—but never the full light of day had it appeared in print. Written as a personality profile of the feisty woman who headed the Natal, South Africa, Anti-Shark Measures Board, it should have been positioned instead as a story on shark biology and behaviorism with Beulah Davis, the uniformed "tiger" of the province, quoted liberally as authority. That's what readers of *International Wildlife* expected. That's what the editor assigned. I got carried away. Because the article was assigned, I received a kill fee; the editor got nothing for his specialized readership. Failure to write to readership is only one of several reasons a story can be rejected or bounced back for major revision.

PLACE THE READER STAGE CENTER

A magazine's use of relationship marketing places the reader—not the magazine, not the writer, nor the editor nor the publisher—at its center. A bond is forged, such that a reader will identify a particular magazine as "my" magazine every time. The magazine is viewed as supportive, advancing and enhancing reader aims. Editorial content and ads are seen as credible, the magazine is perceived as sharing the same value structure and ideologies with the reader. This belief structure allows the California State Automobile Association, through its slick regional magazine *Via,* to increase that relationship (in sales it's called "increasing the sale") by offering its loyal readers travel promotions, discount tickets, special license plates, free traveler's checks and travel books—and an opportunity to buy more service by upgrading the basic annual membership to the more expensive AAA Plus card. It also provides the perfect vehicle for advertisers such as Madrona Manor ("A Wine Country Inn & Restaurant"), Reno's Atlantis Casino and Dr. Wilkinson's Hot Springs Resort in Calistoga to plug into that special relationship by tying their products and services to AAA member interests.

CAN READERS TRUST YOU?

Trust can be violated. I've done it, and my editor allowed it. While a member of the *Audubon* magazine editorial staff some years back, when its readers were mostly loyal birders, I wrote a scathing book review that trashed the biography of a birding pioneer who was a founding father of the National Audubon Society. The biography I reviewed was poorly written, no doubt about it. But I had no idea its subject was almost an icon to loyal Audubon Society members and magazine readers. Neither did the editor: We both misread it.

Days after that particular issue arrived in the mailboxes of subscribers, the irate letters and phone calls began. Readers were incensed. We had violated their trust. Did we indeed share the same value structure? Our credibility fell to an all-time low, and the next issue contained an apology to readers. Thankfully, I kept my job, and so did the magazine's editor. But neither of us committed the same mistakes again. I was so in love with my own words that I failed to put the *subject* of the book in historical perspective. Moreover, I gave no thought to reader interests and concerns. You could say that I failed at relationship marketing.

GET TO A MAGAZINE'S SOUL

To understand a magazine, to get to its soul, you need to determine how the publication has positioned itself to target readership and what its editorial requirements are. After all, you don't want to pour your heart into an idea, package it for a magazine you think is just right, then have your article rejected by the editor.

Do two things first: Obtain a copy of the magazine's guidelines for writers and perform a content analysis on the publication. The guidelines are sometimes posted on the specific web site; almost always they're listed in *Writer's Market* but just as frequently in summary fashion. You can obtain the fuller guidelines by writing or e-mailing the publication. Sometimes the guidelines state the fees to be paid to freelancers for purchase of certain rights to publish the article; sometimes they do not. Almost always the guidelines will indicate length desired for certain types of stories. Here are sample guide-lines sample from two consumer magazines. Both are categorized as religious publications and both emphasize the Christian life. One, however, is slanted to faith *on the job,* the other to faith *in all aspects of life.* Read the guidelines for *The Life@Work Journal* (ceased publication in 2002), then compare guidelines and readership to those of *Charisma & Christian Life,* a magazine about spirit-led living with a self-described charismatic slant.

OUR COMPANY

The primary goal of The Life@Work Co. is to explore and promote the integra-tion of faith and work. For the most part, faith at work has meant "exemplifying character at work" or "evangelizing co-workers" or leading "Bible studies" with co-workers. These are important works, to be sure. But our goal is to provide practical information and real-life examples on life at work from a biblical per-spective. *The Life@Work Journal* was launched in 1998 as a tool for exploring this intersection and sharing what we find with others.

OUR AUDIENCE

We gear our journal to business leaders and other professionals—men and women—who want real answers to real problems and relevant information on important issues. This includes everyone from the home-based entrepreneur to the CEO of a $100 million company. Accountants, doctors, lawyers, bankers, writers, managers, architects, professors and consultants are included in our tar-get audience. In short, it covers just about anyone in a leadership position at work.

OUR CONTENT

We devote about half of *The Journal* to a "theme suite"—a section on a specific topic. Within the theme suite we publish a variety of articles aimed at bringing the subject matter to life. We use features on individuals and on companies that model something specific to the theme. We also use panel discussions, inter-views, news, 18 features and case studies, along with charts, graphs, flow charts and other sidebar stories. Outside the theme suite, we take a "big-tent" approach to the integration of faith and work. We publish information on research, busi-ness trends, technology, humor, mentoring, communication, travel, careers, fi-nances, management, leadership, time management, family and home offices. We also run reviews of everything from current and classical literature to coffee to computers. These areas, which may or may not be connected to the theme suite, contain 200- to 1,200-word articles and are excellent spots for freelance work. Also, if a compelling profile of a person and/or business does not fit an up-coming theme, we will run it outside the theme suite. We strive to be a valuable resource to our readers; thus, we want our articles to have "take-away value"—something practical and useful that the reader can take away and use in his or her everyday life at work.

OUR STYLE

We aim to be a highly practical resource, so our articles should reflect that. Thus, most articles should contain an instructional element, something that tells read-ers how they can apply this particular story to their everyday lives. We want stories to be informative, but not preachy. We look for fresh ideas and fresh ways of approaching stories. We are proactive in our thinking, not reactive. We want to know what's working and what's not working for followers of Christ in the work world. And we want to know why. Our writers aren't afraid to take chances. They write with color. They use vivid analogies, illustrations and anecdotes. We show our readers what works in business and how to implement it, whether it is strategy, principles or technology; and we show them [what] pitfalls to avoid. Not all of our stories have a spiritual theme. Some items might just as easily show up in a mainstream business publication. However, stories without a scriptural element MUST be carried by other elements of excellence— timeliness, creativity, freshness, etc. Readers should gain practical business insights from *The Journal* even if they ignore the biblical message.

OUR PET PEEVES
We're not big on first-person accounts, although we make exceptions for stories written by "experts," for columns and for other stories that are most effectively told in first-person. We reject anything that is moralistic or preachy. We don't mind simple solutions, but we don't want simplistic solutions. We don't want articles filled with religious cliches or articles that overuse or misuse religious language. Although we make certain exceptions, we generally follow the AP Stylebook and we encourage our freelancers to do likewise.

OUR DIRECTIVES
Tell us something we don't already know.

Tell us something we can't get somewhere else.

Ask the hard questions.

OUR SUBMISSION POLICIES
We accept unsolicited manuscripts but prefer that you first send a query. By fax, e-mail or snail mail, send a brief description of your story idea, the valuable information to a *Life@Work* reader. Our stories range from 200 to 3,000 words in length. We pay based on the writer's level of experience and on the degree of difficulty of the story. Manuscripts should include your name, address, phone number and Social Security number. Bible references should come from the New International Version. Include a stamped self-addressed envelope with your query or manuscript. Writers who are new to *Life@Work* are advised to send clips.

In addition to these general guidelines, the individual departments in this magazine have their own. While not printed here, a quick examination of each departmental guideline reveals a great deal about the magazine's editorial formula. The "In-Box" runs 350-word "shorts" on topics such as career, money, Internet ethics and family that "make a connection to the intersection of faith and work." "Wildcards" runs 1,200-word topical features on work trends and innovative practices in a particular organization—information that readers will find interesting or useful. "Reviews" is exactly that—620-word reviews of books, movies, technology, resorts—all of them on business topics and written in a way that reinforces the magazine's role as "trusted friend and mentor" to readership. *Life@Work* profiles four people per issue; thus, the "Life at the Intersection" department focuses on how each of the four applies biblical teaching to his or her job or parts of it. The final department is a guest column.

NOW COMPARE

With a readership of more than 600,000, here's what *Charisma & Christian Life* wants from freelance writers. Note the stress on readers ("our readers want . . ."), and pay special attention to the third category, "Freelancing for *Charisma*":

MEET OUR READERS

More than half our readers are Christians who belong to Pentecostal or independent charismatic churches, and numerous others who participate in the charismatic renewal in mainline denominations. Their media age is 47. Seventy-two percent are married, and 66 percent have at least some college education. Ninety percent of them have been committed Christians for more than five years, and most are active in their local churches.

STUDY THE MAGAZINE

Writers must know the magazine well. A casual examination of a few issues will not be enough. You must study the magazine thoroughly, classifying the articles and analyzing them to discover the elements we typically use. You must catch our vision and get a sense of our readers' interests.

FREELANCING FOR *CHARISMA*

Freelancers write 80 percent of our articles, but we assign most of these to writers who have established themselves with us. In most cases, we only give article assignments to writers with published clips. You should avoid sending teaching articles, interviews, issue-oriented pieces of news analyses: These always originate with the editors. We do not publish sermons, poetry or fiction. We are, however, looking for well-written articles in the following categories:

- Personality profiles. Our readers want to hear about people who are living the Christian life effectively and with pizzazz. Here, we are not looking for complete biographical sketches but "slices of life" that focus on some noteworthy event or story. Stories should include conflict or challenge, resolution, change and consequences.
- Miracle and healing stories. Our readers are interested in accounts of God's supernatural intervention in ordinary human events. These stories must be thoroughly researched and well told. Healings must be medically documented. Pastors and other reference sources may be required.
- Trend articles that discern changes or new directions among Christians or that would be of interest or importance to Christians. Trend pieces must show evidence of exhaustive research. They should be written in a journalistic style and illustrated with anecdotes, facts and quotes from authorities.
- Seasonal articles of all kinds. Our readers enjoy articles that help them celebrate both Christian and secular holidays, including Christmas, Easter and Pentecost, as well as Valentine's Day, Mother's Day, Father's Day, the Fourth of July and Thanksgiving.
- News stories for our People & Events section. We welcome brief (200 to 800 words) and timely stories about people who recently have done something worthy of note or about events that would be of interest to our readers.

Articles must be written in journalistic style and with punch. Facts and quotes must be scrupulously accurate. With the exception of the short news stories, articles should be between 1,800 and 2,500 words in length.

OUR PROCEDURE

Charisma & Christian Life does not accept or reply to unsolicited manuscripts. Writers may send query letters or query e-mails that briefly describe and outline a proposed article. Query letters must be typewritten, either by typewriter or word processor, and double-spaced on one side of 8½" by 11" white bond paper. The author's name, address and telephone number should appear on the top left of the first page. The magazine buys all rights. Payment for articles is negotiable. (Writers may obtain additional information on submission to the magazine by consulting the proper entry in *Writer's Market*.)

CHECK OUT EDITORIAL CALENDARS

Publishers plan their editorial calendars generally four to six months ahead of publication. Seasonal stories, for example, would have to be submitted far in advance of the occasion. For *Life@Work*, a typical year's worth of major editorial looked like this:

Nov-Dec 2000	Balance	booked
Jan-Feb 2001	New Economy	booked
March-April 2001	First Half	booked
May-June 2001	Power	booked
July-Aug 2001	Laughter	booked
Sept-Oct 2001	Partnering	submission deadline 3/19/01
Nov-Dec 2001	Marketplace Grace	submission deadline 5/25/01

ANALYZE CONTENT

Your next step is to determine how these editorial guidelines translate to the printed page. Do this by performing an *item by item content analysis* of at least three and preferably six issues of the same magazine published within the last six months (see the Analyzing Content guide on pp. 32–35). This will give you an intimate understanding of readership and the magazine's formula and purpose in action. Some magazines will mail a writer sample copies gratis; some will charge for back issues. Otherwise, you must purchase the magazines, spend time in the library reading them, or borrow them. It is useful to note that Strang Communications, Inc., publisher of *Charisma & Christian Life*, is adamant that writers know the magazine well. "A casual examination of a few issues will not be enough," says Strang, whose freelancers "must catch our vision and get a sense of our reader's interests."

For instructional purpose, I've chosen a consumer publication with hefty ad content and numerous sell lines on its cover. The sell lines—brief blurbs about an issue's contents written to attract readers—are crucial. *Family Circle,* for example, is sold *only* point-of-purchase, at a store's checkout counter; it has to fight for attention with other magazines on the display rack.

Examine Readership

First, examine readership. The cover of the April 2002 issue of *more* drew my attention immediately. Wearing yellow against a lighter, saffron background, a relaxed Candice Bergen—"having the time of her life," says the sell line—poses for the camera. Beside her these sell lines scream "Buy me!" in bright orange, black and white ink:

Fashion Finds Under $100

Hair Miracles: How To Go from Thin to Thick

Win $5,500 Worth of Great Spring Clothes

Yes, You're Having a Heart Attack: Symptoms Women Ignore

Smart, Sexy, Confident: The *New* Value of Women with Experience

My Mom, Nancy Reagan: How She Keeps It Together

The Good Life: Love, Money, Friends, Adventure

To which reader would this cover be addressed? Which reader may have thin hair and a concern how to thicken it? Which has reached heart-attack years? Which is a woman with experience and looking for love and adventure? Which needs reaffirmation that she's smart, sexy and confident? Which relates well to 50ish actress Candy Bergen? Now continue to assess readership by examining the editorial departments and additional offerings listed on *more*'s contents page. I see three departments—People, Health & Well-being and the Good Life—and two bonus offerings—"Spring Fashion Giveaway" and "*more*'s Model Search." Nothing revealing here—except the title of an article listed under People—"Pregnant at Fifty."

Ads Tell a Lot

Ads tell me even more. On the inside front cover, Estee Lauder cosmetics promises a product that repairs lines, circles and skin dryness during nighttime sleep. The inside back-cover ad features Dove, a soap, states the ad, that "improves and nourishes skin for a healthier glow." On the back cover, a Neutrogena product promises visibly "firmer skin" (another Neutrogena product featured on an inside page promises to "take years off your eyes").

I examine the ads on the rest of this issue's pages. Basking in her "new attitude" toward synthetic hormone replacement therapy (HRT), Patti LaBelle

sings the praises of a Merck and Co. pill that promises to combat the effects of menopause. (The future of synthetic HRT is now in question.) Former Olympic skater Dorothy Hamill touts a product for relieving osteoarthritis. Not to be outdone for the competition in marketing dollars, the State of Texas hawks tourism and adventure with an expensive, multipage advertising insert. I examine the remaining ads and the people featured in them: All except one or two are mature women of the Bergen age bracket.

The Picture Emerges

I now begin to get a picture of the typical *more* reader. In her early 50s or close to it, she's beginning to have health concerns, is active and wants to continue being active, is fairly sophisticated and contemporary in her clothes and lifestyle and still considers herself hip and adventurous. She's married or has been married and likely has children. I look at the table of contents, searching for departments and features; then I examine each. Does the editorial mirror the interests and concerns of this age group? Yes. For example, page 98 begins a six-page piece on celebrity fashion designer Vera Wang; a type of article known as personality profile, it's liberally illustrated with full-color photos of Vera and her husband on each page. The editorial is short—roughly one and one-half pages. The article on hair loss offers more extensive editorial; it's also heavy with photos and bold, pull-me-in graphics, as though losing one's hair is an attractive option of age. Filled with advice on haircuts, camouflage and "medical miracles," that how-to article runs eight pages with no ads. "Looking Good" in the Style & Beauty section features actress and singer Bernadette Peters; "Looking Back" is a series of short-take personal reminiscences dating from the 1950s on remarriage, face lifts, Marlon Brando and the pill.

This issue also contains a first-person mother-daughter narrative on adventuring in New Zealand. Editorial runs nearly three pages in that story; photos grace four of the five pages. The story on Candice Bergen—a brief look at her career and marriages—runs no more than six pages with roughly two pages of written copy.

Examine Editorial

An examination of the actual prose in this issue reveals fairly short articles that employ a range of voices. Patti Davis, daughter of former U.S. President Ronald Reagan and his wife, Nancy, obviously use *my* in speaking of her mother. The writer for a personality profile on actress and model Mariel Hemingway chooses the objective third-person approach, allowing the reader to be part of the story as it unfolds without the intrusion of an unknown observer to interpret for her. The *you* voice characterizes several of the stories, drawing the reader in, speaking directly to her. From time to time, the use of *we* in a story allows the reader to feel she is part of a larger group with many things in common.

Editorial front matter follows current publishing trends: a collage of short-shorts contributed by freelance writers. Mel Gibson leads with six paragraphs, followed by Ivana Trump; singers Pat Benetar, Emmylou Harris and others ("The beat goes on," says the subtitle); a few paragraphs on the return of a well-touted author; and other brief pieces. For the sake of discussion, let's say that *more* speaks to me. Further, let's say that I'm in the Patti Labelle–Candice Bergen age bracket. Let's probe further. Am I a magazine reader? Yes. Am I married with children? No. Am I likely to buy skin replenisher and age-defying makeup? No. Have I some health concerns? Yes. Am I likely to buy at least some designer clothes? No. Do I buy on impulse? No. Do I bow to peer pressure when making my purchases? Sometimes. Am I contemporary in my clothes? A bit. When faced with decisions, do I view celebrities as highly credible information sources? No. Am I a member of a social group, and is it defined by age and lifestyle? No. Am I pretty independent? Yes. Am I looking for adventure? Always.

Based on this very preliminary information, am I likely to become a regular *more* reader? Should *more* alter its relationship marketing strategies to snare me as a subscriber?

Choose a magazine and put each of several issues under the microscope as I've done here. Make sure to do a word count, too. Does the pattern of editorial style and content repeat itself? Do the same advertisements appear issue to issue? If the answer to both is "yes," you now know in intimate fashion who the reader is and how the magazine uniquely answers the reader's interests and concerns. In short, you're clued into the magazine's relationship marketing strategy and have developed the perspective you need to write for those readers. But does the magazine purchase freelance material? Check the bylines—you'll find the byline beneath the title or sometimes at the end of the story—then compare the name with people listed on the masthead, usually staffers and contributing editors. If the story lacks a byline, it was written by a staffer or contributed free by a public relations source. In 2000, *Writer's Yearbook* ranked *more* among the top 100 markets for freelance writers. And could anyone write for the magazine? The April 2002 features both male and female contributors of varied ages.

HELPFUL EXERCISES

The family tree shown here has "foliage" containing spaces for filling in the names of people you know well. These family members can then be profiled on a relationship grid. You'll find gridding helpful in marketing your articles to various magazines. Why? Because each person profiled on it represents a particular group of magazine readers numbering in the many thousands who share similar characteristics. By filling in the tree and later gridding the names, you're learning just how minutely and narrowly a magazine will target its readership—and how precisely you, too, must define a reader so that your article is a match to both reader and magazine.

1. Here's how to use your personal family tree:
   Since you know yourself better than anyone, place your name in the triangle at the top of the tree. Now build your family tree with 8 to 10 people of both sexes

The Family Tree

(square for male, circle for female). Include, for example, your mother, father, siblings, close aunts and uncles, a best friend or two, a cousin or two if you're close, your own children and/or grandchildren if old enough to be magazine players, important people in your life you know well (teacher, pastor, boss or coworker, fellow student, etc.). If you have no parents or no biological family living, substitute the social family you've created for yourself. If you need more space, the tree can be photocopied and enlarged or created on the computer using Pagemaker or Quark Express.

2. Now choose five of the people in your tree and profile them, using the demographic and psychographic data from the list that follows. The data is grouped into six, lettered clusters—A) Vital Statistics and Basic Demographics, B) Income and Occupation, C) Psychographics and Consumer Behavior, D) Lifestyles and Pastimes, E) Information Habits and F) Can Best Be Described As. You can profile these people on a grid such as the personal grid shown (pp. 26–27), or you can simply list the characteristics that apply to each person.

3. Match *each* of your profiled people to *three* magazines and place these on your personal grid or list. The relationship grid on page 28 illustrates how the process works: Specific information from clusters A through F has configured each of your profiled people as a certain type of reader. The relationship grid reveals, for example, that the male on the right at the top is a good candidate for *Suede*, the individual at top center may enjoy reading *Home and Office*, while the woman on the left is a good fit with *Classic Décor*. Lines on the relationship grid that intersect may indicate that dissimilar individuals can enjoy reading the same magazines (for example, *Home and Office*).

To investigate the actual magazines suitable for your five people, go first to the magazines and e-zines (Internet titles) listed in *Writer's Market* and any additional magazines guides you may have available. Scan each magazine's editorial specifics, then double-check those listings against examples of the *actual* publications on library and bookstore shelves. Hint: Do not base your selections on the magazines currently received by your family tree people. Why? Because *receiving* may not equate with *reading, skimming* and *scanning* don't mean that information is *retained,* and magazine buying habits may be just that—tired and outdated, ready to be replaced with a new mirror for the reader's interests and concerns.

THE FAMILY TREE

A. **Vital Statistics and Basic Demographics**

   Name

   Relationship

   Age

   Gender

   Marital status

   Ethnic background

   Religious affiliation

(continued on page 29)

_____

Name

_____   _____   _____   _____

Age   Gender   Marital Status   Relationship

Cluster A	Cluster B	Cluster C

Your Personal Grid

Cluster D	Cluster E	Cluster F

Magazine _____
Magazine _____
Magazine _____

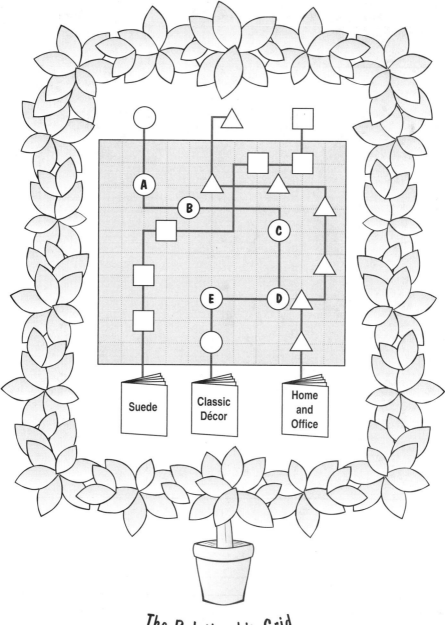

The Relationship Grid

Education level

Ages of children (if applicable)

Political affiliation

Homeowner

Owns second/vacation home

Home or apartment renter

Lives with family members

B. Income and Occupation

Occupation area or industry

Occupational title

Management or line employee

Armed services member (active duty)

Self-employed

Works from home or telecommutes

Retired

Student

Working wife or mother

Makes buying decisions mutually with spouse or partner

Makes own buying decisions

Single-income household

Two-income household

Average annual personal income (less than $30,000; $30,000 to $45,000; $45,000 to $70,000; more than $70,000)

Average household income (less than $30,000; $30,000 to $45,000; $45,000 to $70,000; more than $70,000)

C. Psychographics and Consumer Behavior

Owns one car

Owns multiple vehicles

Favorite store

Favorite type of clothing

Owns and uses computer

Owns cell phone, pager, etc.

Owns pets or likes animals

Most recent big purchase

Likes video games

Enjoys traveling

Travels frequently on business

Recreational traveler

Favorite vacation spot or destination

Preferred method of transportation

Flies at least two times yearly

Prefers organic foods

Likes fast foods

Likes gourmet cooking

Vegetarian

Meat-and-potatoes consumer

Eats out at least once a week

Favorite restaurant/favorite foods

Prefers alternative health care such as reiki, self-healing, homeopathic remedies, meditation, yoga, etc.

Prefers mainstream health care

Makes buying decisions quickly

Likes to try new products

Is slow to try new products or fashions

Has investments (securities/stocks/mutual funds, etc.)

Reads paperback romances

Makes decisions based on input from others

Makes decisions independently of others

Is likely to be influenced by peers

Makes decisions based on input from those in authority/those in social, church or ethnic group

Has a few strong friends

Has a lot of friends and acquaintances

Has a role model or hero (which)

Member of social, professional or fraternal organizations (state which)

D. **Lifestyle and Pastimes**

Outdoor

Stay-at-home

Cosmopolitan

Suburban

Metropolitan

Rural

Rustic

Alternative

Favorite pastime

Favorite entertainment

Frequently buys videos or DVDs

Goes out to the movies at least once or twice a month

Main hobbies or interests

Favorite type of music

Favorite form of recreation

E. Information Habits

Gets most of his or her news and information from electronic or print medium/media or from other individuals

Reads to find out information

Reads mostly to be entertained

Likes practical how-to and self-help information

Would agree with the statement "I'm too busy to read."

Would agree with the statement "I'd like more time to read."

F. Can Best Be Described As

Practical, down to earth

Dreamer/visionary

Thinker—weighs ideas, philosophizes

Middle of the road

Adventurous

Cautious and conservative

Slow to change

Responsive to new ideas and methods

Do-it-yourselfer

Relies on others for tasks

Leader

Team player

Prefers to work alone

Sophisticated

Three magazines suitable for this reader

_____

_____

_____

4. Select one of the titles you chose. Using the Analyzing Content guide that follows, analyze the content of that magazine by examining six consecutive issues in the current year. Your analysis will tell you several things: Have you chosen wisely? Is the magazine a good fit for the reader in your family tree? Can magazine and reader maintain a viable relationship? Don't worry if you've erred. Just remember that in the future you'll be using this strategy to help determine which magazines you want to write for and where to target a particular article you've written.

ANALYZING CONTENT

Title _____

Type of Magazine _____

Specialty Area _____

Frequency

_____ Monthly

_____ Bimonthly

_____ Quarterly

_____ Newsstand or point of purchase (single-copy sales)

_____ Subscription

_____ Controlled (free)

_____ From member dues

_____ Public relations internal or external (free)

Dates of Issues Analyzed

_____   _____

_____   _____

_____   _____

Editorial

Articles, average per issue

% Freelance written (bylines appear under title or at end of article)   _____

% Staff written (names may appear on magazine's masthead)   _____

% Written by contributing editors (see masthead)   _____

% Written by experts in a particular area   _____

% Original articles   _____

% Digested or reprinted (may appear below the article on page one or final page)   _____

Freelance Articles

_____ Accepted on speculation

_____ Assigned only

_____ Published clips necessary with query

Readership

____ Men

____ Women

____ Juveniles

____ Minorities

____ Parents

____ College age

____ High school age

____ Certain occupation(s) _____

____ Certain industry(ies) _____

____ Professionals

____ Blue collar

____ Educational level

____ Single

____ Divorced

____ Married

____ Working

____ Retired

____ Housewives

____ Disabled

____ Other _____

Reader Lifestyle   (Summarize. For example: laid-back American expatriate living in Paris who summers on the Riviera and plays fast and loose with money and women; hippie California dentist who fled San Francisco for a simpler life northward behind the redwood curtain; struggling, single, military mom of three who works as a night-time telemarketer to earn extra money.)

_____

_____

_____

Magazine Slant

____ Help and advise

____ Entertain

____ Inform

____ Other _____

Departments

_____   _____

_____   _____

_____   _____

Types of Subject Matter Covered

_____ % _____

_____ % _____

_____ % _____

_____ % _____

_____ % _____

_____ % _____

Scope of Subject Matter

% National   _____

% Regional   _____

% International   _____

% Local   _____

Types of Editorial Material

% Fiction	_____	% Investigative	_____
% Nonfiction	_____	% Personal experience	_____
% How-to	_____	% Narrative	_____
% Self-help	_____	% Descriptive	_____
% Personality profile	_____	% Info-brief	_____
% Humor	_____	% Essay	_____
% Survey	_____	% Seasonal	_____
% Inspirational	_____	% Sidebars	_____
% Travel	_____		

Length of Average Article (words) _____

Length of Average Info-Brief (words) _____

Average Length of Paragraphs (words) _____

Preferred Attribution (present tense—"he says", or past—"he said") _____

Preferred Leads (story beginnings, one paragraph or a few; see Chapter 8)

_____ Quote	_____ Question
_____ Dialogue	_____ Question/answer
_____ Historical reference	_____ Novelty
_____ Literary allusion	_____ Case history
_____ Descriptive (scene setter)	_____ Anecdotal
_____ Narrative (tells a story)	_____ Action
_____ Summary	_____ Other
_____ Direct address (you)	

Articles Written from Which Point of View

_____ First person (*I*)

_____ Second person singular or plural (*you*)

_____ Third person singular or plural (*he, she, it, they*—objective approach)

_____ Collective (*we*)

Focus of Articles

% Celebrities   _____

% Not well known   _____

% Minorities   _____

% Professionals   _____

% Nonprofessionals   _____

% Housewives   _____

% Retired   _____

% Experts   _____

Articles Substantiated by

_____ Statistics

_____ Opinions from authorities

_____ Indirect or direct quotes

_____ Case histories

_____ Anecdotes

_____ Examples

Photos

_____ Taken by author

_____ Other

Advertisements

Subject matter _____

_____

_____

Percentage of advertising to editorial _____

■ ■ ■ ■ ■

CHAPTER THREE

WHAT IF . . . ?

When brainstorming for story ideas, where do you start?

Try trolling in the waters of "What if . . . ?" I've played this game for many years, often subconsciously. It can net some editorial gems. For example: What if Spanish moss does more than festoon trees in the South and Pacific Northwest? (It does; in fact, this was the subject of my first magazine article.) What if fish can actually walk on water? (To my knowledge they can't, but some can actually walk *on land* when migrating from one body of water to another. According to a news story in the August 21, 2002, issue of the *Daytona Beach News-Journal,* two whiskered catfish, apparently of Asian lineage, were spied by two boys. The catfish were *crawling around on fins* in the driveway of the boys' home in Deltona, Florida, after torrential rains had caused nearby Lake Monroe to overflow and flood the streets.)

And what if colleges aren't just for students? A freelance writer for an AAA magazine, California State Automobile Association's *Via,* asked himself this question. The answer? A four-color, four-page photo essay with limited editorial that focused on colleges as "great places for the whole family to visit." This "What if . . . ?" exercise paid off for Brad Herzog; his photo essay on colleges ran in *Via'*s September-October 2002 issue.

LOOK LOCALLY

You can find such self-generated story ideas in your local area with almost no effort—in your home, within your family and circle of friends, within your job and community, your place of worship and school, associations of which you're a member, the stores and businesses your patronize. How-to articles, for example, a genre popular with many magazines, often begin with ideas and information found locally. Readers want to know how to start a farmer's market or a bed and breakfast, how to do something better or operate more efficiently, how to become a more successful (happier, fatter, thinner) person, how to have more fun, play golf, fish. Seasonal stories, including celebrations such as the Feast of Ramadan, Christmas, Hanukkah, Kwanzaa and Thanksgiving, are always topical. Make sure to query seasonal stories more than six months in advance to make a publication's editorial calendar.

FIND LINKS

Remember, however, that these are just ideas, and ideas have to be within the realm of possibility. You can't write credibly about the world's fastest sport, for example, if you've never been inside a jai alai fronton. Remember, too, that story ideas are only starting points. Ideas must have connections—those crucial links between what you observe and the larger picture of which each may be a part. Without those links, you have no story to develop because your idea doesn't relate to the human condition, doesn't relate to a universal (larger) truth or current trend (and even the trend must be put in perspective of the total), doesn't offer a new take or twist on an old situation.

For example, walking catfish aren't native to Florida; like pollutants, they may actually threaten the food source for native species of fish and for mammals such as manatee. Their possible impact on sport fishing in Florida could have disastrous implications for tourism. Were the original walking catfish simply aquarium escapees grown big and fat on Florida's vegetative largesse? Were they brought illegally to Florida shores from southeastern Asia? Is this situation similar to the giant snakehead fish found in Wisconsin waters—a predatory carnivore as long as three feet that could alter the local fish population and introduce new diseases? Or to cogon grass, a fast-growing, fire-hazardous weed that traveled to America as a packing material and chokes out native grasses? Or even to certain feral mammals now known to carry disease? Ideas also must be current—in the news, talked about, of general concern.

NEWS BRIEFS ARE ESSENTIAL

Newspaper briefs—short news items usually run as a column of stories under a standing head such as "The Area/In Brief" or "News Watch," and calendars of coming events—run once a week in weekly and daily papers, often on Saturdays—are excellent sources of story ideas. The *Daytona Beach News-Journal* ran these two news briefs on a single day—"Biologists name species of box jellyfish" and "Manatee safety zones proposed." Either or both of those stories bear expansion, at least into a news feature if not part of a larger magazine article. For example, further investigation would reveal that cousins of the deadly box jellyfish, including a jellyfish known as the sea wasp, have been painfully stinging swimmers along the world's most famous beach. Biologists cite pollution, global warming and the declining ocean fish population as reasons for the sudden efflorescence of what are called jellyfish "blooms" whose almost transparent bells have begun to appear with frequency and attack swimmers in the shoreline waters of the Atlantic off Florida's East Coast.

Longer news stories and news features can furnish story ideas also. However, I caution you about infringing on copyright (see Additional Resources) by using someone else's hard work or phrasing and passing them off as your own. You should also double-check the accuracy of what someone else wrote even through it was published: Mistakes do get into print, and it happens a lot. Regard these newspaper stories as *pointing the way only;* as a magazine writer, you must do your own research, conduct your own interviews, and write the story using your own words.

DON'T OVERLOOK PR AND ASSOCIATIONS

Here's one of the best sources to net story ideas: the public relations office of a university or college, a governmental agency or a for-profit (Kaiser) or not-for-profit (American Red Cross) corporation. In person, by telephone, by e-mail or snail mail, approach a public relations officer or executive, explain your mission as a new freelance writer and ask that your name be placed on the mailing list (or e-mailing list) to receive news releases regularly. Most places will welcome further opportunities to get their story to a targeted public.

You can also find many news releases posted for free on a corporation's web site. They're not commercial advertising and they're usable at no charge. The staple of most magazines and newspapers, news releases may be run as is, shortened or revised. In fact, it's estimated that news releases comprise one-third of the editorial material in many magazines. These fairly short news stories, most of them run as submitted, are developed and released by a for-profit or a not-for-profit corporation. They contain news and information about the company or organization's products, services, personnel, activities and financial status that are of interest to the readership of newspapers and magazines as well as to the listening and viewing public of the electronic media.

For example, as a freelance writer I learned about the groundbreaking substance bioglas through a news release sent me by a major university's medical college. That substance had been developed by a three-man bioengineering team. Initially tested on animals, bioglas would become grandfather to the dental and bone implants used by surgeons today. I wrote a Sunday newsmagazine story on bioglas after interviewing the research team and watching them as they worked.

Hint: By their nature, news releases are reflective of an institution's point of view. Although magazines run service, product and personnel stories almost without question, it's your responsibility to put other public relations–generated stories into perspective by researching the issue and talking with other sources.

Need to know more about certain industries? Need a starting point? Check out the *Encyclopedia of Associations* in the print or online version (http://library.dialog.com/bluesheets/html/bl0114.html) and check in with any of the thousands of trade and professional associations. They represent everything from undergarment and musical instrument manufacturing to logging, pharmaceuticals, massage therapy, chiropracty, consumer electronics and resort management.

AVOID BEING A COUCH POTATO

Are you a couch potato? Ideas come when you're out and about, noticing things, attending events and meetings such as the annual convention of the National Business Aviation Association, joining clubs, playing games and sports, being both social and observant. The September 1996 issue of *Mother Jones* magazine, for example, ran an article spotlighting the 20 most activist campuses in the United States. "Activist" was identified as those that "pioneered social action and consistently generated students who remain committed to public affairs issues after graduation." Listed among the 20 schools cited for its good deeds was Humboldt State University (HSU); the author of the article was an observant alumna of Humboldt State, Leslie Weiss, who built the article from personal experiences there as a student and member of activist organizations.

CHECK OUT YOUR FAMILY TREE

What about *your* personal experiences and those of others? Have you solved an everyday problem, for example, that others still struggle with? And take a good look at the material you've compiled on people in your family tree. Is your brother John a missionary? Your aunt a trauma therapist? Is your wife or mother a garage sale freak? Are you? Perhaps you paint and refinish furniture or enjoy volunteering for several good causes. Maybe you're a spelunker or a mountain climber. Or perhaps your love in this life is a good game of chess, or raising roses or goats. Something drives you. What is it?

Hint: Personal-experience stories differ from how-to's. Do not attempt to write a personal experience story about yourself or those you're close to. Those stories seldom work in the hands of an inexperienced magazine writer. Instead, use the information you're gathering about people in your family tree only for orientation to a subject or as one of its many building blocks.

A former acquaintance of mine lives in coastal California, north of the redwood curtain and about 80 miles south of the Oregon border. In this isolated area, where rural artists and artisans live and work in the woods, and homegrown microbreweries, coffee brewers and bakers thrive among the rhododendrons and redwoods, personal enterprise, initiative and independence are highly prized. Every Saturday my acquaintance goes to the farmer's market in Arcata to pick out homegrown fruits, herbs and vegetables for her kitchen and to talk with a local vendor they call "the bunny lady." The bunny lady raises her own Angora rabbits and for years has sheared their wool, carding, dyeing, weaving and knitting it into the clothing, shawls, hats, purses and scarves she sells so successfully. Her outdoor stand is a perennial farmers-market favorite for locals and visitors alike.

My acquaintance, a home-knitter herself who we'll call Penny, took a magazine-writing course at the local college and decided to write a personality profile of the bunny lady. Using her personal knowledge of knitting as a starting point, Penny researched Angora rabbits, their care and the uses for their fur, spoke with other knitters and knitting retail shops, and then interviewed the bunny lady at the farmer's market and at the woman's rural home. After a series of interviews, Penny wrote a magazine article that she successfully marketed to a women's magazine.

STORIES FOUND EVERYWHERE

Story ideas are everywhere—even in flyers and notices posted on bulletin boards in offices and retail stores. If there's a need, you can count on the fact that somewhere a solution is being found. The key is to *be observant*. And to *think possibility*. This is particularly true if you have decided to become an editorial expert in certain areas—aviation, trucking, consumer electronics, antiques, forest management, skateboarding, cooking. Monitor what is going on there. Look for improvements and research in the field. Look for people wise in the ways of doing things better. Look for innovative customer service ideas. And how about combining two of your interests—animal science and cooking, for instance? Following a news release tip on a new way to tenderize baby beef before it reached supermarket or table, I wrote a brief feature for a women's magazine that began something like this:

> Fat-free and only slightly marbled, those supermarket cuts known as baby beef are more popular for their budget price than for their bite. Now, a university meat scientist has discovered a shocking new way to tenderize the meat—he gives it the juice. Dr. Roger West reports that a mild electrical stimulation of the carcass relaxes the muscles and tenderizes the meat.

As with all successful stories, I did my field research. I spoke with Dr. West and other meat scientists, observed the beef grazing on the hoof and watched the process of slaughter. As the fresh sides of beef hung on a hook in the slaughterhouse, I spoke with Dr. West, watched as he applied the electric current with a cattle prod and saw the meat shudder, then relax. Unpleasant, perhaps—but an article well worth the effort of field research.

STAY ORGANIZED

Now do what most writers do: Create a story file of ideas you'll investigate later. I use a 3 × 5 file box and put supporting material in manila folders; others create a computer file. Remember that you're just brainstorming at this point. You don't know if a particular idea is viable, over-used or even doable. The key is to remain organized.

LOOK FOR FOCUS

Have you ever held your hand palm open and so close to your face that your eyes couldn't bring your fingers into focus? Try it now if you haven't. Or looked through an unfocused camera lens and found everything a blur? As writers, being unfocused is a very real danger: Nothing we write comes to a point. To be sharply focused, the article must concentrate attention on *one, specific part* of a broad, general field or subject. That part must then be of compelling interest to a particular magazine's readership. It's the difference between writing about weight control and writing about a specific series of exercises for men in their middle years that can trim the tummy in ten weeks without a single trip to the gym.

"CARTOONS, SURE, BUT WHAT'S IT ABOUT?"

Many years ago, while still an infant to magazine writing, I interviewed the proprietor of the world's first cartoon museum, intending the article for the general-interest readership of a Sunday newsmagazine, or readership of an airline inflight or perhaps a travel magazine. By failing to target a specific and appropriate readership for the piece, I committed my first error. I then compounded the error—I failed to check in with the appropriate magazines to determine if the idea had currency. I also failed to research whether a particular publication had covered it previously. My greatest mistake, however, was my *failure to focus.* Overwhelmed by the sheer body of material dating from the 1700s, even awed by the history of it, I could not and did not bring that fabulously interesting material into focus as a magazine article. Rather than concentrate on one aspect, I wrote encyclopedia-style, going on at length about the former newspaper cartoonist who was proprietor of the museum, about the origins of cartoon strips such as "Little Orphan Annie," "The Katz'n Jammer Kids" and "Dick Tracy" and their creators, about the social and political implications of cartoons such as "The Yellow Kid," about single-panel cartoons versus comic books versus comic strips, about the preservation and archiving of all three.

Blissfully unaware how flawed the article was, how lacking it was in focus, I queried editors of various magazines about their interest. After receiving several negative replies, I then "cold-mailed" the article to others in turn. The result? Never published, "Funniest Museum in the World" languishes today in a box labeled "Old Magazine Articles" but better labeled "Learning Experiences." Were I then the editor I am now, my reaction to the article would have been, "Cartoons, sure, but what's it about?"

LOCALIZE, HUMANIZE, MAKE IT SPECIFIC

The story you write has to be made specific—localized, yet at the same time related to the larger picture or overall trend of which it is a part. How does a writer do this? And how does a writer ground a story in the human experience, making it meaningful and relevant to the lives of a magazine's readers? And how can a reader find himself or herself in the article, identifying with the story and the people in it? A magazine is always looking for articles that allow the reader to connect with a story, articles that are simultaneously making a connection between the publication and its readers.

The three tenets of focus—*localizing, humanizing, making specific*—are facilitated by a good writer's use of anecdotes and case histories, direct and indirect quotes, dialogue if the occasion demands it, background research and wherever possible, the use of news "pegs" to ensure the material is current in the minds of readership. To maintain focus, a writer makes sure the material is grounded in a starting point—in an individual, an episode or a theme that illustrates the whole situation. The article is expanded from that starting point, much as a *triangle built in reverse*. Thus, a magazine story you're doing on the dwindling California redwoods (the base of a triangle, reversed) could have begun from this news peg: a syndicated *New York Times* news story reporting in 2002 that California redwoods are facing a new threat. Sheared in the past by unregulated logging, decimated by forest fires, their wildlife habitats destroyed, the redwoods are now falling victim to sudden oak death syndrome, according to University of California researchers. The funguslike microorganism has killed hundreds of forest oaks already.

Is this story on threatened redwoods ripe for the writing? Maybe. Maybe not. Perhaps the subject is too broad. Perhaps it could be better focused on one aspect of the situation. (For example, on shark *predation* rather than simply sharks.) And what specific thing would you plan to say about dwindling redwoods as the organizing principle for the story?

SLANTING TO UNCLE FRED

It's imperative now that you check in with your family tree. Is Uncle Fred interested in a story about threatened redwood forests? And what particular slant can you give this story to appeal to an Uncle-Fred readership? By giving the material a particular perspective or slant, you angle it one way for conservationists, environmentalists and campers; and another for home builders, land developers and the logging trade.

For example, I've written two stories on the Basque sport jai alai so popular in this country. One story was slanted toward twenty-something women interested in "skin" (the Basque players); another was slanted toward a travel magazine and toward readers interested in the world's fastest, most betable and most dangerous sport. Is Uncle Fred a conservationist or environmental activist? Is he a firefighter? A frequent camper? Does he own a vacation home in the woods? Does he regard a tree as a thing of beauty? Or as something essential for survival? Does he contribute to organizations that support wildlife and forest protection? Remember that Uncle Fred may live in a Brooklyn brownstone or a Manhattan high-rise, be interested in art museums yet still be a supporter and contributor to the Nature Conservancy, a member of the National Audubon Society and a regular reader of *Audubon* magazine. Remember, too, that within the broad category of "nature magazines," each publication has its own, unique slant. Your story has to mirror that.

CONSULT MAGAZINES, *READER'S GUIDE*

Is this story feasible? It may appear to interest your uncle and the many thousands like him, but has it been done lately? Now is the time to check in with the three magazines you chose for Uncle Fred, analyzing the current and back issues of each to determine if reader interest is there. Have these magazines covered this subject recently? Have they covered it from the angle you've chosen? If you're forced to choose another angle, would it still appeal to an Uncle-Fred readership? If your approach seems viable, consult the *Reader's Guide to Periodical Literature* to determine what's been covered recently by the estimated 250 magazines listed there. You'll find the book in the library or at the help desk of a bookstore. You'll also find it online, together with other electronic indexes you can consult for what's been published on your topic. Does *Reader's Guide* or one of the other indexes indicate dwindling redwood forests is a hot topic? Or too hot to handle because it's been overdone?

Knowing the answers to these questions and what the competition's been doing lately will save you valuable time and the heartache of writing a story that ends up in the rejection bin. Make sure to pitch this knowledge to an editor in your query letter; it indicates your approach is professional and that you've done your homework. (Chapter 6 covers query letters in depth.)

PHRASE YOUR STORYLINE

You now need a one- or two-sentence *premise* of what the article is about. What specific thing do you plan to say about threatened redwoods that forms the organizing principle for your story? That specific thing—a tight one-sentence or two-sentence *storyline*—is the foundation for your article. It contains a promise and acts as direction finder. It tells the reader where the story is going and tells you as writer if the topic is properly slanted, sufficiently focused and compelling enough to hold the reader throughout. From the statement of storyline springs all else. *If you can't verbalize it, you won't be able to write the story. Never begin an article without first writing out its storyline. And never use that storyline unless you've tightened and refined it first.*

Often the storyline appears in print as a subtitle or blurb; occasionally it will be the actual lead, appear verbatim within the story or even at or very near the end. It need do none of these. The storyline from the article I wrote on South Africa's Beulah Davis appears here, together with some storylines from articles that made it into print:

> Protecting a multimillion-dollar tourist industry from shark predation is a hazardous but necessary job for the woman South Africans call "The Tiger of the Province."

> Euclid Farnham, tireless president of Vermont's Turnbridge Fair, is no armchair executive. At 68, he's a tireless town father who holds nearly 20 positions in town government, civic and religious organizations and is the unofficial local historian. ("Turnbridge's Euclid Farnham," *Vermont Life*, pp. 65–67, 90–91, by Ann Marie Giroux, Autumn 2002)

> Losing a loved one can break your heart, but it can also open your eyes. ("A Stretch of Hard Road" by Sharon Randall from Scripps Howard News Service, reprinted in *Reader's Digest*, pp. 51–54, October 2001)

> When Elaine Kaufman opened her Second Avenue saloon, all she knew was that her favorite, if not most lucrative, customers were writers and that they kept coming back. Four decades later, Elaine's is still a family of regulars—George Plimpton, Gay Talese and Norman Mailer among them—who've drunk, slugged, and hugged with the high-hearted, ironfisted proprietress. (Subhead or blurb from "Queen of the Night," by A. E. Hotchner, *Vanity Fair*, July 2002, pp. 140–156)

> Bathroom décor may take a backseat when decorating. But with the right setup and thoughtful accessories, your bathroom can be a private sanctuary with endless recreational possibilities. ("Suds and Sensibility," in *O, The Oprah Magazine*, March 2001, pp. 140–41 from *Waterworks: Inventing Bath Styles* by Sallick © 2001 by *Waterworks*, Clarkson Potter/Publishers, published May 2001)

> If your backyard and budget are small yet the kids want to swim on those hot, summer days, an above-ground pool is easily and quickly installed at a cost less than $3,000. ("Rules for Pools" by Fran Donegan, *Popular Mechanics*, June 2002, pp. 116–120)

> If you need to be healthier but don't want to grunt through intense exercises to do so, don't despair. Fitness experts say that the perfect exercise for most people

is just to walk. ("Walk, Don't Run" by Christine Gorman in *Reader's Digest*, June 2002, reprinted from *Time*)

The 1994 California earthquake that scored a direct hit on Santa Monica should have been a seismic near miss, say puzzled scientists. But one UCLA geophysicist says he has the answer—a gigantic curve of bedrock in the area that acts like a giant earthquake lens and focuses seismic waves if hit from the right direction. ("The Case of the Displaced Quake," Fenella Saunders, p. 24, *Discover*, December 2000)

If you expect to find unbeatable bargains and save loads of money the next time you're duty-free shopping in a foreign airport, think again. Although airports worldwide are going to great lengths to improve their shopping facilities—making them larger, friendlier, and more attractive—they aren't offering great bargains anymore. (Lead from "Global guide to duty-free," Peter Frank, pp. 46–52, *Conde Nast Traveler*, June 1996)

HELPFUL EXERCISES

Here's how my Beulah Davis story on shark predation could have been narrowed progressively into focus. The story was triggered by a meeting of the world's premier Sharks and Man Conference in Miami, Fla., and a news story announcing it. Davis was a speaker at the meeting. Attending were commercial fishermen, game and fresh water fish representatives, university scientists, biologists, city managers and others. The conference host was the University of Florida SeaGrant program. From *sharks,* the subject of the meeting—far too broad for a magazine article—I progressively narrowed the topic, first from *predation* to one aspect of predation—*economics* (sharks foul up fishermen's nets, shark bites can cause loss of life, predatory behavior of sharks can frighten off swimmers)—then to a single aspect of economics—*effects of shark bites on tourism*—and finally to a concentration on tourism in one country—*South Africa*—and to *one woman there battling to protect* a multimillion-dollar coastal tourist industry from shark attacks on swimmers.

A reverse triangle, such as the one shown on page 46, illustrates the process of narrowing a topic and bringing it into focus.

1. To begin your own article building, choose a broad topic (e.g., sports, insects, pets, money, farming, senior citizens) that should appeal to a person in your family tree. Bring your topic into focus by building a reverse triangle. The base of the triangle—the bottom line of type—should be a specific item (from the news or from a news release, for example) that's part of the broad topic and deals with an individual, an episode, a situation, or a theme. For example, "Woman Leads Fight to Save South Africa Tourism Industry from Shark Attacks" in the reverse triangles on sharks. The broad topic will appear as a single line of type at the pyramid's crest ("SHARKS"). What will be your article's slant? Which magazine could you query? Write a short description of the magazine's readership. Now prepare a suggested storyline for the article.

S H A R K S

Shark Predation

Economics of Shark Predation (Predation Affects Commercial Fishing, Tourism Industry, etc.)

Tourism Industry Affected by Shark Attacks on Swimmers

South Africa Fights To Save Tourism Industry from Shark Predation

Woman Leads Fight to Save South Africa Tourism Industry from Shark Predation

2. Clip or photocopy two magazine articles of lengths varying from one page to four or five. Make sure the copy is substantial compared to any photo illustration. Include page number(s) and the publication information that appears on the magazine's masthead. Make sure to read each article thoroughly.

    A. Define the focus, slant and storyline for each.

    B. Briefly describe each article's readership.

    C. Suggest another way the same body of information in each article could have been focused.

    D. Suggest a new slant for that information, a readership appropriate to it and match both to a new magazine.

CHAPTER FOUR

GET JOE!

Joe R. is the quintessential fact finder. A freelance writer and photographer who also works under contract, this San Franciscan will go anywhere for a story regardless of personal hardship, will interview anyone, will ask tough but compelling questions to get at the truth and will morph from one assignment to another with apparent ease. Editors like his pinpoint accuracy. Joe will tell you: There's simply no substitute for the footwork of research, fact finding and interviewing. Facts document the article and ground it in reality. In making the general specific, quotes humanize the article, allowing the reader to see and hear real people encountering real-life situations.

But how much information should you gather? Where do you begin? How do you know when to stop? When is the information you've gathered enough? Or even too much?

There's a simple rule in magazine journalism: *Gather three times more than you think you'll need.* Do it for two reasons: First, you won't know initially what you'll need or even where the story may take you. In fact, much of what you'll eventually discard is the material you first gathered—material that oriented you to the subject matter and provided a perspective with which to view it. The second reason is more compelling: Information gathered for one article can also serve as background for a second and sometimes a third. That's money in a freelancer's pocket. In fact, my story on shark-battler Beulah Davis, the South African speaker at the premier Sharks and Man Conference, grew out of the research, fact finding and interviewing I did for another and much larger article for which, thankfully, I *was* paid.

"COMMERCIAL FISHERY FOR SHARKS RECOMMENDED"

"Commercial Fishery for Sharks Recommended" anchored Section B of the March 1976 *National Fisherman*, then as now the bible of the U.S. fishing industry. The heavily researched, multisource story ran three tabloid-size pages. Information to build it came from a variety of sources. The Florida SeaGrant

Program and the Mote Marine Laboratory in Sarasota, Fla., furnished research monographs, journals, advisories and other publications on shark behaviorism and predation. Professional fishing-industry associations and the Florida Marine Fisheries Service supplied statistics and other information on commercial saltwater fishing. News stories being run in area newspapers gave the article *immediacy* and *authority*.

What made the story come alive and jump off the page, however, was not the necessary background information but the quotes I obtained from at least 13 sources—most of them interviewed at the conference. These were people who hailed from one coast to another and from more than one country. By profession, they ranged from tough fishermen and fish marketers to marine biologists, oceanographers and representatives of the Florida and National Marine Fisheries Services. Sources also included Beulah Davis of South Africa, and shark-hide tanners, shark-meat wholesalers and packers of shark meat. Also interviewed were restaurateurs, directors of coastal tourism bureaus and investment bankers.

Did I use all the information I gathered? No. Did I leave some information out? Yes, if it wasn't related to the storyline and slant or wasn't pertinent to readership. How did I deal with information that seemed necessary to include but was peripheral to the story focus? I ran it much smaller, used less of it, and paraphrased. Did I use direct and indirect quotes full length? Never. Did I use everything that was said to me? No.

Judging by the numerous letters to the editor, and some that were forwarded to me as well, "Commercial Fishery for Sharks Recommended" resonated with readership. It garnered favorable reaction not only from those in the fishing, fish processing, food and tourism industries but from fish biologists and from entrepreneurs and investment bankers worldwide. In fact, several of the latter called me from other countries wanting more information on how to start a turnkey operation for shark fishing and processing.

COMMERCIAL FISHERY FOR SHARKS RECOMMENDED:
Methods of Control Debated by Scientists and Fishermen

By Nancy Hamilton

Makos, tigers, lemons, hammerheads—sharks are unsafe, at any speed. Relentless cruisers in temperate and tropical waters, they may nevertheless range as far north as the sub-Arctic.

No one knows the worldwide distribution of sharks—experts estimate there are 250 to 300 species—but an accurate census of shark populations has never been taken.

Some are migratory—the blue shark, an inveterate traveler, cruises 1,000 or more miles annually—others are localized. Despite years of scientific research, so little is known about shark behavior that results of experiments on one species cannot be accurately predicted for another—or even within the same.

But commercial fishermen talk about sharks with certainty. They're big—some as large as a 45' whale. They're unpredictable—one year they're concentrated in one spot, the next year somewhere else. And their hunger is costly to men who make their living from the sea.

"I hate the damn things." Thomas Groover is a one-boat man, a bearded mackerel fisherman operating off Florida's East Coast out of Salerno where—ironically enough—Florida's largest shark rendering plant boomed two decades ago and died when Vitamin A from shark liver oil became synthetically available.

Ordinarily a loquacious man, Groover is flinty-voiced when talking about shark predation on his net and catch. "I've seen schools of mullet with no less than 100 sharks feeding. The water was absolutely bloody. Each fish eaten by a shark causes a hole in the net varying in diameter from 6" to one you could drive a car through."

In a three-day period recently, Groover received 91 holes—about 30 hours mending for two people. At $2 an hour to mend an average shark hole, Groover lost roughly one-third of what an east coast Spanish mackerel fisherman can expect to make in season for three days of fishing with no shark interference.

Thomas (Blue) Fulford, who operates off the Florida Gulf out of Bradenton, takes the larger perspective. "We try to stay as far away from sharks as we possibly can. At times they can destroy $10,000 worth of net—I mean quick, too. If a man is going to get 200 or 300 shark bites, it's not worth it. He won't put out his nets if sharks are plentiful."

SEEK PROTECTION

Groover and Fulford have larger concerns than their personal incomes. Groover is treasurer of the Florida Fishermen's Marketing Association; Fulford, executive secretary of the 1,500-member Organized Fishermen of Florida which represents about 15% of Florida fishermen. Both men want protection from sharks.

"We've been hollering for at least five years," said Fulford. "Do something—give us some repellent. Develop some technology small boats can use. We don't want a bulky apparatus to take up our working room."

Experts from the Mote Marine Laboratory in Sarasota, Fla.; from the National Marine Fisheries Service; the Naval Undersea Center in San Diego; and the University of Miami, Florida, oceanography school, say there are none, although some shrimp trawlers report success with an electrical shark shield device protecting the cod end of the trawl.

Sonic signals, fish extracts, electrical fields, bubble curtains, such chemical dyes as "Shark Chaser" that dissolve too quickly to be effective—all fail to impede a shark attack. Through murky water and clear, in shallows and open sea, the big marine animal slashes at the net with four rows of teeth behind the functional row that constantly roll forward to replace those imbedded in boat—or man.

What the actual impact of sharks is on commercial fishing in Florida and around the United States no one knows. The data is lacking. But, says Douglas Coughenower, marine agent for the Fla. Marine Advisory Program, the problems Florida fishermen encounter with sharks are typical. And fishermen take them for granted.

"If we ask the west coast gillnet fisherman in Florida what his problem

(continued)

CONTINUED

is, he'll say, 'Yes, we encounter sharks.' But he doesn't really consider it a serious problem," says Coughenower. "The shrimp fisherman can always cite stories of sharks attacking his bag. 'It's a problem,' he'll admit, 'but it's been around a long time.' The offshore fishermen—the hook-and-liners after grouper, snapper, king mackerel—sharks will take their fish right off the lines and at the same time remove hooks, maybe line. This loss of gear is a problem."

Coughenower continues, "If a fisherman kept accurate records of shark damage, he might be surprised. I think he's looking at anywhere from $500 to $1,000 a year."

The East Coast Spanish mackerel industry is the hardest hit, Coughenower estimates—a spiraling 40 to 60% increase in costs for fuel and nets. Groover agrees: "I think we're approaching a crisis in mackerel fishing. We're expecting to get 17 cents this year; three years ago, I think we got 20 cents. Why? Because the dealers like to make a little extra profit. They claim their light bills went up, so did the bills for the trucks. The fish houses— their light bills went up, and the cost of ice and hired help is more. Everything," says Groover, "falls right back down on the fisherman. That's the last place to push it off."

MUST TAKE CHANCES

Fulford again takes the wider perspective, discounting shark predation as any worse now than it was 30 years ago. But he believes a fisherman may take more chances with his net when dockside values and landing prices for certain fish increase.

"A man getting 25 cents a pound for his fish," says Fulford, "is not as careful with a $1,000 net than if he were getting only 10 cents."

Matched to the $6.7 billion tourist dollars that poured into Florida in 1974, the dockside value of commercial fishing appears small—close to $100 million, estimates Coughenower, although substantially larger as the fish pass through the marketplace.

But Florida fishermen aren't the only ones complaining about sharks— or fluctuating dockside prices. Michael Snodgrass, owner of Snodgrass Seafoods, operates two shrimp boats out of Brownsville, Tex., wholesales in Houston finfish caught in Mexico and shrimp throughout the United States.

"The winch can wind up only so fast," Snodgrass explains. "You'll be pulling in your nets, you'll see them bulging with shrimp, and all these sharks just ripping the nets to pieces. By the time you get it hoisted on deck you have nothing left." Most of the time, said Snodgrass, the net is repairable. But a three-hour trawl time is lost. "I've never put a price to it before," he admits, "but when you're making three trawls a night, well, that's a third you've lost. That's maybe four boxes of shrimp—400 lbs. at $1.75 per lb."

Snodgrass is less concerned about loss of time than he is about the seasonal economics of shrimping. "Right now, shrimp are a good buy—the highest we've ever had—$3.50 a lb. at top count and we're averaging a little more than $2.25." But, says Snodgrass, Texas shrimping comes almost to a standstill during the winter, and he sends out his shrimp boats on a breakeven proposition simply to keep the crew.

"Last year (1974), we went in the hole so much it just wasn't economically feasible to do even that. The expenses involved in sending out boats have tripled, quadrupled. For a while you couldn't make it regardless," he said.

Fulford finds the market for Florida shrimp similar. "Shrimp has gone into orbit," says Fulford, "lobster and crayfish along with it. People pay $3 a pound without batting an eye." Economists tell him he's getting a good buy. But, says Fulford, expenses have gone up. "We're just thankful the market is there."

EXPERTS GATHER

It was the need for marketing help and for some way to combat shark predation that brought Fulford, Groover, Snodgrass and fishermen and seafood wholesalers from across the nation to a two-day meeting in Orlando, Fla., in November. The Sharks and Man conference—coordinated by the Fla. Sea Grant Marine Advisory Program—drew specialists from the Fla. Dept. of Natural Resources, the National Marine Fisheries Service, Mote Marine Laboratory, Office of Naval Research, Natal (South Africa) Anti-Sharks Measures Board, and the Coastal Plains Center for Marine Development Services, among others. It was the first major gathering between shark behaviorists and commercial fishermen.

There, in a man-bites-dog turnaround, Perry Gilbert of the Mote Marine Laboratory and a prime mover of the conference made a landmark recommendation—commercial fishing should be carried out for sharks to reduce predation not only on nets but on bathing beaches in tourist areas.

"Active commercial fishing for sharks," Gilbert told conferees, "is one of the most practical and economic methods of reducing the shark hazard problem."

It was what Snodgrass wanted to hear. "Shrimp boats could easily be rigged up to catch sharks commercially. I'm sure I could handle a large volume for our 200-mile area around Brownsville, and it would be a big boost to the shrimping industry—something to

supplement our crews' income in the winter."

Fulford agrees. "I wouldn't be surprised if a number of commercial fishermen in Florida would turn to sharks if there was enough money in it. It's something you can do on the side—set your trot lines, then come in and fish your nets."

But shark fishing poses three major problems—the danger that intensive fishing would reduce shark populations to a point no longer commercially profitable, the lack of shark processing plants in the United States and the lack of a domestic market for shark meat.

OVERFISHING POSSIBLE

Would shark fishermen outfish their supply? Population data on migratory and local species is scanty.

Stewart Springer, research associate at the Mote Marine Laboratory and former manager-troubleshooter for the defunct shark rendering plant in Salerno, suggests that a continuing shark fishery depends on members of the principal population of sharks—the breeding population usually in deep waters. Sharks lost from the main population, says Springer, are easier to catch but never sufficiently concentrated to make fishing economically feasible—although the principal population is usually possible for short periods only, because of seasonal movements.

The key to maintaining a volume for successful shark fishing seems to be mobility—following the principal migratory populations, rather than outfishing the inshore species. The problem? Sharks have to be washed, iced, bled and skinned within 24 hours to avoid spoilage—and that frequently means on board.

"If I were to convert to shark fishing," Groover says flatly, "I'd want to bring the dead carcass into the dock, roll

(continued)

CONTINUED

him over on the scales or measurement platform and forget about him. Who wants to go out and fish all day long and spend half the night skinning sharks? You'd have to have too big an operation to start with and a 60', 70' or 80' boat. You're talking about probably $75,000 worth of boat adapted to shark fishing. Most Florida fishermen couldn't afford it."

The operation is not only costly, it's smelly. Dale Beaumariage, chief of the Bureau of Marine Science and Technology in the Fla. Dept. of Natural Resources, suggests a way to alleviate both problems—tow a barge to different points along the coastline, a mobile factory that would move along with the fishery to bait, skin and distribute.

SOME GEARING UP

But some fishermen are already gearing up for shark fishing and onboard processing.

William Bell, a charterboat captain from New Jersey, claims that necessity has forced him into shark fishing. "We ran out of all the other kinds," he says. Preston's boat has been adapted to longline shark fishing, and he buys shark from nearby cod trawlers.

James McGee, a young Gloucesterman, now boat captain and part owner of Universal Impex in Miami—an import-export firm with fisheries in the Dominican Republic and the United States—expects soon to be captaining the ultimate—a 78' aluminum longliner which, says McGee, is uniquely designed for shark fishing and equipped with a high-powered winch.

This "floating office" will be joined 90 days later, says McGee, by a 47' vessel, allowing Universal Impex to keep its snapper, grouper and lobster operations separate.

"The vessels are equipped to freeze 225,000 lbs.," McGee explains. "We'll be laying some 30 miles of longline daily, from Port Canaveral down to the Orinoco River delta in Venezuela." The firm currently markets shark teeth and hides in the United States and fins for sharkfin soup in Hong Kong. Meat is exported to South America and Europe through the West Indies and will represent the primary function of both new vessels.

Both McGee and Bell are trying to develop a domestic market for shark meat. McGee estimates that shark meat now brings about half the price of snapper and grouper, but the volume per fish is three or four times larger. Shark specialists say that a shark weighing about 500 lbs. draws about 150 lbs. of usable meat, two-and-one-half pounds of dried fins and 100 lbs. of usable liver.

But the filleted meat yield is not as great as one might expect, averaging about 33% of total body weight. Bell, who currently sells shark meat through a broker to a company in France, is emphatic: "The United States is the only country throwing it away. The problem is, you have to acclimate people to the taste of shark meat."

WASTE EVALUATED

Shark experts estimate the probable value of shark products now being discarded daily by the swordfish fishery in the Southeastern United States is $737 in the Gulf and $362 along the Atlantic Coast. And in 1973, according to the "FAO Fisheries Statistics Yearbook," the United States caught only 500 metric tons of shark as compared to Japan, the leader in world shark fisheries, with 40,600 metric tons.

Why are Americans ignoring it? Used as crab or lobster bait, often discarded by fishermen, if sold to the consumer at under $1 per pound, shark meat is a relatively cheap, fat-free, high-protein source of meat. The protein in a skinned shark is estimated at slightly more than 22% wet weight—nearly on a par with snapper, grouper and mackerel.

In Panama and Mexico, the production and sale of dry, salted fillets—known as **bacalao** and similar to smoked fish—is a thriving industry. Shark fillets grace the tables of European restaurants, often under a variety of names. Dogfish and sand shark comprise the fish in the classic English "fish 'n chips," and sharkfin soup—an Oriental delicacy—not only appears 12,000 miles away in Hong Kong but—ironically enough considering its U.S. origin—reappears as a gourmet delicacy in the finest New York and San Francisco restaurants.

Americans, apparently, are less concerned with protein-power than they are with the mystical energy that accrues from wearing a shark-tooth amulet.

But in the afterwave of publicity from Peter Benchley's bestseller "Jaws" and the graphic movie of the same name, there are hints that shark meat is catching the public taste. Unconfirmed rumors say at least three fast-food chains are test-marketing shark meat in their fish sandwiches.

In New Orleans, seafood wholesaler Preston Battistella this year has sold roughly 75,000 lbs. of finished shark meat to New Orleans and out-of-state restaurants—about 200,000 lbs. of shark in the rough. Battistella is also supplying New Orleans public school lunch programs with 25,000 lbs. of breaded shark fillets. Battistella is emphatic. He wants more shark meat—and he wants U.S. fishermen to supply it.

SMALL FISH PREFERRED

But Battistella, like most seafood wholesalers, wants the smaller, tastier sharks 5' or less in length. And this presents the commercial fisherman with a dilemma—the larger the shark, the better return on his investment. Marketing specialists agree that virtually the whole shark is useful—hide, waste for bait, flesh, fins, jaws, teeth and—in some limited markets—liver oil. The cartilage and offal can be ground into fish meal for cattle, whose systems can absorb the nonprotein urea nitrogen remaining, or used as fertilizer.

But can fishermen find a processor who will handle all parts of the shark at fair prices?

James Heerin is president of Sea Farms in Key West, Florida's last operating shark fishery, now temporarily defunct due, says Heerin, "to a number of economic factors. We made it a policy," he reports, "to buy the whole shark or none in order to discourage fishermen from selling us only the hide and meat and trying to market the fins and teeth themselves. Since the meat and liver oil were and still are weak markets," Heerin explains, "we had to have all the potential products available in order to make the operation worthwhile."

Heerin purchased sharks from the boats on the basis of length and species. An efficient shark fisherman today, says Heerin, could expect an average catch rate of 10% of his hooks, or 40 sharks on a 400-hook line. "Most of our fishermen," he adds, "ran two lines." If the sharks average 8' long and are in good condition, the value of a day's catch to the fisherman would be about $345.

RIG-UP COSTS

Against this income, Heerin details probable expenses: a $1,700 winch, 4,000' of main cable at $1,400 per line, 2,400' drop cable at $600 per line, 400 swivel snaps at $240 per line and 400 hooks at $160 per line with an additional $160 for spare hooks. Costs for bait, fuel

(continued)

CONTINUED

and supplies per 10-hour trip Heerin averages at $100.

Processing sharks is not only messy and tedious but, ways [*sic*] Heerin, presents other problems. "Good shark skinners and flensers are difficult to find. You have to maintain safety and health regulations, and you need a sufficient volume of sharks—and a market—to maintain a steady work force." Most sewage systems will not handle shark waste disposal, and Sea Farms barged it back to sea and dumped it.

Heerin admits transportation was a thorn in his side. Hides had to be shipped soon after bagging in burlap sacks, but many truckers found the smelly moisture from the hides offensive.

With the demise of Sea Farms, there may be only one market for all parts of the shark—Ocean Leather in Newark, N.J., a 50-year-old tannery more in the market for hides than for the fins, meat and liver which it quietly handles as a service to some fishermen.

"It's very difficult to keep track of these other things," admits Chuck Waldes, supervisor of hide purchasing for Ocean Leather. "You don't like to invest your capital and your staff to move it. They generate revenue but," he says, "it's mostly a breakeven proposition to us."

The 600-man tannery sells all of its leather domestically. "Our demand is larger than we can supply," Waldes explains, "and naturally we will do everything possible in order to make sure the fisherman stays in business."

But Ocean Leather buys only large sharks, whose meat is not preferable for consumption—tiger, leopard, dusky, lemon, bull, nurse, valador, sand.

The skinned hide is measured from along the backbone directly above the center of the anal fins. Hide prices are firm, says Waldes—$2.50 to $12 base "to begin a relationship." The tanned leather—tough but supple and virtually scuff-proof—is sold by the square foot for high-priced belts, wallets, luggage, shoes and boots.

But Waldes—like Bell and McGee—would like to develop a domestic market for shark meat. Currently he sells his meat in France for 25 cents per lb.—claims a domestic outlet such as Battistella's would net him 15 cents more per pound.

McGee's Universal Impex operation receives 20 to 26 cents per lb. for shark meat through foreign outlets, about $3.50 per lb. for dried and salted fins and about $40 per lb. of shark teeth. But other estimates of current prices vary: some report an average 10 cents per lb. for eviscerated shark and $1.30 per lb. for fins.

With the weak domestic market for shark meat, the larger dilemma is not whether to fish for the hides or to fish for the meat, but whether to fish for sharks at all. Marine Advisory Agent Coughenower, who still has reservations that fishing pressure might reduce the shark population to an economically unsustainable yield, suggests a net insurance program to offset major losses and that fish prices be stable and realistic.

From the Mote Marine Laboratory, Perry Gilbert recommends that shark fishing be coupled with a subsidy. And others suggest that the tourist industry—particularly in such coastal resort states as Florida where bathing pressure is greatest—should share the cost of shark fishing to reduce the hazards of attack.

Essentially it's a public relations problem—educating the public to accept shark meat as a good source, convincing private enterprise that a fishery is feasible. But it takes capital, know-how, quality control and a fishery itself to start a processing plant, and few seem willing to invest that without an assured market.

John Moore, a New York City investment banker whose firm has prepared a study of the commercial shark fishing industry for less-developed countries, suggests the private sector in the United States should assume another role—entrepreneur and advisor, exporting shark fishing technology to improve the balance of payments in under-developed nations and to help satisfy their protein requirements.

Moore's "turnkey" plant—complete when handed over to the plant operator—would require approximately six months to construct, two boats for fishing and a third for bait and would use mostly unskilled or semi-skilled, local labor except for professional captains brought in to operate the boats.

The cost? About $600,000 to $750,000, Moore estimates.

"Practically all that can be leveraged out or financed on a governmental basis or through one of the development banks," he explains, "either in the country involved or through one of the international development banks."

Moore admits it's a risky venture, not unlike U.S. interests in oil-developing countries. "Sooner or later, even with 100% ownership, the country is going to require local participation." Moore advises that either government or a local fishing cooperative be a partner in the venture from the outset.

But, he adds, "It's not capital-intensive. You don't have to pump in $3 to $5 million to get a good return on your investment."

Many commercial fishermen in the United States would quibble with Moore's suggestion. Why export the fishing technology? If private enterprise can do all that for another country—why not for their own?

SIMPLE GUIDELINES FOR RESEARCHING, INTERVIEWING, WRITING

Before scheduling interviews, you'll need some background information to develop perspective on your topic. I generally start my fact finding with reference works and sources leading to them. These might include the following:

■ The U.S. Government issues a monthly Selected List of U.S. Government Publications from which you can purchase pamphlets, publications, video and audio files on subjects ranging from home gardening to coin collecting to health, plumbing and hydroponics. To order the list and the monthly catalog of U.S. Public Documents, go to the U.S. Government Online Bookstore at http://bookstore.gpo.gov. In addition, check the U.S. Government Organizational Manual—your library should stock it—for a list of agencies that might have additional material relevant to your article.

■ Uncle Sam's Reference Shelf, officially known as the *Statistical Abstracts of the United States* and also available on CD-ROM, is a national data book that contains statistics on economic and social conditions in the United States. See www.census.gov/statab. The abstracts also can be found in your library's reference section. In addition, check www.statistics.com. This is another good source of statistics, most of these posted from the government and other public sources.

■ Check out the U.S. Census Bureau's Online Shopping Center for information on education, housing, business, foreign trade, geography, people, and so on. Go to www.census.gov and click on Catalog Home.

■ Created by an act of Congress, The U.S. Small Business Administration (SBA) operates in local areas to offer financing, training and advocacy workshops for new business start-ups. Contact the local office through the yellow pages of your phone book or through the national SBA web site, www.sba.gov.

■ The U.S. Chamber of Commerce can be accessed through www.us chamber.org. You also can contact local Chambers of Commerce and various state agencies such as those concerned with development, travel and tourism, conservation and natural resources, parks and recreation, labor and transportation.

■ Almanacs, atlases and encyclopedias provide instant facts in brief on a variety of topics. Typical of the almanacs are *The World Almanac* and the current year's *Information Please Almanac*. However, you can find a wider range of almanacs on topics as diverse as farming, sports and spousal abuse simply by going online to www.infoplease.com. You'll also find an atlas and an encyclopedia there. Don't forget to check road atlases and road maps, gazetteers and publications of the various national and regional offices of the American Automobile Association (AAA). Encyclopedias often provide initial information in a bit more depth. Find most of these on CD-ROM in your library. In addition, www.britannica.com not only offers the full text of the *Encyclopedia Britannica* online but allows you to read the first sentences of each article without charge. (There's a monthly fee if you want to access the full text.) The Britannica web site can guide you to other Internet resources in your subject area. You'll find such goodies as video and audio clips and a thesaurus.

■ For what's been written on your topic, check out *Books in Print,* a listing of books by author, subject and title. Your reference librarian has it on computer. So do bookstores.

■ *Reader's Guide to Periodical Literature.* Found as a reference book in the library, it's also available on a CD-ROM database. Updated monthly, *Reader's Guide* will give you a good idea of what's being written on your topic by major magazines. Also helpful are indexes such as the *Index to Periodical Literature, Standard Periodical Directory, Magazine Subject Index* and various specialized indexes found in the library.

■ For a general reference, try www.researchville.com. Researchville lets you search multiple sources simultaneously with just one query. The University of Michigan Internet Public Library site is also valuable. It provides links to other reference materials through www.ipl.org.

■ Medical information can be found at www.intelihealth.com and at www.mayoclinic.com. For queries on brand-name and generic pharmaceutical drugs, try the U.S. government's www.nlm.nih.gov/medline/plus/drug information.html and the nongovernmental web site www.rxlist.com.

■ For biographies, try these books: *Current Biographies, Webster's Biographical Dictionary* and the *Dictionary of American Biography.* Also check out *Who's Who,* a very helpful series of biographical books broken down by region, country and topic; for example, *Who's Who in Medicine.* Online, there's www.biography. com which provides a wealth of articles on living and historical figures.

■ Northern Light, at www.northernlight.com, is a Web-only collection of individual articles, most of which were published in newspapers and in the lesser-known magazines. Anyone can read the abstracts of these articles, but to read the full text you must become a paid subscriber.

■ The *New York Times* Article Archive and the *Wall Street Journal* index are indexed issues of news stories run by both these daily papers. Except for current issues in the library's reading room, you'll find the stories either on microfilm, microfiche or through computer access. Don't forget to check out your local newspaper's library as well.

■ Check to see if your library provides access to a CD-ROM system that stores articles full text or in abstract that were published in hundreds of newspapers, magazines and journals. Nearly 5,000 databases of articles ranging from Native American issues to those in the biological sciences are stored on such a system. Choose the one you want.

■ A major online service, www.lexis-nexis.com, available through your library, allows you to quickly access articles in full text plus the complete transcripts of broadcast news stories. In addition, www.dialog.com will put you in touch with hundreds of databases covering a full range of subject areas.

■ Also see *Facts on File: A Weekly News Digest*

■ Want to know how something works? Check out the handy online source www. howstuffworks.com. If it's a gasoline engine you're after or a process such as heating with a flat-plate solar collector, HowStuffWorks will provide you with descriptions, photos and diagrams for more than 2,500 different entries.

■ If you've encountered an acronym, abbreviation or set of initials you can't decipher, try finding the explanation at www.acronymfinder.com. This web site provides more than 242,000 definitions. If a technology-related query, you're better off consulting TechEncyclopedia's www.techweb.com/encyclopedia. You'll find definitions here of more than 20,000 items.

Directories can point the way for you. Check out these:

■ *Chase's Calendar of Events* lists more than 12,000 events by day, week and month.

■ Available online and on CD-ROM, *Gayle's Directory of Associations* has a database of more than 35,000 association records. The database for Associations Unlimited is also valuable. It can be accessed through the online library resources of many universities.

■ *Standard Rate and Data Service volumes* for the various news media contain advertising rates and other publishing data.

■ *The Foundation Directory,* listing more than 41,000 foundations that make grants. See also the online edition at www.fconline.fdncenter.org.

■ *Standard and Poor's Register of Corporations, Directors and Executives.* Remember that companies, trade associations and manufacturers can provide you a wealth of information through their public relations and public affairs arms.

■ The *Thomas Register* lists specific manufacturers and can be accessed at www.thomasregister.com. Look up European manufacturers at www.tremnet. com.

■ *Standard Directory of Advertisers.* See also the American Advertising Federation web site at www.aaf.org for its governmental affairs publications, news bites sections and news of its legislative activity. Access the Public Relations Society of America (PRSA) through its web site at www.prsa.org.

■ *Editor and Publisher International Yearbook,* with its encyclopedic listing of all dailies worldwide, as well as North American weeklies, is the bible for the newspaper industry.

THE INTERVIEW

Use common sense when conducting an interview. Make an appointment first, be on time and avoid scheduling a session right before lunch or late in the afternoon right before quitting time, when your source may rush the interview. Allow your source a few days to prep: This gives him or her time to think about the topic and to gather materials that may be helpful to you. Don't go into an interview cold: Know something about the topic. Know why this individual's comments are important to it. Know something about your source by talking with people who know him or her. Make sure you know the full name and proper title of your source. Dress appropriate to the setting and occasion. Your clothes, your attitude, even the items you carry should not fight with your surroundings, overwhelm your source or compete for attention. Let nothing distract from your mission. Make sure to get your source's work and home telephone numbers: You'll need them when it comes to verifying of clarifying information in your notes.

The choice of interview site may be as crucial as the time of day. Interviewing sources on their own turf can yield valuable background information and reveal give-and-take between sources and those around them. At the same time, on-site interviews hand power to your sources. More relaxed, mutually agreed-on sites such as a conference room, garden or restaurant may loosen tongues and yield more information; they also neutralize a source's power. Hint: If the source offers to pay for coffee or lunch, politely decline; you dare not compromise your objectivity by taking favors. If the situation dictates that you must consume something, eat very lightly.

Go into the interview armed with a written list of crucial questions to which you know you need answers. Ask these—but listen closely and be alert to answers that may suggest questions you hadn't even thought of. In the course of conversation, a source often digresses to reveal more about an issue than you were aware. Follow up on this new information by mentally formulating additional questions as the source is talking. If he or she digresses into clearly unrelated terrain, gently ask another question to pull the source back to the issue at hand. Keep good eye contact during the interview: It's both encouraging to conversation and nonthreatening. Use words such as "Yes," "I see," and even "um-hmm" to keep the source talking during those moments of note taking when you can't look up. An article needs what writer Jimmy Stewart (see p. 61) calls "flesh and bones."

Most stories benefit when you take the time to build people *round*, or in depth. During the interview, look for anecdotes that reveal something about the source, pay attention to the surroundings, listen to the way a source speaks and observe how he or she interacts with others. Do some scene sketching when you write, the better to build reader identity. (See Chapter 10 on personality profiles.)

How you ask questions during an interview and the order in which you ask them can influence the response you get. Ask only single-item questions, and keep them short. A source asked to respond to two questions in a single sentence gives a single response only—usually to the last item or the easiest question. Begging the question—"You don't want that smelly fish, do you?"—bags a dishonest response: The source tells you what he or she thinks you want to hear. Try to ask open-ended questions. The alternative—yes-no questions—can stop an interview: The source answers "yes" or "no" without elaborating. Immediately follow a yes-no answer with, "Would you explain that?"

Interviews can end abruptly or the source cease to cooperate if controversial questions are asked too early in the session: Establish rapport first with milder questions that ask for a factual response. Says Al Tompkins, faculty member at The Poynter Institute: "Subjective questions usually begin with phrases such as 'Why . . . ,' 'Tell me more about . . . ,' or 'Would you explain. . . .' Objective questions produce factual information. . . ." (From "The Art of the Interview" by Al Tompkins, Fall 2002 *Poynter Report,* pp. 21–22.) For example, "How many people died in car accidents last year?" is a factual question. Decide the purpose of your interview and tailor the phrasing of your questions accordingly.

To avoid getting only a formula reply, Tompkins suggests using silence. Look a little puzzled, he says, as if you don't quite understand the canned response. Then wait silently. The person you're interviewing is likely to jump in with a clarified statement that is much better than the first one. And here's a trick I've used often to get a source to elaborate on a comment: I feign ignorance and surprise. "Oh—really? I had no idea. How (interesting, courageous, noble, kind, etc.)."

The insider's secret to asking good questions may be this advice from Tompkins: Choose a word or phrase your source used, then use the word yourself in asking the next question. For example, had one of the businessmen I interviewed for the *National Fisherman* story described commercial shark fishing as a "sweetheart deal," my follow-up question would have been, "What do you mean by a 'sweetheart deal'?"

If the interview leads you into a sensitive area, ease into it with questions that are delicately worded. Perhaps you'll even want to ask permission to discuss it at that point. Remember that interviews are neither adversarial nor confrontational: Keep them objective. Don't inject your personal feelings and biases nor react belligerently if you don't agree with a response. Should a source refuse to cooperate when you're trying to set up the interview or is hostile to questions during it, remind the person that your article has to cover both sides of the situation and just how essential his or her viewpoint is. Tell the source that this would be an opportunity to set the record straight. You should think of the interview as *relationship building.* Be polite. Be conversational. Establish rapport by mentioning some things you and your source may have in common. Get the source to relax.

When interviewing, use a tape recorder only if absolutely necessary and then, only if your note taking accompanies it. Rely on your notebook; transcription of tapes is time-consuming. Some interview sources are uncomfortable being recorded; ask permission first. Tapes sometimes snarl or break in the middle of an interview, too. Furthermore, use of a tape recorder can lull you into a false sense of security. How? The mind reasons that if it's all on tape, why should you bother to clarify a fact you may not understand or ask the burning question you would have asked as follow-up? When I tape an interview, I find a notebook helpful in another way: I annotate the notes as I go along, underlining an important fact or direct quote, placing a checkmark in the margin next to it along with the recorder counter number. This allows me to note which facts are essential to the article and to retrieve a quote immediately when transcribing.

Be aware: Often the best comments come just as you've put away your notebook and turned off your tape recorder. It's logical—your source is now more relaxed. When that happens, store the information in your mental file bank. Back in your car, your office or residence, quickly jot down or tape those last-minute comments. While the interview is still fresh, type all of your hand-written notes, transcribe your tapes or take notes from them as you replay the interview. Hint: It's always best to keep your tape recorder running until you've left the interview.

Did your source intend those last comments to be *off the record*? Was anything said about it? If not, that material, like the rest of the interview, is yours to use. Avoid getting into an off-the-record situation. If you agree to it, the material obtained can't be used in the article. Better to thank the source for his or her time, terminate the session and find someone else who can furnish the material and comments you need. *Remember the rule of the game: A source who agrees to the interview and doesn't say "off the record" automatically agrees to it being printed.* If a source tells you at the conclusion of an interview that it was all off the record, you are not bound to comply.

Don't throw away your notes. If there is a problem pre- or postpublication from editor or readership, if you don't understand a particular quote or a source denies saying something, your notes give you the ability to recheck or rebut. Keep them for a year or more after publication. Don't just file away your notes: It's too easy to lose or misplace them. Instead, categorize what you compile *as you compile it* by data heading (e.g., fishnet holes or Blue's quotes), source, date obtained, file heading (fishermen complaints) and location of file. Your computerized master sheet will look something like a bookkeeping spreadsheet. Thanks to my master sheet, I was able to rebut a reader's angry complaint that I incorrectly interpreted statistics and some State Department information in the investigative article I wrote on migrant agricultural labor for the Washington monthly, *Washington Scene.* My rebuttal became a second article, and I was paid for that as well.

WRITER SAYS E-MAIL, INTERNET RESEARCH, CRUCIAL

E-mailed interviews are also an option. A word of warning: They're blind. E-mail can't substitute for your eyes and give you those valuable, visual clues to a person's character, personality or surroundings so useful in a personality profile. In addition, you can't be absolutely sure that the person you've e-mailed is the same person responding. Rely on e-mail for nonemotional, noncontroversial material. Use it to make initial contacts, set up interviews, seek basic information and do interview follow-ups.

Writer Jimmy Stewart finds e-mail and the Internet indispensable. Stewart, managing editor of *Charisma & Christian Life*—an independent, non-denominational consumer magazine with a worldwide circulation base of

Jimmy Stewart

more than 225,000—entered an epic, seven-page, heavily researched article on Goth culture in the 2002 Florida Magazine Association's annual Charlie Awards competition. He won second place. The assignment to produce the article began during an editorial meeting. Board members, deciding the magazine needed stories that would engage with pop and underground culture, handed Stewart a nearly impossible task: Debunk for our readers the myth that all Goths are part of a brooding, Marilyn Manson–Columbine youth cult. Write a story exploring this dark side of youth culture. Let *Charisma* readers discover Goth music, literature and culture through the words of the Goths themselves. (The name *Goths* is a take-off on the first-century barbaric group known as Visigoths, the first independent, barbaric nation within the Roman Empire. Contemporary Goths defy any resemblance to that group.)

Sink or Swim

It was a sink-or-swim situation for Stewart, 48, who was "fairly clueless about Goths." He had to learn fast. He had no solid information, no real leads, just a few names of people he had never met and a single e-mail address. "I started out with a seed," he said, "that's all." Who were these Goths? Why did they live on the fringes of society, dress in black leather and heavy metal T-shirts, chains and spikes? Were they believers? Satanists? Followers of the Antichrist? Neopagans? Stewart would soon find out. He began to gather information, to develop and pursue leads. The journey would take him four to five months.

"I spent a lot of hours on the Web," he said, "using it much as I would a library. There were literally hundreds of web sites dealing with Goth culture." Since Stewart believes sources on the Internet to be "faulty at best," he had to weed out sites that contained misleading or inaccurate information or information authored by people who couldn't be verified or authenticated. At least 50 sites remained usable, and some of those were linked to others. Over time, he winnowed the usable ones to three.

Would They Cooperate?

Forewarned that the Goth community was closed to outsiders, Stewart expected to encounter suspicion. He turned to e-mail for his initial contacts, hoping to set up in-person interviews, some of them on-site. He sent e-mail

GOD IN A TEXAS BARRIO • PERSECUTED CHRISTIANS IN FRANCE • APOLOGIZING TO JEWS

The Magazine About Spirit-Led Living

Charisma

& CHRISTIAN LIFE

www.charismamag.com

A TRUE CHAMPION, PAGE 64

August 2001 • $3.95

Don't Be Afraid of the Goths

They love black clothes, black lipstick and dark music. Who will take the gospel to America's Goth culture?
PAGE 38

U.S. $3.95   Canada $5.99

08

0 74470 92374 9

Members of the Goth community in Northampton, Massachusetts

letters to those thought to have a Christian ministry to Goths and to individual Goths themselves, both Christian and non-Christian. He was, said his e-mail letters, trying to conduct interviews with those who "would be willing to be interviewed and quoted in print as to their views of being a Goth in modern society and how they are treated by Christians or by the mainstream church in general, and how you believe that should change." Included with the initial e-mail were 20 questions he asked to have answered, together with a request to quote the person in the *Charisma* article.

■ ■ ■ ■ ■ ▬▬▬▬▬▬▬▬▬▬▬▬▬▬▬▬▬▬▬▬▬▬▬▬▬▬▬▬▬▬▬▬

STEWART'S 20 QUESTIONS

1. How long have you been a Goth?
2. What prompted you to embrace the gothic culture, as opposed to another culture?
3. Do you enjoy Goth music? Favorite bands, styles?
4. Do you enjoy other kinds of music? Favorite bands, styles?
5. Favorite books, magazines, TV shows, movies?
6. What are some of your favorite "Goth-like" things to do? (Sorry if this sounds trite or corny. Just wondering if there are specific things you enjoy doing that you'd consider to be more gothic than other things.)
7. Is there anything in particular about your appearance that would let others know you are a Goth? (Again, sorry if this seems like a stereotypical question. It's not meant to be. In making a few Goth friends, I've learned that some of them enjoy having either more or less of a "Gothic look" than others.)
8. Do you believe Goths are stereotyped by mainstream culture; i.e., by the media, by religious groups, by other groups?
9. If so, what is or are the most common stereotype(s) you encounter as a Goth? (These could be ones that are applied to Goths in general or ones you've experienced individually.)
10. Would you agree or disagree that any of the stereotypes are valid?
11. Do you consider Marilyn Manson to be a Goth? If not, why not?
12. Do you believe there are core reasons or common reasons why people embrace the Gothic culture?
13. How are you generally treated by people who are not Goths?
14. Do you know any Christians or have you encountered any Christians since you've been a Goth?
15. If so, have you been treated differently (as a Goth) by them than by people who don't call themselves Christians?
16. Do you consider yourself to be a Christian?
17. Have you ever met Goths who profess to worship Satan or who practice black magic or occultic arts?
18. Do you know any Goths who are into vampirism, and if so, have you ever met any who drank blood ritualistically?
19. Is there anything in particular that you'd like non-Goth people to know about being a Goth?
20. Are there ways that Christians can improve in the way they treat Goths or think about Gothic culture?

BRIEF WRAP-UP QUESTIONS

1. May I quote you in my story?
2. Do you have a Goth nickname you go by or like being called by? How would you like to be identified in the story (name)?
3. May I use your last name and age in the story, city/state or occupation? Thank you!

Responses to his e-mail request were favorable. Elated, Stewart knew it was time to immerse himself in Goth culture. "I had to have a live, visual experience," he said. "I was dealing with a worldwide youth counterculture movement that had been around since the late 1970s. It had a well-established history and a dark image somewhat similar to a Renaissance/vampire culture with a Bella Lugosi visualization." Somehow, Stewart had to present enough of that history to allow his readers to identify with members of the Goth movement. He began to schedule interviews.

Dressed entirely in black to blend into their surroundings, he waited.

It was night when they met him. Wearing fishnet and black leather, dark capes and dog collars and walking in high lace-up boots, they appeared to Stewart more suicidal than homicidal despite their tattoos and heavy unisex makeup. They spoke with him where they frequented—in fringe churches and on dark, dimly lit street corners in California; in the bars, clubs and back alleys of South Florida; and in the dark recesses of a Goth bar in Boston so noisy that Stewart couldn't use a tape recorder and had to conduct interviews outside, in below-freezing temperature. "My fingers became too numb to hold a pencil," he recalled. A further interview, conducted by telephone to a Goth in New Zealand, yielded additional information.

Eventually, Stewart developed 25 usable sources—most of whom he interviewed—directly quoted 16 of them in the article and compiled copious notes. However, the size of the feature "well" for his story permitted only 2,800 words. In what Stewart now recalls as "a long weekend without sleep," he wrote and edited the entire story on deadline, ruthlessly downsizing his first 6,000-word draft by slicing away every redundancy and every bit of information, every quote, every word and every comma not entirely essential to his storyline.

■ ■ ■ ■ ■

DON'T BE AFRAID OF THE DARK

By Jimmy Stewart

A young woman is checking IDs on a Saturday night outside the Kitchen Club in Miami. In the glow of moonlight, her wan face radiates against the coal black of her lips, eyeliner, hair and clothing. Darkly accented patrons drift by her to be frisked before vanishing into this Goth club situated along a main street of the tropical city.

Everywhere inside the cave-like club there is black—on the floors, the walls, the ceilings. Jet black clothing shrouds hundreds of Gothic allies of the night who are here after midnight. They are adorned in capes, hoods, wings, spikes and chains or veiled with leather, lace, wool, fishnet, vinyl and velvet.

A young man and woman—slim, androgynous and decorated by huge shimmering fairy wings on their backs—glide like a pair of Gothic pixies along a twisting bar tempered by dim ruby light and draped with scarlet curtains. Beyond, it's so dark you can't see your feet.

(continued)

CONTINUED

Wham! wham! wham! goes a strobe light against the eyes, stabbing the blackness of the dance floor with thrusts of white. Figures caught in its eerie flash go jerking by—appearing, vanishing, reappearing.

"The bats have left the bell tower / The victims have been bled / Red velvet lines the black box / Bela Lugosi's dead / Undead! Undead! Undead!" cries a song from the P.A.

Like one fluid form, a black mass of people move to the music in a dramatic underworld exhibition of how the "dead" can dance.

A young woman snakes with arms held high in the ethereal atmosphere. Black lace-up boots reach above her knees, and she wears a shiny black-vinyl miniskirt. She is shirtless, and only black tape shaped like *Blair Witch* crosses covers a scant portion of her upper torso. Nearby, a young man dances in a tight black skirt that hugs down to his ankles, and a woman in a black top and clear miniskirt pushes through the crowd.

Wham! wham! wham! against the senses goes the unceasing strobe, and the music cries again above the macabre regale: "The virginal brides file past his tomb / Alone in a darkened room / Oh, Bela / Bela's undead!" [*sic*]

CELEBRATING DARKNESS

If you think the kind of Saturday night fever found in Miami's Kitchen Club is uncommon, guess again. From Bondage A-Go-Go in San Francisco to Straightjacket in New York City to Release the Bats in Germany to The Blood Coven Bar in Brazil—similar scenes are everywhere.

Welcome to Goth culture.

Today, students from the country's most elite universities gather at Goth nights called "The Crypt" and "The Fuse" in Cambridge, Massachusetts, in the sprawling ManRay Club only a few blocks from Harvard and MIT. They hang out below a giant mural of bats that covers an entire wall lit by black lights.

They dance to Gothic, industrial and synthpop music within spiderweb partitions made of chains. They shoot pool and drink while bloody vampire movies play on ceiling-mounted televisions.

Such clubs are a fixture—but only one—of the subterranean Goth culture that has emerged in the United States in recent years. Goths tend to see beauty in what society considers morbid—a pallid look, skull and skeleton designs, coffins, graveyards. Their tastes lie outside the mainstream—and that's how they like it.

Beyond the glint and glare of everyday society the Goth subculture has spawned its own music, arts, fashion and distinctly alternative way of thinking. Since the 1970s, "Gothdom" has grown from its British grassroots into an international taproot for counterculture youth.

Bands old and new such as Christian Death, London After Midnight, The Electric Hellfire Club, Alien Sex Fiend and many others power the important musical side of the scene. They can be found in assorted record stores or in extensive catalogs such as the U.K.'s Nightbreed Recordings.

Contemporary novelists Anne Rice (*Interview With the Vampire*) and Poppy Z. Brite (*Lost Souls*) as well as 19th century dark muser Edgar Allan Poe are but a few literary favorites. Some Goths prefer comic-book series, such as The Sandman (Neil Gaiman) or Johnny the Homicidal Maniac (Jhonen Vasquez).

Gothic films hawking the imagery abound: *The Crow, The Nightmare Before Christmas, The Cabinet of Dr. Caligari, Nos-*

feratu the Vampire (1922) and a slew of other vampire films. A staggering Gothic network exists on the Internet with newsgroups, listservs and chat rooms.

You might spot Goths by their dress—a classical Renaissance style with elaborate medieval-style shirts, gowns and topcoats—clothing that many of them make themselves—or the sharper-edged look of vinyl, PVC polymer, latex, or black leather fixed with metal studs or spikes. At The Inkubus Haberdashery in Miami's eclectic Coconut Grove district you can pay $300 for a black trench coat made of PVC, $120 for a latex miniskirt, or $200 for a fierce-looking "armor" ring of silver and turquoise shaped like a talon.

Today's Goths, who generally tend to be in their teens and 20s, have nothing to do with the Germanic Visigoths of Europe in the third and fourth centuries A.D.

Instead, they derive their cultural identity from bands such as Bauhaus, Siouxsie and the Banshees, The (Southern Death) Cult, The Cure, Ministry, and Sisters of Mercy, some of whom revolved around London's Batcave Club during the late 1970s and early 1980s. These musicians launched what became known as a "darquewave" musical style that originated in punk music but stood out as a campy response to the happy image of disco that was popular at the time.

British band Bauhaus, named for the German architectural design school whose credo was "less is more," is considered a progenitor of the subculture. Formed in Northampton, England, in 1978, Bauhaus debuted in 1979 with its spooky single, "Bela Lugosi's Dead," and the gaunt atmospheric guitars and creepy Buddy Holly-like vocals raised a generation out of the shadows.

Says Todd Mayville, 36, of Northampton, Massachusetts, a high-school teacher who's been a Goth since 1984:

"In college I saw David Bowie's The Hunger, and it opens up with Bauhaus singing 'Bela Lugosi's Dead,' and I just got chills. I was like: 'Oh, what is this music? I need to have all of it!' "

WHO ARE THESE PEOPLE?
The growth of the Goth movement in the last two decades has spawned a few misconceptions and misguided stereotypes—specifically, that the Columbine killers were Goths, that Goths worship Satan and that they all believe they're "vampires" who must drink blood.

Goths bristle when it's suggested they hold the same beliefs that prompted the killing spree at Columbine High School in Littleton, Colorado, in April 1999. Anders Mar, an administrative assistant in his 20s who lives in Portland, Maine, blames the stereotypes on posers who don't authentically represent the subculture.

"I can speak for the true Goth population as a whole: The fact that these fakes have ruined our good name is a source of great anger to us," he says.

"Each group has its bad seeds," says Seth Gooch, 24, of Kalamazoo, Michigan. "Columbine doesn't represent Goths as a whole."

"We've really gotten a bad rap because of the Columbine massacre," says Julie Peterson, 29, of Madison, Wisconsin. "Those who don't conform are stereotyped as bad."

David Hart, 51, a former concert promoter in Southern California for Christian artists ranging from Amy Grant to Stryper, has been a pastor to Goths in San Diego for close to 15 years. He says they are more likely to be passive and artistic than aggressive, more the type to sit in a room with candles and talk about literature.

"Their parents tend to be the opposite," Hart says. "Goths tend to come from homes of two-career parents who

(continued)

CONTINUED

Churches on The Edge

Three unique pastors are reaching Goths for Jesus.

With his 6-foot-1-inch, 295-pound frame topped by purple hair, tattoos and facial piercings, Steve "Pastor Freak" Bensinger, 41, couldn't look less like your everyday pastor—except maybe when he's also behind the wheel of the black 1985 Cadillac Hearse he drives.

"When you look like I do, you've got to know what you're talking about," he quips. So he studies 10 to 20 Bible chapters a day as pastor of Come As You Are Church in Kalamazoo, Michigan, a 50-member congregation he founded four years ago. A gentle giant, Bensinger holds four martial-arts black belts and used to smash bricks inscribed with "S-A-T-A-N"—a fitting skill for someone who says his ministry gift is breaking demonic bondages.

Bensinger represents a growing number of Christians who work outside of tried-and-true ministry traditions to reach an increasingly diverse, non-Christian American culture. Bensinger's church—like The Refuge in St. Petersburg, Florida, and The Church on the Edge in Huntington Beach, California—specialize in ministering to people who don't fit in most churches.

People such as the Goths.

Bensinger—with his son, Steven, 18, and church member Seth Gooch, 24, both Christian Goths—minister to the Gothic subculture by way of a "medieval outreach" held Thursday nights. They welcome Goths of all backgrounds, including Wiccans, and provide a meeting place, a meal, and medieval-style hobbies such as sword-play and dancing.

Bensinger began his ministry after first being denied ministry credentials with the Church of God (Cleveland, Tenn.) because he wanted to start a church much like he has today.

are aggressively pursuing the American Dream. If anything, Goths are more likely to be suicidal than homicidal. Many are from families where they were parented from the philosophy of: 'I'm too busy. Here's $50. Go to the mall and let me work.' The kind of thing that was going on with the Columbine killers."

But surely all that black garb Goths wear means they're evil. After all, the Columbine killers wore black trench coats.

And Goths are Satan worshipers, aren't they? Most Goths scoff at the notion that they worship the devil.

Mayville grew up in the Episcopal Church and was an altar boy. His DJ name, D'Arcangel, is a play on the term "dark angel" or "the archangel."

"My baptismal name is Michael. My DJ name is an homage to Michael the archangel. So I find it ironic with these Christians going off on me, saying you must be a devil worshiper."

He also has to defend himself, as many Goths do, against accusations that his dark clothing means he's evil.

"People will say: 'You dress in black. Do you worship the devil?' And I'll say: 'Well, priests dress in black and so does Johnny Cash. How come I can't?'"

Peterson echoes: "I've never in my life met anyone who worships the actual being, Satan. Satanism is, in fact, humanism—the worship of self."

Also exaggerated, Goths claim, is their shadowy reputation as "vampires." Most members of the subculture

"We need to understand that God says don't judge by appearances but by godly judgment. God wants us to look like Jesus," he says. "I respect the Goths. God died for them just like He died for me. What will God think if they don't want to come to Him because Christians offended them?"

Hundreds of miles away, Bruce Wright, 40, a former Youth for Christ staffer, founded The Refuge in St. Petersburg, Florida, eight years ago to minister to kids rejected by churches. He reaches out to Goths through concerts, coffeehouses, Bible studies and a weekly church service.

He often teaches them from the books of Ecclesiastes and Psalms because they identify with the books' themes of emotional pain and the difficulty of knowing God.

"Goth kids relate to suffering," he says. "They identify with the disaffectedness, the vanity that Solomon felt with . . . his materialism and addiction."

A similar ministry approach is taken by Joey Roche, 46, who pastors the 150-member Church on the Edge in Huntington Beach, California. He's married with five children but is a self-described "scary-looking guy with lots of tattoos" who plays in a punk band and preaches a strong repentance message.

His church is "living for God straight-up" and resembles a "Noah's Ark thing," he says. "A grandma will be sitting next to a kid with a blue Mohawk. It's radical."

"Church on the Edge is made up of believers who are fed up with the traditions of men," Roche says. "No one is ever turned away because of how they look, talk or live before they come to the knowledge of the truth."

And that includes Goths. A married Gothic couple lead worship at his church, where ministry is done through hardcore-music concerts, anti-abortion counseling and feeding the homeless.

"People have looked at me and said, 'That's the pastor?' and *boom!* left right then," Roche says. "But Jesus never told us to look right. He told us to live right."

are quick to say vampirism is a sideline interest or a fetish embraced by a minority within their ranks and that it is practiced nonviolently.

Those who do engage in it sometimes do so through a "live-action role-playing game," or a LARP. Some players use a guidebook titled *Vampire: The Masquerade,* a sophisticated volume of genealogy and role-playing that reveals how to play a vampire or victim. Players at times will share blood in a ritual called a "Vauldrie," which is used to create covenants or allegiances.

Frankie Guell, 23, of Miami, has witnessed the exchange of blood between friends on several occasions. He has never participated in the act, but he has been intrigued by vampire lore he says since his childhood when actor Bela Lugosi, who played one of the first Count Dracula roles in film, appeared to him in a dream.

"I've seen people cut with razors or using syringes—consenting partners—never nothing that would hurt another person," he says. On such occasions, blood would be put into cups and shared, he adds.

"There is something very sexual about it," he says. "It's almost like you're sharing yourself completely because your essence is going into someone else."

Yet, deep below their outer trappings of music, fashion or fetish, Goths define themselves primarily as being those who possess the "soul" of a Goth.

(continued)

CONTINUED

Searching for Lost Souls

David Hart is known as a godfather of sorts in Goth evangelism.

Pastor David Hart, 51, of San Diego often dresses in Gothic clothes and heads off into the night to befriend kids who are immersed in the city's Goth subculture. Nothing unusual about that. Hart's been doing it since the 1980s.

That's how he met Lythia several years ago. She was about 14 then, and she was conducting a vampire ceremony for friends outside a Gothic dance club late one night.

Hart watched as she cut herself, drained her blood into a cup and passed it around for her friends to do the same. When it came back to her she did an incantation and sent it back around. Each person took a sip this time, and when the cup reached her again she drank and ended the ritual.

Lythia was practicing magic, trying to turn herself and her friends into vampires. Afterward, Hart attempted to befriend her.

"You're that pastor who's invaded our club," she said. "There's no sense talking to you. You'll just freak out about the occult and demons."

"That's not where I was going at all," Hart answered. "I was just curious . . . how are you going to keep from getting AIDS?"

As a young teen, Lythia hadn't yet fathomed that possibility. Hart's concern led to a friendship between the two, and he still sees her sometimes in his role as pastor of The Sanctuary in San Diego, a church he founded in 1986. He was just ending a career as a concert promoter in Southern California and started the church to reach heavy-metal kids.

Today, among his many roles, he's pastor for MCM Music, a Gothic music label that's home to Christian artists Saviour Machine, Rackets and Drapes, and Eva O—formerly known as Evil Eva of secular punk-Goth band Christian Death. He's the author of *It's All*

"Most [of us] consider it internal," says Steven Bensinger, 18, of Kalamazoo, Michigan, who works for a national Gothic retailer called Hot Topic. "I don't dress strictly Gothic. If I did, I wouldn't be a Goth if I didn't have my clothes on."

Though Guell initially was drawn to the scene by a fascination with horror, the friendships and acceptance he found appealed to him more. The desire for relationships, Mayville notes, is a greater key to the subculture's attraction than its mysterious side.

"One of the universal aspects of the Goth subculture is that we're very accepting as long as you're being true to yourself," Mayville says. "We don't care if you're a Christian, a Jew, a Muslim or a pagan. It doesn't matter if you're gay or straight. Be who you are, and we'll accept you for who you are."

Some Goths believe they are born with distinct Gothic personalities. Peterson believes that a person is born with an affinity for the subculture but chooses to embrace its dark aesthetics.

Hart has counseled many Goths who have been abused verbally, emotionally, sexually or physically. He says the "Gothic personality" tends to bury emotional suffering and that the style of dress sometimes is meant to reflect inner pain.

"Goths tend to be intelligent, sensitive and deeply introspective. They

Rock-n-Roll and the founder of Rock Talks Ministries, through which he lectures at schools, churches and youth camps on such topics as "Getting Goths to Christ."

Hart says Goths are summarily misjudged by society.

"Goth kids are intellectual," he says. "[They] are well-read, artistic and passive. They mull and brood. Whereas metal music is more about banging your head on the wall, Goth music is more about staring at the wall."

They tend to be dark on the outside, he says, because "they focus on reality and think life is painful and that we're all shooting toward death. Most Goths have been told they're fat, ugly, stupid. The most common wound I hear is, 'I'll never amount to anything.'"

To combat that rejection, Hart goes out of his way to build relationships with them. He went once with a group of non-Christian Goths to a Marilyn Manson concert and ended up being less offended by the concert than by the behavior of Christians who picketed the show.

Says Hart: "[The Christians] screamed at me that I was going to hell if I went in that show. All I could think was: *You don't understand. I'm going to hell if I don't go in that show—woe to me if I don't preach the gospel.* They had no idea who I was or what I was doing. They were just screaming."

Hart admits he sometimes feels isolated in ministry, and young pastors out of Bible colleges tend to think he's too old to understand youth culture.

"I feel like the old Indian fighter in the Westerns—where the young cavalry lieutenant is telling the old scout how it will work. I've done youth work for 30 years, and I'm not naive," he says.

That dedication won Lythia's heart. After two years as Hart's friend she gave her life to Jesus. After another year, she led her boyfriend to Christ. Today she's free of vampirism.

"She looks like a gypsy princess," Hart says. "She's the happiest she's ever been."

For more information about The Sanctuary, San Diego, log on at www.webpulse.com/sanctuary/.

tend to hold their pain inside for a really long time and let pain define their lives—which is why some of them dress the way they do. They see their lives and their souls as tattered and dark, and they dress accordingly."

"We are misunderstood and need an outlet for our intellect and creativity," Hannah Syfritt, 25, a wife and mother in Phoenix, says of her subculture. "We need to be accepted for our emotions and style of learning and not just put on medication."

RUNNING FROM THE TRUTH

Goths are outcasts who are desperately seeking acceptance, and they are running from established Christianity into the arms of Wicca, a neopagan religion of witchcraft and nature worship. Most Goths already have given up on absolute truth and are atheists. But the majority of the rest of them are Wiccans—most of whom were reared in Christian churches.

"A large percentage of Goths have come out of highly ritualized churches—Catholic, Episcopal, Presbyterian," Hart says. "Because of this many are predisposed to the ritualistic nature of Wicca."

Despite what they believe about God, Goths tend to be very spiritual, and sometimes this leads them to religions other than Christianity that promise power, something many Goths have lacked in life, Peterson says.

(continued)

CONTINUED

Invading the Heart of Darkness

One evangelist from New Zealand is taking the gospel right into Goth clubs.

As a Christian musician and evangelist, David Pierce, is more than "outside the box"—he's literally "outside the coffin." His exit from one of these postmortem props is the climax of an avant-garde rock opera he performs in Gothic clubs with his evangelistic band No Longer Music (NLM).

Pierce is the executive director of Steiger International, a ministry he founded in Amsterdam in the 1980s to reach the city's punk and anarchist subculture for Jesus. The Minneapolis native now lives in New Zealand, and Steiger has expanded its ministry boundaries to include the United States and other countries. It continues to focus on taking the gospel to youth countercultures wherever they may be found.

NLM puts on an extreme thereafter performance set to Gothic-punk music. The drama's grand finale is Jesus' death and resurrection communicated in modern motifs. To symbolize the crown of thorns, cross, dark clouds and tomb, the band uses a torture helmet, knife, fire, flashing lights and smoke-filled coffin. "Jesus"—Pierce's character—is knifed to death, placed in a coffin and resurrected by the power of God.

"We try to show the horror of the cross in order to break the cliché that the cross has become," Pierce says.

On a recent tour of hardcore Goth clubs in South America, NLM led Goths to faith in Jesus inside bars where they performed. Club managers allowed the band to play in the occultic venues only because they liked NLM's act.

One site was a three-story facility that included a bar where books on Satan worship, sadism, sexual depravity and torture were sold. Elsewhere, in a district of discos, gay bars and what Pierce calls "sleaze mafia clubs," NLM played a venue where occul-

How then has the church lost such a sizable portion of its youth to the lure of unbelief, dark aesthetics and romantic paganism? Some say it's because too many Christians aren't willing to change with the surrounding culture.

"Culture changes, but the Scriptures do not. Yet the mainstream church's mentality is: 'I want you to have my cultural experience of Christianity,' " Hart says. "Goths come from a different framework and won't have it."

Bruce Wright, 40, a former Youth for Christ staffer and pastor of The Refuge in St. Petersburg, Florida, goes a step further. He thinks youth subcultures such as the Goths have no taste for Jesus because the U.S. church has diluted the Word of God.

"The Bible is sanitized and sounds like fairy tales to them," he states. "They perceive that life is easy and that Christianity is a lifestyle that is prosperous and has no struggles.

"They expect those who know Jesus to be unselfish, but they see the church as a politically right-wing, elite social club who call themselves pro-life yet won't help the poor."

Horrific as the visage of Gothdom can be, there are some Christians who aren't afraid of the dark. Outside the glint and glare of everyday Christianity they have spawned their own music, Internet life, and evangelism for Goths. They can be found in Christian Goth bands, on Christian Goth Web sites and even in churches for Goths, such as the

tic symbols covered the walls, patrons dressed like witches or vampires, and the manager called himself "The Devil."

The owners of another site practiced witchcraft and voodoo and had attended an international vampire convention in New Orleans. During the evening, Pierce says, chimes were rung at the club to welcome demonic spirits.

During one performance the crowd grew increasingly hostile as NLM acted out Jesus' execution. By the time the other band members placed Pierce in the coffin, he feared for the group's safety.

"As I lay in that coffin it felt it felt like I was in hell. It was like hearing the cries of demons all around me. People were manifesting [demons] and screaming foul, obscene things about Jesus," he says. The crowd—not realizing a resurrection was part of the drama—grew quiet when he burst out of the coffin, he says. In the lingering quiet caused by the impact of the scene he preached the gospel.

NLM concluded another performance by singing a worship song, which stunned that crowd as well. Again, Pierce says, he took advantage of the moment and led some 80 people to a room where he and NLM members told them about Jesus. About 15 Goths prayed for salvation while the rest yelled obscenities.

"It is extremely taxing going to these clubs," Pierce told *Charisma*.

NLM has performed in satanist bars and anarchist clubs in Europe and Asia, hardcore heavy-metal festivals in Siberia, and a host of similar venues where they have been threatened, spat upon, jeered and cursed for preaching Jesus. Still, they prefer playing in demonic strongholds to "preaching to the choir."

"The way to reach Goths is with the cross, not by being subtle with the gospel," Pierce says. "The cross is the power of God for salvation. There is power when you lift up Christ and Him crucified [*sic*]."

For more information about Steiger International, log on at www.steiger.org.

First Church of the Undead in Orange County, California.

Most of them are just everyday Christians—such as Melody Bailey, who attends an Assemblies of God congregation in Slidell, Louisiana. Besides being a greeter at her church and a leader in her youth group, she reaches out to non-Christian Goths with friendship.

She's also one of several people *Charisma* interviewed who became Goths after they became Christians. Bailey did, in part, because she "always liked to be different" and because Goths "were way nicer to me than other people," she says.

Dan Chick, 26, of Minneapolis, an Internet database developer, was a Christian when he became a Goth two years ago while attending the Cornerstone Christian music festival in Illinois, where he met Christian Goths.

"When my life started falling apart a few months later it was the Christian Goths who were there for me when none of my other Christian friends were," Chick says.

Peterson is a Christian stay-at-home mom who homeschools her four children. She attends a nondenomenational church in Madison, Wisconsin, and is taking a hiatus from a ministry she started for Goths called Ex Nihilo.

In the meantime, she leads an Internet ministry called Xnetgoth that provides a way for Goths to network with one another and fellowship online. Like those she ministers to, Peterson is unashamedly Gothic.

(continued)

CONTINUED

A Radical Departure

*Derek Corzine was kicked out of his church because he chose
an unorthodox approach to reach his Goth friends.*

Nineteen-year-old Derek Corzine became a Goth for the "wrong" reason. After all, it's normal to become a Goth if you're drawn by the music, the dark fashions or the relationships. But Derek became a Goth because God told him to.

Wrong reason—according to some of the Christians Derek grew up with in Denver City, Texas.

Derek was raised in one of the local Baptist churches but drifted from his faith. In junior high he rededicated his life to Jesus, was filled with the Holy Spirit and began attending an Assemblies of God church.

By the time he reached high school his best friends across the nearby border in New Mexico were Goths. They dressed in black, got drunk, cut themselves with razors and said the Goth lifestyle was the only way they could "feel human."

Derek wanted to tell them about Jesus. After praying about how to, he says God told him to become like his friends. "I became a Goth to minister to Goths," he says. My motive was 1 Corinthians 9:22—becoming all things to all men that I might win some to Jesus."

So Derek grew his hair long and wore black leather, chains and spikes. He carried his Bible with him to school and shared Jesus with classmates. He wore Gothic makeup in a style that portrayed a hidden personality trait, as many Goths do.

His makeup, however, symbolized his unseen mission: "I wore my makeup like war paint, because I was in a spiritual battle," he says.

Because of his conservative Christian background and his radical outward change, "people were tripping out . . . people freaked," he says. One day his pastor told him he would have to stop wearing Gothic makeup, because it was "not ethical in a Christian church."

Derek disagreed, saying that Christian mimes wear makeup for a similar purpose when they evangelize with skits. He tried to explain by quoting 1 Samuel 16:7, Galatians 2:6 and Matthew 7:1-2, but Derek's pastor ordered him to leave the church and not come back.

Derek remained a Goth for three years and stayed true to his mission, though he calls that period "the hardest time of my life." He led a Goth friend and several classmates to Jesus.

Today Derek still wears his hair long, but he dresses in baggy jeans and heavy-metal music T-shirts. He attends a nondenominational charismatic church in Lubbock, Texas, and plays with a Christian-metal band called Syringe, a name he chose for the symbolism of a needle injecting healing below the outward surface.

Says Derek: "Sinners will be sinful until they accept Christ. Get to know them—and say what God wants you to say."

"People stop and stare when I go grocery shopping with my kids. I wear all black. I wear dog collars and lots of silver jewelry," she says. "I love to sit in the graveyard and contemplate life. I like to light all the candles in the house and dance to The Cure in my living room." Syfritt, who attends a house church in Phoenix and whose parents are former Foursquare pastors, says Christians need to learn to embrace more than "just the happy people staring at the back of your head every Sunday morning. It boils down to this: We are here to love God and love each other. If we do not . . . then we do not know the heart of God."

Syfritt and a growing minority of unorthodox Christians apparently have decided that if young people in the Goth subculture are going to hear the gospel, then believers must be willing to light a candle in the dark to reach them.

ATTRIBUTE, VERIFY, QUOTE ACCURATELY

Double-check the accuracy of every information source and every quote you obtain, verifying it by other means. Don't blindly assume that information you find in a magazine or e-zine, a newspaper article, news release or on a web site is accurate simply because it's printed there. For example, who sponsors the web site? When was it updated last? Does it contain fact? Or opinion? In the case of interviews you conduct, that may mean verifying with another person the quoted information or perspective your original source gave you.

Information generally well known and in the public domain need not be attributed to the source. But information obtained from another printed source such as a magazine or newspaper must be attributed. You must also attribute all direct quotes you find there and all quotes, both indirect and direct, from interviews you conducted personally. (Hint: For the sake of accuracy, get the source to say the same thing to you that was printed elsewhere.) When attributing, rely on that old standard "he said" and "she said." Anything else, such as "he averred" or "she maintained," detracts from story flow and can't hold a candle to good sentence wording. Some magazines prefer the immediacy of "he *says*" to "he said." "He *says*," however, also connotes impermanence. I suggest you defer to the magazine's style. Remember that a person who is coughing or laughing is not simultaneously speaking; for example, "I don't like it," he coughed, is invalid. Better: He coughed. "I don't like it." (Good advice: Don't end a sentence with a partial quote and start the next sentence with a full quote; it's confusing and destroys reading flow.)

When quoting directly, stick to a source's exact words and the context in which they were uttered. (Exception: It's okay to clean up incorrect grammar unless that's indicative of a person's circumstances.) When a quote is used indirectly or paraphrased, be careful not to distort its meaning. Partial as well as complete quotes are acceptable. You need not use quotes in the order something was said; however, you can't use them out of context or alter what they refer to.

Your meaning must be absolutely clear to the reader. To avoid story confusion, don't mix quotes from more than one person in the same graf: Start a new graf for the next speaker by identifying the source first, then following it with a direct quote. As a general rule, when a new person talks it indicates the story is now delving into another aspect of the situation.

Stewart believes a news story is better paced when direct quotes balance exposition and narration. But when is it appropriate to use a direct quote rather than an indirect one? When should you paraphrase what's been said? Said Stewart, "In a direct quote, I look for something that immediately illustrates what's being written about at that particular moment in the story. It has to have a bit of a zing to it. If I have a weaker quote but the point is important, it can be rewritten [as an indirect quote] and come across better."

When writing an indirect quote, Stewart tries to keep the language and flavor of it as close as possible to his source's wording. He takes extra care when paraphrasing. "I'm very careful that I don't add meaning or take away an important point, that I don't exaggerate. I try to keep it true to what a person said to me, at least to the spirit of it."

Reserve direct quotes for the most important points in the story. The best direct quotes either punctuate a statement of fact or are self-explanatory. Well-chosen, a quote should stand alone without the writer jumping in with a paraphrased explanation, much as to say, "This is what he really meant."

Too many people introduced and quoted within a short editorial space dilute your points and overwhelm the reader. Limit the 200- to 800-word info-brief to one or two sources, only one of whom you'll quote directly. When introducing a source in a longer feature story, try to stay with that source for at least four grafs. Why? Readers need time to absorb the information. They're also more likely to remember that source later in the story when needed. Unless deliberate repetition makes your point, don't run quotes from different sources that say the same thing.

It's more effective—and timely—to quote what a person *says* than what a person may have *written*. Freshen the story by approaching this source with new questions. The payoff may be fresh insight.

It will help to remember that you have only one editor. That person works at the magazine where your article will be published. Although some people may disagree, I suggest you avoid letting a source read your manuscript before submitting it. If you mistakenly grant this privilege, a source can deny what he or she said, change your wording and even your conclusions. If you've taped the session, try settling the matter by playing back for the source the section of tape in question. Best advice? Offer to get back to the source as you're writing the article with any questions and to verify the accuracy of what was said. Remember: If anything is unclear to you during the interview, clarify it immediately, on the spot. This isn't ignorance: Common sense says that you can't write what you don't understand.

MORE INTERVIEWING TIPS

The Poynter Institute's Tompkins has this to add about interviewing: Keep your questions short. "Short questions produce focused responses. Long, rambling questions produce confusing replies." Tompkins also advises keeping questions simple: "The more information journalists put into questions, the more information interviewees leave out."

DID YOU PARTICIPATE?

Is it ever acceptable to be a *participant* observer rather than an *unbiased* observer gathering information? Is it ever acceptable to put yourself in the story even when the story isn't about you? Many travel writers do that, giving readers their own personal reaction to a certain place or experience. My suggestion? Reserve this approach for the first-person narrative or personal experience story (see Chapter 11). After all, good writing should never depend on the writer's presence in the story to make it more readable. Best advice? Be practical. If a magazine has certain preferences, be guided by them.

The late anthropologist Margaret Mead interacted as a familiar with her subjects when she field-researched them for her benchmark book *Growing Up in Samoa.* Did she sacrifice objectivity and skew the results? Most people agree she did. By becoming a participant, wasn't she actually becoming part of the sociocultural fabric of Samoa and in some way altering it? Wasn't New Journalist George Plimpton, the perennial writer-cum-insider, more than an observer when he became a professional football quarterback with the Detroit Lions to gather material for a *Sports Illustrated* story and later used it in his 1966 book *Paper Lion?* Did he sacrifice objectivity by becoming "one of the locker-room boys"? Or did he choose total immersion as a way of commenting on the *process* of major league ball playing—the why and the how, not just the what? (Plimpton, author of nearly 30 books and editor of *The Paris Review,* made his writing career by participating as an amateur in such professional sports as boxing, baseball, football, and golf and writing about them.)

When I covered migrant agricultural labor for *Washington Scene* magazine (see Chapter 5), I quickly learned that the easiest way to get cooperation and respect from the different ethnic groups was to work as hard at my job as they did at theirs. Unfortunately, I overstepped the line when I picked cherries for a day with migrant fruit pickers in California. The work was arduous, backbreaking. I had to move heavy wooden ladders three times my height from tree to tree. Moreover, I had to fill the same quota as the others did of so many cherry-filled flats per day. For the migrant workers, this was serious business. For me, it was merely a day's hard labor and I had to stop frequently. I was an outsider trying to be an insider, and from the hardworking migrants, I received no quarter or cooperation. I had squandered my sources of information.

Immersion, of course, is only one type of research. It makes no claim to objectivity and assumes no responsibility for putting a situation into unbiased perspective. Newspaper reporters, on the other hand, must be objective. The nature of their deadline work, however, often dictates they cover stories and conduct interviews by phone. On-site reporting, interviewing and in general, observing and asking follow-up questions, become expensive premiums. (Thanks to the Internet, reporters can now go online quickly to mine the additional data they may need to put a situation into perspective.)

The technique of *observation,* however, permits a magazine writer or newspaper reporter to retain objectivity when doing research. I covered solar energy systems for a business magazine some years ago. For part of my research, I went on-site at the state prison to observe the construction and installation of flat-plate solar collectors that would be used to partly heat the main building. In the process, I interviewed convicts and spent some time with lifers in the solar-heated prison greenhouse, reporting, interviewing and in general, observing and asking follow-up questions.

As an on-site observer of the situation, I could let the people and surroundings cue me to discover and ask additional questions. At the same time, I could avoid the *participant* mode with its obvious pitfalls. Information I gathered this way provided me with valuable insight and a strong slant for the article I later wrote.

The three research techniques I've discussed—field research, which usually also includes interviews; library and Internet research; and telephone research and interviews—almost always are used in combination by good magazine writers to find and check facts. On the Internet, using a search engine such as Dogpile.com or Yahoo.com will save you considerable time; just type in one or two keywords—*stem cells,* for example—and let the computer fetch data and web sites for you. Remember to double-check everything, including the credibility of the web source, when doing Internet research. When researching through the library, you'll find it easier to use library networks such as Lexis-Nexis than to hunt and peck by individual entries.

Other aspects of interview behavior will be covered in Chapter 10 on personality profiles.

HELPFUL EXERCISES

1. Drawing from a mixture of shelved and online material, use at least five library and Internet resources to determine whether the topic, storyline, slant and focus of your proposed article make it timely and marketable for the readership and magazine you have chosen. In précis, or summary, form, explain the material you've found, where it was found and cite each resource used to locate it. Based on this preliminary research, is your idea viable for the market? Explain why or why not and, if necessary, how you might change your approach to be saleable; for example, converting a consumer how-to story on building your own kitchen cabinets into a profile of a cabinet maker for a business magazine.

2. Compile a preliminary list of people you can interview for the article. Beside each name and title, explain your reason(s) for speaking with that person. Remember that personal interviews must be doable in terms of time, access and location.

CHAPTER FIVE

"I DID IT; SO CAN YOU"

Personality profile, how-to, first-person narrative—what type of story should you write? Many possibilities exist; you can read about them in this chapter. Your decision will be based partly on the storyline you've drafted already and partly on the types of articles, and their respective lengths, run by the magazine you've chosen. (See the Analyzing Content guide and the family tree in Chapter 2.) It also depends on your point of view toward the subject and that favored by the target magazine and its readership. For example, do you believe it's frivolous to invoke the Endangered Species Act for a two-inch species of fish? Or do you view the species' imminent demise with such alarm that you write an alarmer-exposé? Be sure to maintain your point of view. Should you find your attitude—your approach—changing, should material creep into the manuscript that doesn't support your point of view, you must be willing to re-examine it.

Pay close attention to the editorial guidelines for each department of the target magazine. *Charisma & Christian Life,* for example, offers writers a tantalizing opportunity to write 200- to 800-word shorts for its "People & Events" section. Articles there range from personality profiles to straight news stories with a summary lead. The "Features" section of the same magazine offers writers a chance to do personality profiles, personal experience stories and historical pieces. Each of these feature-length articles is accompanied by related sidebars that are assigned and almost always are written by another freelance writer. Why? The magazine uses sidebars as though they were feature-length stories. Do all magazines do this? No. Do all magazines run sidebars? No again.

On assignment from a statewide business magazine, I wrote a feature-length sidebar to accompany another writer's cover story on solar energy. The sidebar profiled Austria-born Erich Farber, world's solar energy pioneer, commenting on the state of the art. Editor Jimmy Stewart's cover story on the Goths, however, contained four short sidebars totaling two-and-one-third pages of copy. Stewart wrote the sidebars himself, shunting material to them that he felt would overload the article and disrupt its narrative. "I wanted to keep the main part of the story lean and well paced," said Stewart, "without bogging it down with people and destroying reading flow." Stewart used his sidebars to concentrate on people in a lengthier fashion. Each sidebar was a short profile that gave key sources a chance to tell their own stories in greater depth.

ANOTHER VIEW OF SIDEBARS

Sidebars come in all shapes and sizes; your use of sidebars is as much dictated by the magazine's format as it is by the material you're writing. Traditionally, sidebars house statistics, lists, names and addresses, directions and other supportive and useful information that would be obstacles to reading ease if placed in the body of the article. Today, there's a definite trend among major magazines to pull feature copy directly from the narrative of the main story and to highlight it as a sidebar on a colored tint block. This graphic technique effectively reduces the main story to a shorter, quicker read while adding a few smaller stories we once called sidebars. However, no hard-and-fast rule currently exists in magazine publishing. An article in the May 2002 issue of *Ladies' Home Journal,* for example, illustrates that. Pages 124–135 featured a health story entitled "The Best Doctors for Families—Coast to Coast" that consisted of an introductory graf, followed immediately by a lengthy, multipage, regional list of physicians. Interspersed on the list pages were two related sidebars on tint blocks—one a half-pager that asked "When Is It an Emergency?" and the other a one-third pager detailing "Common Health Mistakes Parents Make." Both sidebars were written by freelancers; the body of the article was compiled by a staffer.

Written succinctly and airtight, a sidebar contains backup material helpful to story comprehension. It can also build reader identification by humanizing information. However, a sidebar risks becoming a dumping ground for material if you don't stick to storyline and focus. Think of the sidebar as a small dormer window permitting access to a part of the larger image. By focusing attention on one small aspect of the material, the dormer window, or sidebar, draws the reader in and adds to knowledge and experience.

The choice to run certain material in a sidebar is generally the editor's. However, if your research has uncovered information you believe should be highlighted, then by all means put it in a sidebar.

FORMULA APPROACH?

Is there a formula to follow for each type of story? A certain way to approach and structure the material? A structure to include certain items in a how-to article, for example, but to leave others out? Is there, as Michael Shapiro notes in the November/December 2002 issue of the *Columbia Journalism Review*

("The Curse of Tom Wolfe"), "a disquieting trend in the magazine trade: a dullness, a numbing predictability, a growing sense of stories crafted less with a desire for greatness than with an eye for avoiding mistakes"? Have editors, publishers and writers fallen slave to what market research reveals readers want? The answer is yes, no and maybe. Without doubt, you'll find it safer and easier to stick to a prescribed formula for a particular story type than to deviate and risk losing a sale. Without doubt, writers who use a mix-and-mismatch, cobbled-together styles do sell today, but their confusing material is not very readable.

Still, there is room for experimentation. Purists at first scoffed at such mid-1960s to 1970s New Journalists as Tom Wolfe, Joan Didion and Joe Eszterhas who scorned nonfiction form and sacrificed their editorial objectivity in pursuit of a personal imprint. Their technique was to eschew journalistic technique entirely. Simple subjectivity—total immersion in a story—ruled. The "I" was always the implicit voice, but rarely was it stated. For these writers, *the challenge was not the subject matter itself but the journey experienced in getting it.* Reporting that journey became the story, and New Journalists borrowed liberally from fiction techniques such as dialogue and scene-sketching to make that story come alive. Although most of today's nonfiction magazine writers employ some fiction techniques and put some thought into viewing the subject matter as an idea, they can't afford all-out literary experimentation. With their eye on the bottom line, most publishers won't run what they consider too avant-garde for readership. Your challenge? Avoid cookie-cutter journalism and involve the reader in a good story that simply can't be put down.

ARTICLES THAT DOMINATE THE FIELD

Two types of articles continue to dominate the changing field of magazine publishing—the personality profile and the how-to story with its self-help variant. Together, they account for an estimated 72 percent of magazine feature material. Although Chapters 9 and 10 cover how-to's and personality profiles in greater depth, the following breakdown and brief description of all article types will suffice to get you going. Hint: Pay particular attention to the discussion of *voice* in this chapter.

Personality Profile

This popular type of article profiles a contemporary or historical person, community, nation or state, company or association. Although most profiles are written in the objective, third-person voice, in the hands of an accomplished writer—and very often a known one—the first-person "I" may be the perspective used for a personality profile when the writer has personally experienced the subject. However, *the most successful personality profile allows the reader to experience the story directly without having to filter that experience through the "I" of an unknown writer.* Despite this common-sense perspective, many magazines today prefer the "I" approach for personality profiles. Gerald Grow, a journalism professor at Florida A & M University, suggests why: "More magazines may favor the 'I' approach," he says, "because they're trying to simulate a personal relationship with readers by addressing them directly. It's not personal, of course," says Grow, "but many people seem to project personal relations into their favorite media and advertisements." Use of the term *profile* may be a misnomer: Today's magazine articles range from painting a person in "the brief"—in silhouette or outline—to a story that paints a person round, in his or her many facets.

Your first task is to decide what the magazine wants and why the reader should care about this subject. For example: Does this community exist despite the odds? Has this person overcome extreme difficulties or a handicap? Hint for new writers: Don't attempt to compromise your objectivity by writing a personality profile on someone to whom you're closely related or with whom you're closely associated. The article will not sell. Why? The story won't ring true. Not only will your bias and assumptions show through, you'll tend to put words into the mouth of your subject. (See Chapter 10.)

How-To

Easily the most popular and the shortest and easiest to write, the how-to article with its self-help variant gives instructions for how to do or be something or how to do it better (build a tree house, improve your social skills or relationship, treat old-age spots, lose weight, change your career, save for retirement, meditate). Because it mandates you give instruction in a logical fashion—for example, step one, step two or first, next or the equivalent—it binds you to a repetitive style in which each paragraph sounds like the previous one and the whole risks reading like a recipe. You'll discover some remedies for this in the following pages. The self-help/how-to article is hallmarked by clarity, conciseness and simplicity and by carefully chosen nouns and verbs that paint precise mental pictures.

Hint: The new writer must be careful to teach the subject in nonteaching fashion such as, "I did it; so can you. Here's how and here are the happy results." This article need not—but often does—switch voice, *acceptably* breaking a cardinal rule in magazine writing: *Choose a consistent voice throughout.* The voice you choose for *any* type of article will depend on your viewpoint. Is this something that happened to you, the writer? Then choose the "I." Are you speaking from an experience or an emotional, spiritual or physical state you share with the reader? In that case, I suggest you start with the "I" (or "we") and switch to the "you" as you share. However, if you want to impart information in an impersonal fashion, choose the objective, third-person singular voice of "it" (see "Flies 'R' Us," discussed in the Survey or Informative Article section).

You'll also use this objective voice (or its "he, she, they" variant) in writing the narrative/descriptive article, survey article, service story and personality profile. Another viewpoint—the omniscient—assumes a God-like, know-everything-everywhere-for-all-time visage. Rarely used, it fails to build a relationship with the reader. At least one magazine of my acquaintance divides its feature stories into various categories. The magazine's editorial guidelines specify which point of view and voice to use in each category.

Survey or Informative Article

The survey article can be term-paper dull with research or vibrant with well-thought-out images, quotes and colorful description. This type of article surveys a field such as sports medicine, solar energy, or breast cancer and in timely round-up fashion tells what's going on there. It needs a strong, organizing focus and storyline—something that speaks to the human condition. To write about fruit fly research, for example—and one woman did (Karen Wright, "Flies 'R' Us", pp. 26–27, in the April 2002 issue of *Discover* magazine)—would seem boring and "fruitless." But this article gave us a novelistic rather than an ordinary look at a bunch of agricultural pests that have wings. Wright used quotes liberally from different researchers to illuminate passages of exposition. She crafted an attention-grabbing lead. And, like the language in the rest of the story, that lead had punch.

> After three decades of stalking fruit flies in the wild, Theresa Markow has honed her technique to a fine art. Her weapon is a long glass tube with a gauze trap in the center. "You sneak up on the flies and suck," she says. "Then you blow them out into a vial."

The short sentence following the lead balances it perfectly.

> *Most folks would just grab a flyswatter.*

Alarmer-Exposé

A *Reader's Digest* staple, the alarmer-exposé is designed to alert and move the reader to action. Well-researched and heavy with documentation, it takes a stance and adopts a particular point of view on a timely and often controversial issue. Its purpose is to expose what's wrong there. Simultaneously, it covers—but quickly dispatches—alternative viewpoints. This article is best written by an established writer who's skilled in reporting an issue and building a case without flagrant—and apparent—bias.

Expect to encounter some opposition—possibly even hostility—in researching and writing this type of article. I did. Years ago, I covered migrant agricultural labor coast to coast for a magazine then known as *Washington Scene.* From Florida to northern California, I spoke with migrant farm workers from various ethnic mainstreams and foreign countries, at one point even working alongside them. I went inside the labor camps where they lived; I spoke with them on-site in the fields, the groves, the packing and processing plants. In California and Washington, D.C., I met with leaders of Cesar Chavez's Farmworkers Union. I spoke with crew bosses in the fields, agricultural company heads in their corporate offices. Despite permissions to interview and look around, I often was spied on and surreptitiously followed by crew bosses and company representatives. Sometimes these people angrily confronted me; sometimes they turned me back. Occasionally I was accused of activities that never occurred. After studying U.S. census data and other government documents, I spoke with people at the State Department and the Immigration and Naturalization Service (INS). I even went on raids in Arizona with the Border Patrol. When the article was published, a well-placed government official accused me in print of misinterpreting and misrepresenting census figures. Using the same census figures, I was able to rebut this reader in a second story for *Washington Scene.*

Narrative

From an Agatha Christie cliffhanger to Hansel and Gretel, almost everyone likes a good story—particularly when it's true. Witness the popularity of the *Reader's Digest* "Drama in Real Life" section—loads of human-interest material that puts the reader in the story. Remember the books you read when you were little? The stories your parents told you when you couldn't get to sleep at night? I remember begging my mother to tell us another story about "when you were a little girl (and your cousin would wet the bed when you slept together, and how you pantomimed *Silas Marner* that day at the school assembly, and the scar you had on your back because you were standing on the sidewalk below an apartment-house window the day a little girl tapped on the pane with a penny and the broken glass came crashing down)."

The narrative uses fiction technique to recreate the tension, the setting, the emotion—the drama—of something that actually happened. The article must have implications and ramifications that are meaningful to a reader. It must be relevant to what's going on today—one event that relates to the larger whole. It could deal with a hang-by-the-nails crisis. It could be an inspiring, even a historical, event. By using narrative technique, you've re-created that something in the *now,* as though the reader were there and part of it. As the episodes unfold and the story progresses, the reader is carried along.

Narratives are best told in the third-person "he" or "she" voice; to place yourself in the story as its writer will only prevent the reader from fully identifying with the situation and main characters. If in doubt about voice, apply the "which-is-more-important" test—the subject of the story or your reaction to it? Reserve the "I" voice for an "as-told-to" or personal experience story. A word of caution: Be sure to start your narrative by jumping into the middle of the story, usually near the crisis point, then backtracking. You'll lose reader interest if you try to tell it chronologically in "once-upon-a-time" fashion.

Although not technically a narrative—some articles are legitimate hybrids of several types—this excerpt from a personality profile in *Today's Viewpoint* on jai alai player Bolivar illustrates both points. It starts by jumping into the middle of the story with action, and it illustrates a way to handle your "I" without being intrusive.

> They call him Cancha King, the 22-year-old *macho pelotari* of the Florida jai alai circuit who turns the toughest returns into points, and he loves it and lets the hushed adulation of spectators outside the huge wire cage sharpen his concentration and distract his opponents. But this afternoon the rubber grin and the braggadocio strut were gone. Spectators in the Tampa fronton clutched their quinela tickets and sensed it. Jose Antonio Illoro known to fans as Bolivar had a beef.
>
> "He is nervous," confided the wife of another Basque as we watched him sit apart from the other players on the sidelines bench, moodily strapping on the white helmet. "Always they pair him with a weak backcourt partner, and he is going to play a special *partido* with two players from Miami who are watching and he doesn't want to look bad."
>
> The seventh team lost, and Bolivar took the front court, the center position where he dominates play like no other, and waited for the opposing team's serve. The ball slammed into the front wall and rebounded high, and his Basque temper got the best of him. He snatched the ball from the air in his hooked *cesta*, whirled and smashed it in a two-shot against the side wall, watched in frustration as his partner lunged for the ball on the second return and missed, the point going to 30-year-old veteran, Gorrono.
>
> Bolivar shrugged and walked off the court in disgust.
>
> "He is always like that," said the woman as we walked through the parking lot behind the fronton. "He can't stand to be under anybody else."
>
> The player's door opened, and Bolivar exited alone in a red windbreaker, dark hair plastered against his forehead. He turned to the girl waiting for him at the door and frowned. "You go home!" he thundered. He walked to his car and drove moodily home. (Excerpted from "Cancha King" by Nancy Hamilton and Katie Bartolotti, *Today's Viewpoint*, Nov. 1975)

A second way to handle that "I" is not to mention it at all. It's understood that the woman is speaking to someone, presumably to the writer.

> "He is nervous," confided the wife of another Basque. Bolivar sat apart from the other players on the sidelines bench, moodily strapping on the white helmet.

"Always they pair him with a weak backcourt partner," she continued, "and he is going to play a special *partido* with two players from Miami who are watching and he doesn't want to look bad."

Do you like the first or the second version? Why? The article could have been constructed a third way, also, without using the woman and her quotes. In that event, you would have to find another way to put the situation into perspective.

The following city magazine narrative, reprinted from the April 2002 issue of *Ocala* (but without its excellent photo illustration), conveys charm and information—but only if the reader is particularly motivated. The story fails on several counts, starting with its "once-upon-a-time" approach. ("Our room with a view offered a bonus tonight. . . . Soon we would be out there too. . . .") The narrative also fails the "which-is-more-important" test for voice. Employing *three different voices* for three points of view and see-sawing at random among them, the story begins with the "we," switches once to the "you," then segues to the objective "it," returns again to the "we," then to an implied and an explicit "you," thence to "us" and again to the implied "you." Reader confusion about viewpoint gives rise to other questions. Why does a Florida-focused publication run an article on Quebec City? Why does it fail to identify that location until graf four? And then, why does it become a guessing game? ("Where were we? Paris? Strasbourg? Chamonix? Not even close.")

■ ■ ■ ■ ■ ■

QUEBEC CITY AT ITS FINEST

By Vinod and Linda Chhabra

Our room with a view offered a bonus tonight. It was a Courier & Ives landscape come to life—of parents lugging wooden sleds, the children on them looking like stuffed mittens, horse and buggies ferrying dinner guests, Golden Retrievers frolicking in the deep, feathery snow that blanketed the park overlooking the river.

Soon we would be out there too, at the cozy restaurant Le Saint-Amour, in a 300-year-old stone cottage for a dinner more memorable than any we've had in Europe. Our attentive waiter was classically Gallic. So was the menu from which we chose a steaming pot of mussels poached in wine and herbs, grilled breast of duck napped with a pepper-cream sauce, a leafy salad with wild mushrooms and home-smoked salmon, a different wine with each course, crepes bulging with pears in maple syrup, the sweetness softened by a cloud of fresh cream . . .

After dinner at 9, the city was just coming to life, and we strolled beneath the looming chateau, past candle-lit bistros and stylish shops tucked in stone buildings, to sip cappuccino and watch the city lights glittering in the river. In the distance, accordion music and laughter warmed the cold night air.

Where were we? Paris? Strasbourg? Chamonix? Not even close. We were in North America's most European city, where 90 percent of the 500,000 residents speak French, and enjoying an elegant French lifestyle at less than half the cost of Europe.

Quebec City is a charmer, in ambiance, culture and gastronomy. But it's a lot closer and a lot more affordable than you may expect. It's close enough as a getaway over a long weekend, and with the US dollar fetching $1.60 Canadian, it's a bargain!

Bert Heuser, of Lighting Unlimited in Ocala, illuminated our path to his favorite hideaway—Room No. 1 in the cozy Chateau de Lery. This charming little 19th-century-style European hotel sits in the heart of historic Old Quebec (Vieux-Quebec), a few steps from the grand Chateau Frontenac, the view from our bay window looking over the magnificent Parc des Goueverneurs (governors park) and the Saint-Lawrence River. It was a steal at less than $70, including breakfast.

If you're like us and love the snow, Quebec City is it, with its famous winter Carnival in February, sledding at the base of the mighty and magically frozen Montmorency Falls, skiing the 56 slopes at Mont-Ste.-Anne less than 40 minutes away, or clopping around town in a caleche (horse-and-buggy), bundled in blankets with a bag of hot chestnuts warming your hands.

Instead of hibernating, the Quebecois break out of the winter doldrums in February with the 15-day Carnival de Quebec. As always there are some silly ways to have chilly fun—dogsled races, snow sculpture competitions, music and dancing in the snow, curling, even sliding down the long icy chute on a wooden toboggans [sic] at supersonic speeds (well, okay, 40 mph).

However, this is a city that is alive in all four distinct seasons and the most enjoyable way to get here is by Canada's excellent railroad, VIA Rail, that glides up along the scenic south shore of the

Saint Lawrence from Montreal, about 180 miles west, in less than three hours (a three-course meal and bar drinks in luxurious first class).

North America's oldest fortified city, Quebec exudes the charm of old France without the hauteur that is often encountered there. Indeed, it is so unique that the entire city has been designated and protected as a World Heritage by UNESCO. It's a place for walking and browsing and an easy place to spend time soaking up the ambiance, history, and delicious food.

The city's modern history reaches back to explorer Jacques Cartier, and the establishment of the settlement in 1608. The French, British and Dutch fought right here over who would control the New World.

The historic Plains of Abraham, just minutes from our hotel, is where the French and British clashed. In a battle that lasted 20 minutes in 1759, General James Wolfe defeated the French. Both generals—Wolfe and Montcalm—were killed and are honored at the Parch des Gouverneurs [sic]. The victory also sealed British control of the region and consolidation of Canada.

Today, the Plains of Abraham are part of the city's huge Battlefields Park where people hike, bike and picnic, and the Citadelle is home to Canada's decorated Royal 22nd Regiment.

The city is in three parts, two of them in the old city. Following the European tradition of walled towns, Vieux-Quebec is defined by its original fortifications and narrow, steep, winding steps—the steepness the result of its location on an enormous promontory overlooking the mighty St. Lawrence River.

As we entered, the city's charm immediately took over. Part of the charm is that in Vieux-Quebec there are no skyscrapers, only cobblestone streets,

(continued)

CONTINUED

refurbished stone buildings, and old-world ambiance.

We took our time discovering the two parts of the old city—upper and lower, a steep walk or 360 steps connects the two. The easiest is a glass-enclose [*sic*] funicular ride (about $1) that takes a few minutes.

The lower section, Place Royale, with its Vieux-Port (a popular destination of cruise liners), gorgeous railroad station, and such landmarks as the grand Notre-Dame-des-Victoires church, is a labyrinth of narrow alleys, the old stone buildings converted into intriguing art galleries, cafes, bistros, and antique shops. Merchants, traders and artisans gathered in the village below the cliffs, while clergy, military and government leaders chose the easily-defended plateau above.

Take a 20-minute boat ride across the river to quaint Levis or to Isles d'Orleans, a virtual open-air museum of rural Quebec life.

From Port Royale, you look almost straight up the cliffs for the city's most impressive landmark, the hotel Chateau Frontenac—a wedding cake of gables and turrets topped by weathered copper roofs, built back in 1893 and heads of state, stars, and to the merely gracious-wealthy (and yours, for less than $100 a night) [*sic*].

This is definitely a walking city, and it's clean and safe even in the dead of night. People were everywhere, crowding the terrace outside the Frontenac to view Place Royale and the imposing river, angling for tables at the inviting cafes, crowding the alleyway of Rue de Tresor to see the artists' paintings and etchings. Street musicians, bakeries, boulangerie, bistro serving sublime fare, restaurants offering table d'hote (full dinners at a set price). Music and aroma filled the air. Shopkeepers greeted us in French, then graciously switched to English. The street chatter was lyrical—and thus our room with a view went unused most of the day.

The exchange rate—$1.60 to US $1—is only part of the attraction. The shopping here is Eurocentric, stylish, whimsical, and we shipped home to Ocala two original oils by artists who have since established a major presence worldwide.

For us, though, a highlight was food—the Quebecois take great joy and pride preparing it and serving it, as if you were the long-awaited guest.

Le Cochon Dingue (on Boulevard Champlain)—where a lunch for two, including a salad loaded with maple-smoked salmon—set us back around $15 . . . the Initiale, on Rue St.-Pierre, with its eight-course grand menu with wines would set you back close to a grand in Paris, but got the two of us change from a $100 bill . . .

Don't pass up the restaurants on Rue St. Louis—especially the Restaurant Aux Anciens Canadiens . . . or the La Peite Italie (average price US$8–$12 per person!), the lovely La Cremaillere on Rue St. Stanislaus. And duck into La Marie-Clarisse, in a 340-year-old building.

Try the Le Saint-Amour (Rue Ste-Ursule) with its two-foot-thick stone walls make it the perfect winter space [*sic*] and the Arctic char with fennel is memorable . . . At the Metropolitan (Rue Cartier), dinner for two $40. The food is Japanese, the menu French, the sushi distinctly north-of-the-border, and this fusion is served up by wispy French waitresses to a young, glitteringly hip crown [*sic*].

Cafe du Monde (Rue Dalhousie)—brunch for two, $25—a boisterous, engaging bistro . . . The Bar St.-Laurent in

Chateau Frontenac, a genteel, marvelous place to breakfast or dine with a view, as cashmere-clad women sip port by the stone fireplace and a chamber quartet plays softly in a corner.

Unlike some European French, we found the Quebecois to be extremely warm and friendly. While strolling past La Petite Italie, the owner caught our eye and smiled. Where we were from [sic], he asked.

"Florida! Welcome . . . be my guests for a glass of wine!" (We not only ended up staying there for dinner but he, graciously and without pointing it out, knocked 25 percent off our bill and sent us desserts with his complements [sic].)

Our favorite streets were in the lower city—Rue St. Paul and Rue St.

Pierre—with their numerous, world-class art galleries, antique shops, and small, stylish cafes and restaurants.

Soon it would be time to leave. But there many of reasons [sic] to return to this charming city that uplifts the mind and inspires the palate. As the famous Winter Carnival winds down, the warm season begins and the city is alive with festivals celebrating food, wine, artists and musicians, fireworks, balloonists, concerts on the rolling lawns overlooking the river.

All will peak with the brilliant fall festival, celebrating the harvest, the brilliant foliage . . . And soon the air will be filled with the aroma of wood fires once again.

Personal-Experience Narrative. It could be your story or someone else's you're telling, but the personal-experience narrative gets its support from a strong story line. In this story type, something must happen—a revelation, a life's lesson—that changes the protagonist in some way. Such change must be implicit from the beginning. As the story unfolds, fiction techniques are used to build the momentum of suspense, drama, danger—even disappointment. This type of narrative uses either the first-person or the third-person voice. My advice to newcomers? I'd avoid personal-experience narratives until you are . . . well . . . *experienced* in the writing game. Most magazines don't run these types of narratives, and even an accomplished writer knows that most experiences aren't exciting enough, tragic enough or sufficiently revelatory to be told. The events of September 11, the tragic explosion of space shuttle Columbia, are, of course, exceptions. Even then, avoiding the repetitive "I" takes great skill.

If you're tempted to write a lighter personal-experience narrative with a humorous approach, remember that humor often falls flat for two reasons: It either relies on insider jokes to which only insiders can relate, or it makes the reader the butt of the humor. Successful humor requires that *you*—not the reader—take the fall. (See example in Chapter 11 and the use of dramatic technique in the personal-experience narrative.)

Personal Essay

Publishing opportunities for the personal essay are slim, even for experienced writers. This essay requires deep, thoughtful writing—and readers who have time to invest. That's why most so-called "popular" magazines don't run them. You'll find them in *The New Yorker* and *Esquire*, among others, and *Reader's Digest* occasionally runs them. *Reader's Digest* is a good place to start your search for personal essays. The piece may be a *Digest* original, or it may be a reprint or condensation from another magazine. In fact, the *Reader's Digest* may have purchased that story originally, "placed" it in another magazine through contractual arrangement, then reprinted or condensed it in order to retain the digest image. Another good source of personal essays is *The Best American Essays* series. The 2002 anthology, for example, featured essays from such sources as *Harper's Magazine, Vanity Fair, The Missouri Review, The New Yorker, The New York Review of Books, DoubleTake, National Geographic Adventure* and *Esquire.*

Written from the "I" point of view, the personal essay is an *inward look* and personal *commentary* on some situation or feeling familiar *to readers.* This is not a soap-box opportunity. Think of the personal essay as a voyage of discovery for both you and the reader—a trip to understand life through the eyes of a new perspective. Sometimes that trip can be humorous. Often, its tone will be serious.

In either event, a personal essay can be challenging to write. How do you make thoughts and feelings that are so emotionally charged and compelling to you, interesting enough to grab and engage others? How do you keep from rambling and losing sight of the reader in the article's equation? It can also be agonizing. Writing the personal essay forces you to look deep into yourself to explore life connections that may be painful to make. The exploration is usually triggered by some incident in the present, perhaps even by a casual comment. It reaches down into your psyche and causes you to think. Over time, you start to make connections between what just happened or what was just said and your feelings and reactions from another, usually preexisting situation. Examine your feelings about both situations. How did you react? How do you feel now? To get a perspective on the *preexisting* situation, you have to connect it to your feelings and reactions from the *present* one. After finding and developing the perspective, or relationship, that unites both, connect it to a universal theme—one with which readers can identify.

This nonfiction writing requires your creative best—a strong lead and storyline, a compelling conclusion, a body with main points fully supported and language and pacing that propel the story. I strongly suggest you reserve the personal essay for the time when insight, inspiration and experience with the subject matter have reached maturity in your mind.

It reached that stage for Erika Sheppard, whose agony and grief over the Columbine massacre became the personal essay, "What Was Mine." Published in the Spring 2003 online *DoubleTake* magazine, it was her first, and to date her only, magazine submission. The essay began in a composition class at Colorado State University. Her grade on it? B–. She reprised and revised the essay when she later took a creative writing course. Result? This instructor liked it and suggested she submit it to *DoubleTake.* She did, "and the rest," she said, "is history." Not a writer or journalist by profession, Ms. Sheppard teaches Spanish-speaking children in the Colorado public school system.

WHAT WAS MINE

By Erika L. Sheppard

I am upstairs in the bathroom, staring out the window at the field of prickly pear cactus and thistle that borders my parents' house in Colorado, where I spent my high-school years. On the far side of the field, a pile of dirt rises as high as the house. The dirt came from the parking lot of my old high school in 1995, when the school was being remodeled and a team of construction workers lowered the parking lot by eight feet. A committee agreed to dump the extra dirt in the field, where it could serve as a sledding hill in winter and part of a track for the cross-country running team in the warmer months. The last time I stood on top of what my peers nicknamed Mount Columbine, I could see all the way to Boulder. I haven't been up there for months now; it's a place of mourning that I haven't had the nerve to visit. It doesn't belong to me anymore.

The fifteen wooden crosses that once stood on top of that hill—including the two that people cut down after writing phrases like "May God have mercy on your soul" on them—are pictured in my May 3, 1999, issue of *Time* magazine. So is a picture of a blond-haired girl cupping her face in her hands as she tosses her head back, sobbing in that quiet way that people do when something hurts so much that sound won't come out. She is standing in my front yard. When my mother first saw that picture, she told me the girl was in shock and was having a hard time choking down the juice my mother had given her to drink.

"She couldn't even call her parents to let them know she was O.K., because she had difficulty speaking," Mom said.

I'm in college now, and every month or so I take out that *Time* magazine, with its cover framed in red, and I have the same reaction as the blond girl. When I look at Eric and Dylan surrounded by their victims' black-and-white photos from the Columbine High School yearbook, under the words "The Monsters Next Door," the pictures get blurry and I shut the magazine so that the wet saltiness from my tears won't ruin the pages.

I soak in my anger at Eric and Dylan for taking my mother away from me that morning. She didn't have time to talk about the test I had just flunked, the fun date I had had with my boyfriend the night before. Instead, she was busy cleaning up the killers' mess.

When I open my mouth and try to speak, nothing comes out but a quiet rush of air, as if someone had cut out my voice box. My throat gets tight and makes me gag on my silent sobs. After I am done crying, the apples of my cheeks are a bright pink, burnt from the salt water. I put Lubriderm lotion on my face to soothe the burned skin and get ready to go to class or work.

Today is different. Today, I don't have the magazine with me. I am curling my hair in the bathroom, thinking I should dye it "Champagne Blonde" again, as my roots are beginning to show. My

(continued)

CONTINUED

mom and I are about to run some errands before my little sister and brother get home from school. They both go to Columbine now. I stare out the window and look at the spot where the fifteen crosses used to stand.

I think about my little sister, Laura, in Spanish class with no safe exit if someone wanted to pick up where Eric and Dylan left off. And I picture Joe, my little brother, in science class somewhere upstairs, near the rooms where kids couldn't reach 911 on their cell phones because their parents were calling them, trying frantically to locate their children.

In the distance I see Joe and Laura walking home together, past Mount Columbine and through Clement Park, their backpacks shifting with every step. Joe gestures as though he were making fun of Laura, and she shoves him away from her. I guess everything must have been O.K. at school, or else they wouldn't be acting so normal. "Get a grip, Erika," I whisper to myself.

Mount Columbine used to remind me of a morning toward the end of my senior year when I trudged to the top of the hill with four girlfriends. All five of us wore our pajamas. We spread out a fuzzy yellow blanket and brought along thermoses of hot chocolate. Some of us would leave for college in about three and a half months; I was going to Colorado State in Fort Collins, Corrie to the University of Colorado in Boulder, Darcie to Puget Sound; the next year, Angela would head to the University of Denver, and Colleen to Metro State College in Denver.

I was so scared to leave home. I didn't want to be away from my close friends. I told the girls this and learned that they were equally scared. We promised to remain friends and keep in touch throughout college. Then we just sat awhile and stared out at the sun rising over the foothills of the Rocky Mountains. It was a morning to look ahead and realize that life does go on, no matter what happens or how scared you are.

About a year later, on April 20, 1999, I realized that life does not go on for all people. Now I know how lucky I am that Laura, who was inside Columbine High during the shootings, is still among the living. When the shooting began, she managed to escape down the grassy hill outside the school's science wing. (Later she told me she went to a friend's house and then to a church.) And I am grateful that my family was able to open up our home to the true victims, who had holes in their sides that formed human fountains spurting blood on my front lawn. I thank my mother for tying our bedsheets and bath towels around those kids to keep them from dying before the paramedics arrived.

My family had to live through that while I was eating lunch in my dorm room at Colorado State flipping through the channels on my little TV. I just wish I could have been there with them, because now I feel like I am on the outside: I didn't have to hear the glass breaking and the small *booms* that rolled over the field and caused waves in our pool. Now I feel I have to protect them, help them talk about it.

Eric and Dylan took Mount Columbine away from me. Now, instead of conjuring up images of that morning with my close friends, the sight of Mount Columbine invokes a picture of mourning, antlike figures moving slowly through the snow, up the path to the peak of the hill, to visit the crosses.

Our community was fortunate to have a place like Mount Columbine to grieve. But what about my earlier version of Mount Columbine? Am I allowed to reclaim it as my own, or is that selfish? I want to look at that heap of dirt (because that's all it is, really) and realize that I will be O.K., and that even though a tragedy happened in my backyard, it's O.K. for my life to go on. I feel a responsibility to quit chewing my nails, resume my life, and encourage those around me to do the same. After all, we were fortunate enough to be spared the pipe-bomb shrapnel and bullets. To stay in mourning forever would be to give in to the pain that Eric and Dylan intended to cause.

Sasha, my dog, is in the backyard whining to be let in. I look down at her through the bathroom window. She turns and gazes toward Mount Columbine, which hides the high school behind it. Then she stares up at me. I run downstairs and open the sliding glass door. Sasha bolts in and through the house, panting and wagging her tail, which is reddish-brown and curls up at the end. I follow her to the front door. I open the door and reveal the source of her excitement: my little brother's lanky, boy-turning-man figure is loping up the driveway. His oversize pants hide his skinny 130-pound body. Laura is right behind him, and her white-blond hair flashes as she follows him through the door. She smiles at me as she passes.

"Hey, Erika!" Joe shouts, as if he isn't already indoors. "Let's take Sasha for a walk up to Mount Columbine. I think she needs it. She has way too much energy!" Sasha is barely able to contain herself at the word "walk," and she begins chasing her tail in tight circles. Three pairs of eyes wait expectantly for my answer. But I'm not ready to go back up there yet.

"Actually, I have to go shopping with Mom, but I'll see you when we get back. Maybe we can take Sasha then."

Laura and Joe seem satisfied with my answer, and I holler for my mother to see if she's ready to go. "Mom, I'm ready when you are!"

"All right, all right, Erika. Just let me get my shoes on," Mom says from downstairs in the basement, where she's been working at the computer. Soon she emerges in the stairwell and runs her hands through her thin, honey-blond hair as if she's the Breck Girl. She locates a pair of size-ten white Keds sneakers that have holes in their toes. The left shoe's lace breaks as she tries to pull it tight.

"Let's stop at the mall to get you some new shoes, Mom."

"What, do I embarrass you when I wear these ones?" she asks me in a mocking tone. I shake my head and say nothing. *It's not the shoes, Mom, it's when you start yelling at Laura and Joe and me in the middle of the grocery store. Or when you start crying while we're standing in line at the bank.*

Mom's changed since the Columbine thing (as my family calls it). I think she wants to talk, but everyone's too afraid of upsetting her. She was in therapy for a while. She brought in pictures that she'd painted, and her therapist asked permission to show them to an art therapist. Now they're going to be published in some book as classic examples of trauma-victim expression. They have black and red focal points and defined brush strokes with white space between them. Mom uses lots of muddy reds and browns that resemble blood. I hate those boys for taking my real mother away from me, the one who wouldn't yell and cry in the middle of the grocery store.

My mother smiles at me and cups the left half of my face in her hand. I instantly feel guilty for being embarrassed by her fragile state. I want her to get better so that people won't look at us with

(continued)

CONTINUED

expressions of pity when we're in public. I want her to be able to hold me and listen to my feelings about April 20; I want her to know how scared I am to talk about it, because I know I shouldn't feel this upset since I wasn't the victim. I didn't get back to Littleton until seven o'clock that night, eight hours after the shootings began. Mom had told me to stay in Fort Collins, but I needed to be with my family and friends. The police had confined westbound traffic on Bowles Avenue to a single lane marked by red flares, so I had to drive five miles out of my way on a detour through another neighborhood and approach my house from a different direction. Then I had to tell the police where I was going and why before they would let me through.

Mom and I hoist ourselves up into the front seats of our charcoal-gray Ford Aerostar minivan; she turns the key in the ignition and backs us out of the driveway. On Peakview, the road that leads us out of our neighborhood and onto South Wadsworth Boulevard, we pass several houses that boast gigantic blue-and-silver ribbons on their front doors. On Wadsworth, a tan Chevy Suburban changes lanes and is now in front of us. It has a Texas license plate and an assortment of bumper stickers. One says, we are *all* columbine. Immediate anger makes my hands turn into fists so tight that my fingernails dig into my palms. I daydream about rolling down my window and shouting to the driver, "Was *your* little sister scared to go to her own prom because she thought someone might try to kill her? Is *your* mom cracking up because she had to keep those injured kids alive until the ambulances could arrive? Only when those things start happen-

ing to families like yours will we *all* be Columbine!"

Instead, I shake my head again in slow motion. Mom is staring at me; I can tell because I see her face out of the corner of my left eye. I don't acknowledge her, but instead pull my legs up onto my seat and rest my forehead on top of my bent knees. My jaw tightens and my teeth begin to hurt.

Mom turns onto West Bowles and then into the mall parking lot. We park and climb out of the vehicle, locking our doors behind us. Dillard's department store is our destination, so we use the entrance by the movie theater. Directly ahead of us is the sunken court where elementary-school choirs sing and kids sit on Santa's lap at Christmas. Various lengths of colored paper hang from all of the second-floor railings. They are covered in phrases like "Our thoughts and prayers are with you," and "You are in our hearts." Some are surrounded with signatures and resemble gigantic yearbook signature pages. Others are framed by second graders' handprints made out of tempera paint in primary colors.

"Why can't they just leave it alone?" is the first thing out of my mouth. "I mean, it's cool and all, but can't we go anywhere without being reminded of it?"

"They're just trying to help. What do you want them to do, Erika?" Mom says, sounding upset.

"I don't know. I just want to go somewhere without having to think about it. I just want to be able to move on. Not forget, but just continue. It has to happen sometime." Mom sighs and walks ahead of me toward Dillard's.

I feel my eyes getting hot again, and the anger makes my hands shake.

"Mom, can we do this another time?" I call after her. She turns around and walks back toward me. She takes hold of my sweatshirt-clad arm and we walk to the van in silence. On the ride home, I wait for her to ask me what's wrong, but she says nothing.

After my mother turns off the ignition, she says, "I'm going to take a nap." She goes directly upstairs to her bedroom and shuts the door behind her. Sasha follows her and scratches at the door to be let in, but the door stays shut.

Laura is standing in the foyer, studying my face for a reaction. "What's with Mom?"

"Don't know," I reply. But I do know, and Laura can tell. The Columbine thing. Laura gets my message that I don't want to talk about it, and hugs me instead.

"Erika?"

"Yeah?"

"I'm glad you came that night," she says, "even though Mom told you not to. It made me feel better."

I smile at her and then hug her back so she can't see my eyes, which are starting to water again.

"Hey, you wanna take Sasha for a walk now?" I say, after regaining my composure. "Let's get Joe and go." She runs off to get him.

I don't want to trudge up that gigantic pile of dirt, see the holes in the ground left by those crosses, but I know it's time for me to move forward and reclaim that spot. I get Sasha's leash out of the coat closet. As soon as she hears the jingling, she runs down the stairs and sits at my feet, excitedly nipping at the leash while I clip it to her collar.

Service Article

One can argue that *all* articles are—or should be—of service to the reader. View the service article, however, as a short filler. In one-and-a-half to three-and-a-half pages of copy—about 600 to 800 words—it offers the reader a few kernels of suggestion or good advice—nothing more—and helps to cement the "being-helpful" relationship between reader and publisher. The beauty of a good service story is its portability: It can travel to a variety of magazines that don't have strictly overlapping readership. "Ten Tips to Good Car Care," for example, could go in *Woman's Day* as easily as it does in a AAA magazine. This article emphasizes choices, costs, reassurance, guidance and advice. Remember that any information furnished you from or by another source must be attributed. Here's a good example of a service article. "The Healthy Way To Donate Blood" appeared on page 21 of the January-February 2002 issue of *Natural Health* magazine.

THE HEALTHY WAY TO DONATE BLOOD

By Cheryl McGrath

More than 1 million Americans donated blood in the six weeks following the September 11 terrorist attacks. But blood is always in demand. The next time you give blood, following these tips to keep your energy level high:

(continued)

CONTINUED

Two weeks before: eat more iron-rich foods to boost your intake of this essential mineral, says Mars Mallari Apherisis, supervisor at the Stanford University Blood center in Palo Alto, California. Women age 19 to 50 should already be getting 18 mg a day; women over 50 and men should be getting 8 mg. A cup of cooked spinach has 6 mg of iron. Also take 100 to 500 mg of vitamin C a day, which helps your body absorb the extra iron, and avoid high-fiber foods, which block iron absorption. Steer clear of foods high in saturated fat; doctors may reject fatty blood.

Five days before: If you are temporarily taking a synthetic blood thinner like Coumadin (warfarin), ask your doctor if you can skip it until after you've donated. (Long-term users of this type of drug can't donate blood.) Taking supplements, even vitamin E, known to thin blood, is safe.

The day before: Drink ten 8-ounce glasses of water; giving blood dehydrates you.

During: to calm yourself, try this: Inhale deeply just before the needle is inserted, and exhale fully as the needle is inserted. Exhaling relaxes your muscles and makes inserting the needle easier. While your blood is being drawn, focus on the rhythm of your breathing. Exhale fully again as the needle is removed.

Immediately after: Focus on your breathing for five minutes before you get up. For the next few hours, eat plenty of nonacidic fresh fruit (like apples or pears), which will agree with your stomach better than acidic fruit, or dried fruit (like apricots) to replace lost blood sugar.

For one day after: Avoid vigorous exercise.

For three days after: Continue your increased iron intake and drink lots of water.

Don't confuse the service article with the sometimes equally short or shorter magazines pieces found in the graphically noisy front of many magazines. These shorts—actually departmental fillers designed to attract advertising and pull readers into the magazine—can be considered mini-articles and are notable for quotes and human interest. When printed, they tend to range from a ponderously long single graf to three.

Other article types include the humor story; nostalgia article; religious or inspirational piece; backgrounder—this provides the how, why, who of a timely subject or situation so readers can understand it better; essay or commentary piece; business story; travel article; and the general-interest story providing information on a timely subject but not in narrative fashion. Remember, however, that many articles are hybrids, resembling each other in parts if not in approach. Various chapters in this book discuss key article types in greater depth.

BUSINESS MAGAZINES HAVE SPECIALIZED REQUIREMENTS

Business magazines, formerly called trade publications and both horizontals and verticals (see Chapter 1), offer writers a wealth of untapped opportunity.

However, an article written for, but rejected by, a specific business magazine usually can't be submitted to another magazine without considerable revision. Rarely do readerships overlap, and editorial requirements can differ dramatically. It's probably safe to say that business-magazine writing must be tight, short and targeted. Articles must be useful in the reader's industry or profession, focusing on industry trends, new products, job advancement and ways to do the job better. That's all the reader wants from this magazine—and that's all the time he or she has to spend within the pages. Whether the magazine is *Aviation Week* or *Florida Realtor,* adhere to these general guidelines.

- Give the article a timely news peg.
- Don't meander; quickly get to the storyline.
- Write *concisely,* not just briefly: To write *briefly* is to skim the subject and gyp the reader.
- Use simple, direct sentences. Using the jargon of the profession doesn't guarantee clarity—or a sale. Avoid jargon; it's usually edited out anyway.
- Personalize and featurize articles whenever possible; human interest guarantees readership, and that's what the editor wants.
- Assume the reader already has the background to evaluate a story; don't waste words by rehashing it. Get to the point.
- Do your research, but confine it to what's needed for your own comprehension. Readers rarely have the time to go into depth.
- Write conversationally, the way you speak. Think of yourself as *dialoguing* with the reader, not talking down to him or her.
- Before you begin, analyze in depth the magazine's readership and editorial requirements. See how this is worked out in the pages of the publication.

WRITING FOR THE INTERNET

You probably skim, scan and otherwise surf the Internet on a daily basis, stopping only briefly to read something. You probably don't even read every word. And you tend to read screen copy slower than you would copy in a printed magazine. Think of the reader as doing the same thing. To hold reader attention, you need to write with extreme clarity and precision—in other words, concisely—and do it in what is usually an extremely small space—roughly 150 words—on a horizontal layout that doesn't favor long text. Any sidebars to a main story will not appear with it on the computer screen; the reader will be directed to click on one or more smaller items or subtexts. Thus, *each sidebar must stand alone* as a complete story. In preparing Internet copy, use short sentences and pay close attention to your word choice: Choose words that can be quickly digested. Paint precise mental images with verbs that are in the active voice and nouns that are accurate, meaningful and easy to read. To forage among adjectives and adverbs is to risk losing the reader.

Few people will read to the end of long articles online, reports Ned Desmond, executive editor for Time Inc. Interactive. As a result, People.com—the Time Inc. online edition of *People* magazine—is shortening everything. A regular 800-word, two-page piece in the printed version is typically reduced to 400 words online. In fact, some of its online articles contain only two paragraphs. However, says Desmond in an interview with journalism professor Gerald Grow, those two grafs have real content and get real readership.

Reading is always an adventure in *National Geographic Magazine.* That venerable publication tells stories in greater depth, and readers expect to spend more time with each one. Since articles in *National Geographic*'s online edition don't have the space restrictions of the printed, bound magazine, stories can actually run *longer* online, says Lesley B. Rogers, senior editor for *National Geographic Magazine.* "Tone is another major difference," she says. "Some, but not all, of our online writing is informal, with more humor and quirkiness. The first-person accounts of experiences in the field by authors and photographers are examples of this. However," she cautions, "this is fairly raw copy, carrying a caveat saying these articles have not been edited or researched." At *National Geographic*'s online magazine, editors don't make new writers fight for a voice. "Less experienced writers have a chance to write online articles," she continues. "They wouldn't have this chance otherwise. Our hope is that after being edited, their copy will be the same caliber as in the print magazine."

Since editorial requirements for a magazine's print and its online editions may differ, it's always wise to check writer's guidelines carefully.

HELPFUL EXERCISES

1. Using a variety of magazines, clip or duplicate, then label, an example from the following article categories: how-to or self-help, narrative-descriptive, service, survey and personality profile. From which viewpoint and with which voice is each example told?

2. Clip or duplicate an article that has no sidebars but seems to lack detailed information a reader could use. Using Internet sources, printed materials, perhaps even quotes from your own short interview, research the subject of that article for those additional details. Using those results, write a sidebar that could accompany the article.

3. Using another article that lacks sidebars, read it thoroughly, then highlight in sidebar proportion some interesting copy in the article that could be featured on a tint block to humanize the story and entice readers.

4. Using library resources, read an article or chapter from a book written in the mid-1960s through the early 1970s by New Journalists Joe Eszterhas, Joan Didion, Tom Wolfe, Norman Mailer, George Plimpton, Nat Hentoff, Herbert Gold, Gloria Steinem, Hunter Thompson, Truman Capote or Gay Talese. What did you find most interesting about the style? Least? Would today's magazine journalism find this style acceptable or controversial?

■ ■ ■ ■ ■

CHAPTER SIX

THE ROAD TEST

Are your slant, storyline, focus, viewpoint and voice appropriate to the material, to readership and to the magazine you've chosen? Is your research on track? It's time to road test all six aspects through the query letter. Since the editor is the first person the writer must sell, the query letter becomes a major factor in the relationship-marketing equation. Write the query well, write it concisely and conversationally, direct it to the interests of readership and you'll hurdle the first roadblock to writing success. In fact, writing the query letter is your main opportunity—sometimes your sole opportunity—to receive a "yes, send it" response. Occasionally an editor will give you a provisional reply, suggesting that you make certain course corrections to the article, then indicating willingness to see the story when it's completed. Sometimes you'll receive a rejection letter. Lucky is the writer who receives a rejection letter *and* a form checklist indicating why the article isn't suitable for that magazine. Consider it a lesson learned.

The query letter should come after you've conducted preliminary research—enough to determine what documentation you'll need and which sources you'll be speaking with. Ideally, you already have conducted several interviews.

Never wait until completion of the article to query an editor. And don't put your interviewing, researching and writing on hold just because you haven't heard yet from the magazine you queried. The query may have to pass through several editorial hands before it reaches a decision maker. It may take a few months for a response.

SHUDDER FACTOR

Some writers shudder at writing queries. Most editors shudder to receive them—an estimated 60 queries *per week* at one magazine. By industry estimate, *only two percent* of query letters submitted ever pan out into published articles. Much of the failure, editors will tell you, lies with that query letter. Directed to the appropriate editorial staffer (see the magazine's guidelines), the query has to accomplish several objectives simultaneously—and all in only one page.

■ It has to hook the editor immediately, tantalizing him or her to read on. Remember that most editors can scan the first few lines of a query letter and tell immediately whether it's worth reading to the end. The all-important first graf of the query usually is written compactly in one or two sentences, and these must encapsulate the storyline or main point. While the storyline is the focus of a query letter, many writers use it verbatim, backing it up with some details in later grafs. The storyline may be part of the hook, or it may come in the second graf. Many writers use their story's lead—if they've written it already—as the first graf.

■ It has to tell why the article is important to readership, usually by citing a news peg, a trend or other timely relationship. Make sure to include some documentation—what the competition has been running on the subject, for example, and a clear statement detailing why your story puts the subject in another perspective (or covers another aspect). *Never* tell an editor it's a "hot topic." Show the editor *why* it is. The query must outline the scope of the article so an editor can judge whether it will be complete or not.

■ It must indicate the type of article, the slant and the focus.

■ It has to contain a line or two on your background and expertise in the subject; for example, if the article is about fishing, mention that you've been a sport fisherman for 15 years and have won several angler awards.

■ The query letter must authenticate the article by citing the interviews you're conducting and what your research sources are doing. Try including a quote or two.

■ It must use short sentences that vary in length, verbs that are active rather than passive and phrasing that paints instant—and accurate—mental pictures. These essentials of good writing also characterize the full article. *Remember: Good writers know how to connect with readers by showing rather than by telling.*

■ It has to look like and sound like a mini version of the article without giving away the whole story. Remember that the best query letters show *substance, style and cohesion*. To show *substance* the query should contain enough details to indicate that the writer has the ability and resources to deliver on the storyline. *Style* mirrors that of the article—tone, pacing, rhythm, viewpoint and voice—all of which give the article its distinctive flavor. And a query letter must have *cohesion*, each paragraph growing out of the wellspring of material in the graf preceding it; thus, the letter itself almost blueprints, or outlines, how the article will be structured.

Some years ago, I wrote two articles on jai alai from the same body of research. One was a survey article on the world's fastest sport; the other, discussed in Chapter 5, was a personality profile on Bolivar, the premier Basque player on the East Coast jai alai circuit. The opening grafs of both query letters sounded much the same as the leads. Although the lead on the survey story was poor exposition, I used it as a run-on sentence with fast-paced action verbs. That action, that forward momentum in the lead of both stories caught the rhythm of the sport—and the editors' eyes. Both stories sold on first query. Following publication of the personality profile, *Today's Viewpoint* asked me to be a contributing editor. (Coauthoring these articles was Katie Bartolotti, a journalism student at the time and a Tampa resident. Familiar with the sport and the Basque language, she knew Bolivar and later married a Basque jai alai player.)

Let's look at some query letters that resulted in publication and one that didn't. From a former student, Nicole Keele, here's a query letter that produced "yes, send it" results from the editor of a business publication for city planners.

(Her address and date)

Ms. Sylvia Lewis, Editor
Planning Magazine
122 S. Michigan Ave., Suite 1600
Chicago, IL 60603

Dear Ms. Lewis:

Finding a low-cost, eco-friendly way to treat raw sewage is a problem for almost every city in America, but a small town in northern California has found a solution. Arcata, Calif., (population 15,000) treats its sewage and reclaims lost wetlands at the same time.

In fact, these series of man-made marshes also serve as a wildlife refuge for more than 200 different species of birds, including the endangered peregrine falcon. The treatment center's series of man-made freshwater marshes are filled with plants, algae and bacteria—all which aid in the water's clarification process. At the end of a 35-day period, all the raw sewage has been removed from the water, and it is chemically free. It is now at EPA drinking-water standards. Currently, there are 17 successful marsh projects in 10 different states.

I am writing an article that will describe the benefits of such a sewage treatment system and will give a detailed description of how any city in America can build its own. The cost of building an entire system such as Arcata's is substantially less than the $50 million for a conventional sewage treatment system for a town of comparable size. Because the marsh also is a popular tourist spot, the total cost of this system is less than the conventional way of treating sewage.

I am in the process of interviewing Bob Gearheart and George Allen, co-founders of the Arcata Marsh Project; Dan Hauser, the local congress-man who helped gather support for the financing of the project; and Steve Tyler, Arcata's director of environmental services. I am also contacting city planners in Orlando, Fla., and Hillsboro, Ore., for information on their successful projects.

As a lifelong resident and graduating college senior in Humboldt County, I have done considerable work in regard to the Arcata Marsh and Sewage Treatment Center. In addition, I have participated as team member in gathering chemical and biological background information for World Wide Web pages being developed by the engineering department at Humboldt State University.

Would you be interested in seeing my article? Thank you for your consideration. I look forward to hearing from you.

Sincerely yours,

[signature]

Nicole R. Keele

Enc. SASE

Here's the first graf of a query letter that, to my knowledge, failed to receive any response at all from the targeted magazine. Note that graf one is vague and uses such unsubstantiated phrases as "incredibly less expensive." The letter is wordy, verbs tend to be passive and state-of-being, and faulty grammar could have been rectified had the letter writer read it aloud. In addition to the letter's failure to pin anything down with facts and figures, story-line and focus fail to appear until the second graf. Will the editor or reader wait until then? Despite the subject—the interesting and ecologically sound building material known as *cob*—prospects for a sale went down for the count after the letter's first sentence. (Underlining is mine.)

> Using recycled materials <u>not only slows</u> the demand for virgin building materials, it <u>is</u> also incredibly <u>less expensive.</u> Fresh building materials <u>are</u> harvested at <u>an unsustainable</u> rate from <u>every corner of</u> the globe. This is unfortunate because <u>many</u> people do not realize <u>that</u> there is an abundant supply of <u>reusable</u> materials <u>that</u> could be <u>used</u> instead.

Here's a query letter in conversational style that I really like. It needs some minor editorial revision and a note on which sources are being interviewed and why, but writer Fernando Rodriguez, a non-native speaker of English, made the subject come alive and put the editor-reader in the picture from the first sentence. Note that the second graf indicates his credentials for writing about the subject. The last graf could be more to the point by adding a completion date and anticipated length for the manuscript. In writing your query, you can use this letter's format. Make sure to double-space between grafs, single-space the body of the letter and use one-inch or one-and-one-half-inch margins all around. Editors prefer block-formatted letters rather than paragraph-indented ones.

(Use several lines here for writer's postal and e-mail addresses and date. Phone number is optional.)

(2 line spaces)

(Editor's name and title, followed by name of magazine and address)

(2 line spaces)

Dear (editor's name preceded by Ms., Miss, Mrs. or Mr.):

(2 line spaces)

"I'm a pretty naive artist," says Sam Gregerson, 43, of Arcata, California. An untrained furniture designer, he made kitchen cabinets for 15 years in this last hippie community before deciding that something else awaited him. Today, this unsophisticated man is surprised that his fanciful wood furniture is selling to the elite in California and featured in galleries and museums from Berkeley to Brussels, Belgium.

I first saw Gregerson's work at Plaza Design, one of the finest furniture shops on California's North Coast. I immediately thought of art I had seen in some of the foremost furniture shops in Madrid, Spain—my hometown—and in San Francisco, Los Angeles and other major U.S. cities. Apparently, so did a customer. Margaret Atwood, author of *The Handmaids Tale,* keeps in the foyer of her home one of Gregerson's best-selling pieces, a whimsical mixed-wood "demi-loom" table.

I'm writing a personality profile on Gregerson called "Sawdust of the Redwoods" which explores his naive discovery of the art world, his personal understanding of how wood expresses his unique vision of what is art, and his interest in northern California environmental issues. Currently he is working on an extended catalog that will display some of his best pieces as well as those of other fascinating artists on the west coast.

Would you be interested in seeing my article when it is completed? Thank you for your consideration. I look forward to hearing from you.

(2 line spaces)

Sincerely yours,

(4 line spaces) [signature]

Fernando Rodriguez

Enc. SASE

Heeding certain *dos and don'ts* in a query can save you heartache. *Don't* tell the editor that you're *considering* writing an article on the subject. Amateurs *consider*; writers *write*. (A proper phrase would be, "I am writing an article on. . . .") *Don't* tell the editor you have an *idea* for an article. Editors buy well-researched *articles*—not ideas. *Do* tell the editor how long the article might run (800 words, 1,500 words, 6,000, etc.). Flattery will get you nowhere: *Don't* tell the editor how much you like the magazine and what a good job the staff is doing. Such gratuitous statements waste space. However, if you have an actual connection with the magazine, briefly say so early in the letter.

QUESTIONS AND ANSWERS

Q: Should I re-query the editor if I haven't received a reply in the response time reported for that magazine?

A: Yes and no. Yes: After two months, send a short follow-up letter that describes your original query and the date it was sent. You might also include a second printout of your manuscript and a self-addressed, stamped envelope (SASE) for the manuscript's return or a stamped postcard for reply. No: Move ahead to another magazine with similar readership. But to be safe, wait the recommended period of time, then send a polite note to the first magazine as a memory-jogger and advise the editor that if there's no interest in your article, you'll be sending out other queries. You might include a self-addressed, stamped postcard. Wait a week to ten days for the editor's response; if no reply, query the second magazine on your list. Note: *Do not call or e-mail an editor to inquire about the status of your query.*

Q: Can I query more than one magazine at the same time?

A: This can be unwise. After all, you can sell first rights to only one magazine; what happens if two magazines reply "send it"? If readership doesn't overlap, simultaneous queries (and submissions) might be acceptable. Make sure to tell the editor that another, noncompeting publication will receive the same article. However, *a magazine that buys all rights has every expectation of receiving an "exclusive."*

Q: Must I query short subjects, particularly those targeted to a particular department of a magazine?

A: Perhaps not. Check the editorial guidelines to determine this.

Q: Should I use the specific names and titles of people I'll be interviewing?

A: Yes, if you know them. To know them by both name *and* title is a measure of your thoroughness.

Q: What if the publication wants a disk as well as a hard copy?

A: Fine. Send both, but make sure the disk is a *copy* and that you retain the original.

Q: Should I tell the editor I'm an inexperienced writer?

A: No.

Q: Should I say I'm a college student?

A: No again—unless your student status fleshes out your credentials for doing the article. (See the Nicole Keene query letter on p. 101.)

Q: I've been published before. Should I state this?

A: Yes, but the statement is stronger if you've published in the subject area of your article. Don't send newspaper clips or magazine tearsheets unless specified in the magazine's editorial guidelines. If those guidelines specify e-mailed queries, you have choices for sending clips: as attachments to the basic query—that may result in lengthy downloads—as attachments to a second e-mail message you've told the editor to expect—or, with formatting loss, as .txt or .rtf files.

Q: Should the query letter include the title of my article?

A: It can, if it's a working title that is strong and encapsulates the flavor of the article. If you're unsure, don't include it. Remember that your title probably will be changed by the magazine to meet editorial or layout requirements. (See Chapter 13 on titles.)

Q: Do I query by e-mail or snail mail?

A: Editorial guidelines will state whether the magazine wants an e-mailed or a snail-mailed query letter. If by postal service, make sure to enclose an SASE for reply.

Q: Do I use the same format if I query by e-mail?

A: No. Common sense dictates certain format changes. Don't include your postal address; at the end of the query, include your name, telephone number if you wish and e-mail address. Don't include the address of the publication. Do address the query to the editor by name and title, followed by the name of the magazine. Get to the heart of your query without preamble, and avoid double-spacing unless absolutely necessary.

Before printing out your query letter, check it over for typos, spelling, grammar, punctuation and other errors. Do the verbs have punch? Are there enough specifics to convince an editor? Do paragraphs follow logically, each expanding on the previous one? Is additional information needed? Don't hesitate to revise. Now read it aloud. Does the writing flow well, or do you stumble over phrasing? Aim for a well-paced query letter that's rhythmic with its own music.

Hint: Only an amateur would request a copy of writer's guidelines and a sample issue of the target magazine *within the query letter*. It indicates the writer hasn't carefully researched the magazine.

HELPFUL EXERCISE

Draft a letter to your target magazine querying the editor's interest in the article you're writing. Read it aloud and revise as necessary. Then make a copy of the query but leave off your name and address. In group forum, blindly exchange the query with someone else. Acting as the editor receiving that person's letter, decide whether you would give a "yes, send it" response or a "no, sorry, here's why" reply. Substantiate your decision. Based on what you've learned in this fashion about your own query letter, revise and send it off.

CHAPTER SEVEN

GROWING THE STORY

If you're overwhelmed at this point by background information for your article, statistics, observations and copious interview notes—*don't write a word.* Your first task is to organize the material into main points and substantiation for each, then to blueprint or "map" the story, giving it a structure and a direction that both you and the reader can follow.

Before you map your story, try clearing up the clutter. Related material can be color-coded using a selection of highlighters and placed in color-coded file folders. To the top folder in each stack, append a printed statement of that particular main point. Depending on the length of your article, you'll probably develop two to four main points, supporting them with quotes, facts and figures, anecdotes, case histories and other material—all of this placed in color-coded file folders. A printed item that contains information relating to several main points should be duplicated if possible, important sections highlighted appropriately and placed in the appropriate folders. If duplication is not possible, then leave a note in an appropriately coded folder indicating in which folder the other material can be located.

Organizational methods are not graven in stone—you could do it all on the computer, for example, although paper files allow you to see all your material at once—but tight organization is absolutely necessary. You need good order and a good grasp on your main points in order to develop a map, or outline. While writers differ on the need for an outline—some say it destroys creative inspiration; others say outlines make stories dull, predictable and lifeless—unseasoned writers take note: If you don't know what your main points are and where you're going with them, neither will an editor. There's no second-guessing on a magazine's part: You just lost the sale (or failed the staff assignment).

A short article of 200 to 800 words will sell without elaborate outlining. For a how-to or a service story, for example, you might simply list the steps or suggestions in order, then write a few lines about each, fleshing out the story with more information when you sit down to write. For a short article that fits neither type, simply list the one or two main points you're making, then back each up with substantiating material—a few telling quotes, perhaps, or perhaps an anecdote that perfectly expresses the storyline, perhaps a few statistics or a case history. As with all outlines, main points may be listed as brief items or in one or two full sentences.

THE OUTLINE

Start your outline with the article's working title. Follow it with your story-line, then write out your lead, or opening. (See the discussion on leads and endings in Chapter 8.) These elements will launch you into your main points and backup material for each. Backup substantiation could range from quotes and anecdotes to case histories, statistics and other facts. The story's ending completes the outline. Remember that points should flow logically into each other with the most important (or the most telling or the most shocking, etc.) point leading the outline. For long stories, a proper outline requires that one main point be followed at least by a second, that there be at least one subpoint and preferably more for each main point and that subpoints offer at least one element of substantiation apiece and preferably more. Thus, in outline language, a *I* requires a *II*, an *A* requires a *B*, and both *A* and *B* require at least a *1* apiece. If your outline appears to be unbalanced—top-heavy with main points or bottom-heavy with too many substantiating elements—*rethink your outline and in particular, your main points.* Novice writers tend to confuse main points with subpoints or even with backup information. Check out the outlining function of Microsoft Word for help in formatting.

An outline for my *National Fisherman* story on sharks could have looked like this:

Working Title: Unsafe at Any Speed

Storyline: Commercial fishermen hate them, swimmers fear them and entrepreneurs want to market their meat and hide. The simple fact about sharks is the complexity of the problem: No one can agree on how to control shark predation and do it economically, without over-fishing the population out of existence.

Lead: Makos, tigers, lemons, hammerheads—sharks are unsafe, at any speed. Relentless cruisers in temperate and tropical waters, they may nevertheless range as far north as the sub-Arctic.

  I. Shark predation on commercial fin fishing and shrimping
     A. Nets destroyed, income lost
        1. Interviews with Groover, Fulford, Snodgrass for fishermen point of view
        2. Interview with Coughenower (Marine Advisory Program) for national perspective (possibility of fishnet insurance program)
     B. Effect on wholesale fish prices

II. Shark predation on swimmers, coastal tourism
  A. Statistics on shark attacks and human mortality (coastal Florida, United States, South Africa)
    1. Background from shark behaviorist Gilbert, others—Mote Marine Lab, Sarasota, Fla.
    2. Information from B. Davis—Anti-Shark Measure Board (S. Africa)
  B. Concerns of city and state tourism officials regarding lost income
    1. Interview with tourism heads in Daytona Beach and State of Florida
    2. Interview with B. Davis, Anti-Shark Measures Board

III. Entrepreneurs' solution: develop market for shark meat by development of commercial shark fishing industry
  A. Weak domestic market for shark meat
    1. Interview with New Orleans restaurateur, others, regarding dining on shark
    2. Statistics from Hong Kong and other worldwide locations
    3. Costs of shark fishing
      a. Interviews with Perry Gilbert—Mote Marine Laboratory, others
      b. Coughenower concerns regarding shark over-fishing
  B. Interview with investment banker John Moore regarding development of turnkey operations to export shark fishing technology overseas

Ending: Many commercial fishermen in the United States would quibble with Moore's suggestion. Why export the fishing technology? If private enterprise can do all that for another country—why not for their own?

THE HARDEST PART

A good story sounds as though it just grew; a poorly written one sounds as though it were merely cobbled together in chunks, without flow and organization. Think of the growth of an article as you would that of a tree. The roots at its base provide foundation and take in nutrition. The tree's trunk provides structure and acts as a conduit for food and water flowing through xylem and phloem. Branches spread upward and outward from the trunk; from their nodes spring buds, leaves and fruit. Growth occurs naturally, without interruption: *Each element stems from the element preceding.* By analogy, nothing in an article should interrupt reading flow; nothing should be merely dropped in without reason.

How do you decide what you use and what you don't? *Charisma* editor Jimmy Stewart calls it "the hardest decision of all." Stewart first sits down and does his best to categorize the story by thinking "here are the elements of the story I absolutely have to have—my A list of elements."

The elements are people, topics—elements that are absolutely critical to expressing the story; in other words, you have to have the things you know that you can't do without. I think that's a bit instinctive. Beyond that, it has to be stuff you will keep in order to fulfill the angle of the story—what you've been assigned to write, what your story is supposed to say and to whom it's supposed to say it. I look for the things that will most strongly give the story flesh and bones—a personality, a voice, a sense of expression that is *not* Jimmy Stewart's but this person's or that person's or these people's story. Aside from that, I look for the kind of thing that will grab the reader's attention. That might mean by a shock effect. If something shocking happened, that's reality and I'll use it. I also try to give a story a sense of place. I want readers to feel as though they know where this story has come from, why it's being presented to them and why it's written in such a way that they're drawn in. I'll keep in anything I see in my notes and other materials that I think supports this.

How do you decide the most effective way to organize your story? How do you decide when to present a particular quote? How do you decide that case history A belongs *within* the story but that B belongs at the beginning? "You can have wonderful information," said Stewart, "but if you don't put it together right, it may not say much. Without structure, I'd feel lost." Stewart's Goth material almost defied organization. He wanted to open the story with something visual because Goth communities, the wild dress and the culture itself, are strongly visual. He chose the place where Goths congregate and "do their thing"—the clubs.

It was bizarre yet very intriguing. As quickly as possible, I wanted to segue into the people, the Goths themselves, and what they had to say. But aside from the visual opening, most readers would be like me at the very beginning: "Aren't they the ones who like Marilyn Manson music? Aren't they the kids who shot up Columbine?" I had to give readers some framework—a perspective on what this movement is—*before* I launched into the individual people themselves. It made for a long story opening. I tried other ways but couldn't seem to get it all to mesh and make it work. Finally I said, "Okay. I'll go with a visual opening to draw in the reader. Then I'll explain it to the reader using narrative exposition: This is who they are, this is where goths came from, here are the folks you're getting ready to read about. Then I'll launch into the rest of it."

LINK YOUR PARAGRAPHS

Each paragraph expresses a thought—sometimes written as a topic sentence—and each thought is an outgrowth of another. In the brain, thoughts are fluid—protoplasm traveling by osmosis from one point to another; on paper, the relationship between one graf and the next must be clearly linked and revealed. With linkages, or *transitions,* story organization flows smoothly. Without them, readership slows, then dissolves in confusion. There's a way to avoid this. Think of your story as a succession of related thoughts, thoughts that literary convention tells you must be packaged into word groups called paragraphs. Paragraphs may contain as little as one sentence—sometimes even one word—or they may contain as many as four or five sentences. Each graf will express and enlarge on a single thought. The transitions from one thought to another, one graf to another, signal shifts in time, space, place, speakers and action, making the story understandable because the connections (connective relationships) among the grafs are clear.

In this sense, the computer function known as cut-and-paste is *not* your friend. Instead of forcing you to do the hard part—rethinking, revising and rewriting—the ease and speed of cut-and-paste allows us to move paragraphs and other blocks of type from one place and drop them in another all too easily and too frequently. Our absorption with this timesaving function can destroy story organization because it destroys logical progression of thought via smooth transitions. Witness the choppy stories in many of today's newspapers.

TRANSITIONS BY ANY OTHER NAME

Certain words, phrases and types of sentences help a writer transition from one connective graf to another.

The *echo transition* takes a key word or phrase used in the first graf and repeats, or echoes, it at or near the start of the second. Thus, the last sentence of the graf you've just read and the first sentence of this graf maintain the relationship by echoing the word *connections* (*connective* is a variant). From a short piece on chocolate in the January-February 2003 issue of AAA's *Via* on pages 61 to 62 comes this lead for "Truffles and Flourishes."

> Leave it to a scientist in California, home of heart-healthy merlot and medical marijuana, to discover that chocolate is good for you.
>
> Chocolate, says Carl Keen, a professor in the department of nutrition at UC-Davis, is rich in flavonoids, the same components that have made green tea and red wine famous as health-enhancing beverages.

Note that graf two amplifies the graf one statement by explaining *why* it is good for you. Having introduced him, the second graf also sets up the reader to expect a quote or two from Keen, the nutrition professor. Had it been forthcoming in graf three or four, it would have been a *transitional quote.* Like a paragraph of exposition, which also can transition to the next thought by introducing another aspect, the quote belongs in a graf by itself.

The *question transition* is another useful device to link thoughts. I've used it often in this book to keep you thinking and to vary sentence structure. The question transition typically is used when one paragraph sets up a situation that the next graf must answer. Thus, from the November-December 2002 issue of *Via* on page 11 appear these two grafs.

> Five years ago, most hotel room rates were fixed. Not any more. One guest may pay $99 for his room, while the guy across the hall is shelling out $175.
>
> Why the discrepancy? In recent years, many hotels have adopted a more fluid pricing model that helps them fill rooms and maximize profits.

Certain key words and phrases act as *transitional alerts*. Among them are *meanwhile* and *at the same time* (for more or less simultaneous action going on elsewhere), *in addition* and *also* (when explaining another aspect), *however, on the other hand* and the ubiquitous *but* (when qualifying what you've just said), and the much-overused transitions found particularly in how-to and service stories—*first, second, next, now* and *later*. As with any transitional devices, avoid frequent use of the same transitions and the appearance of artificially using them.

HELPFUL EXERCISES

1. Clip or duplicate a magazine article that runs two or more pages. Highlight, then number and label by type, each transition you find in it. On an attached sheet of paper, briefly write out the main points you believe this article contains.

2. Transitions have been deleted from these examples published in the January 2004 *Men's Journal*. For each example, write a word, phrase, sentence or sentences, perhaps even a researched short graf, to carry the reader through a change in thought.

   > Denim used to be a symbol of rugged individualism, and the only decision you had to make was zipper versus button fly. Today jeans are a fashion necessity, and one pair just won't do.
   >
   > First, know that a good fit means more than nailing the waist and inseam measurements. When you try jeans on, suggests Rich Rodriguez, a spokesperson for Levi's, "ask yourself, 'Do they feel good in the thigh? Is there enough room for me there?' " If they're too tight, try another pair. . . . (From "Denim Jungle" by Marion Maneker, pp. 68–69)

   > I stood in my driveway, eyeing my cross-country skis with skepticism. Though it was the middle of winter, the temperature at my home in North Carolina was in the 60s. The chances of spending the weekend carving ski tracks into the highlands of northeastern West Virginia with my buddy Alan were looking slim. But I chucked the skis into my truck anyway.
   >
   > There are 350-plus trail systems spread across North America, many of them close to major cities, and a few below the Mason-Dixon Line. . . . (From "Easy Gliding" by T. Edward Nickens, pp. 14–16)

2. Using the working title, storyline and main points for your own article, map the course you'll be taking by constructing a working outline. *Do not* add lead and ending to the outline at this point. You'll want to read Chapter 8 first.

CHAPTER EIGHT

BRANCHING OUT

As *Charisma*'s Stewart reveals, a lead serves a purpose—to attract and hold, *to hook,* reader attention while leading the eye into the body of the story. Choose your lead with care and discrimination: The first 100 or so words of your article make the difference between keeping the reader—and editor—hooked and letting him or her off the line. *Don't* think of it as writing your creative best; *do* think of it as writing a contract or promise—a promise that you won't *mis*lead the reader. The opening you select must be appropriate, matching body and conclusion in tone, style, slant and content. In that sense, a lead—like the metaphorical trunk of a tree—grows out of the material and the storyline that root it. The rest of the story—branches, buds, leaves, fruit or flowers—flows from the lead.

Study your notes and outline. Put yourself in place of the target reader in your family tree. Will a surprise opening or a startling statement attract and hold that reader's attention? Maybe. But will either satisfy your slant and storyline? No? Then what about an opening that issues a specific challenge, or one that asks the reader a pointed question, presents a problem or provides a solution to a situation that impacts this reader and thousands, perhaps millions, of others? Warning: If your lead ends up a gimmick that fails to flow into the body of the story logically, rhythmically and without strain, *rethink it.* If the body of the story is serious in tone but the lead you've written is light or humorous, *rethink the opening.* If the opening is an anecdote or case history (see pp. 117, 119) that is *atypical* of your storyline and doesn't bear on your focus or slant, *choose another.*

A LEAD THAT DIDN'T MATCH

The best lead I've ever read came from an article run in a golfing magazine. Beautifully crafted, the nostalgic anecdote ran perhaps five paragraphs. Since I was hooked almost immediately, logic says that I should have read the entire article. But I didn't. Why? The lead wasn't representative of the story; in fact, it had almost nothing to do with the storyline. As a beginning writer, make sure to avoid such tacked-on leads that promise one thing but deliver another. Lead and story that follows must grow from the trunk of *the same tree*. Regard exclamatory sentences or useless questions—wherever they appear in a story—as throwaway games and gimmicks.

A good lead also must satisfy the **TIPPS** criteria:

Timeliness (the topic is on readers' minds)

Immediacy (it's happening now)

Proximity (topic is near to the reader emotionally or geographically)

Punch (crisp, on-target words, concise phrasing that gets to the point quickly)

Specificity (narrowness—nails down the focus with who, what, where, etc.)

In addition to the foregoing, a good lead offers a range of choices that may employ such additional elements as conflict, comparison and contrast, and surprise.

Most writers begin to feel comfortable with their material after they've written the lead. I think of it as a morning cup of coffee that jump-starts my writing. By the time I've mentally chewed on possible leads—this could happen overnight but usually takes days or weeks—I pretty much know how I'll map the rest of the story. When I sat down to write about jai alai star Bolivar, I had to accomplish two purposes with my lead—*put the reader into the action immediately* by use of pacing and scene sketching and *build reader identification* by describing something of Bolivar himself. I did the latter through the eyes of a spectator.

TYPES OF LEADS

Like the various types of articles, leads fall into different typologies. Their use isn't rigid: Several types of leads could fit a single story and still match the storyline, slant and focus. For example, I could have started the sharks story with a *quote lead,* then followed up immediately with identification of the speaker and the situation. Instead, I chose a *summary lead* and withheld for several grafs that single, spit-it-out quote from Groover, the one-boat man. For a quote to work as a one-or-two-sentence story opener, it must strike the right tone, get right to the heart of the situation, put the reader immediately into the picture with vivid language and be the best quote you have—clear, punchy, short, direct and representative of the situation as in this example:

"I've seen animals do things in my backyard you don't get to see on *National Geographic*," says Barbara Thuro, whose garden in Vista, California, is a sanctuary for a variety of creatures, winged and wild. Dragonflies perform aerial acrobatics over the pond. Raccoons sleep under her deck; at night, they join skunks, opossums, and other prowlers rustling in the bushes while crickets serenade them. (From "Gardening for Wildlife" by Loren Bonar Swezey and Sharon Cohoon in *Sunset*, Nov. 2002, pp. 77–80)

This one works as well.

"You'd have a difficult time finding a room here this week," says Hilton Hotels CEO Stephen Bollenbach, sitting in the company's flagship Waldorf-Astoria in New York City. Of course, he's managed to snag a rather nice one.

In fact, getting his hands on hotel rooms, say an additional 10,000 this year, is Bollenbeck's mission at Hilton, a company he hopes to turn into a hot property again. ("Boom at this Inn" by William Dowell and Greg Fulton, *Time*, July 8, 1996, pp. 42–43)

Choose the most appropriate lead for your story from a range of opportunities—not only quote leads, but those employing dialogue, action, question, question-and-answer, conflict, comparison and contrast, startling statement and single word, historical or literary reference, description, narration, case history, anecdotal, direct address, summary, figure of speech or play on words, teaser, parody or irony, prose-poetry (purple), composite, blind, sensory, and hybrids of these. For our article on Bolivar, for example, we chose an *action lead* that immediately set up a conflict: Bolivar competing against another player, Bolivar battling with himself. The first conflict was a metaphor for the second. That thread runs throughout the personality profile and helps to define the character and personality of the man. *Conflict leads* are big interest-getters but must be sustained by the rest of the story.

With the late J. Clarke Weaver, an expert in voice and personality, I wrote "How to Sound Younger" for *Modern Maturity* magazine some years ago. Employing the *direct address* of a self-help piece (the writers speak to a "you" or an implied "you"), the story's lead not only presented a problem and defined a solution, it also contained a composite person and was presented as such to readers (by means of the asterisk). Why a composite? The explanation is simple: Carl Folks didn't exist by name—but he shared demographics and personal concerns with those of *Modern Maturity* readers, and we wanted to use him.

People are always surprised when they meet Carl Folks*, a semiretired realty agent from Phoenix, Arizona, who does much of his business by phone.

"From your voice, I thought you were much younger!" clients exclaim.

Folks, a vigorous 69 with a firm handshake and a likeable smile, is lucky: He has a voice that keeps you listening.

Had there been a reason, we could have used that lead "blind." *Blind leads* (like blind anecdotes and blind case histories discussed later in this chapter) involve an actual individual (or town, business or other organization) who cannot be or chooses not to be fully identified in print. To do so might put this person in danger or perhaps subject him or her to public ridicule and humiliation. In a blind lead, make sure to *partly identify* the person in order to build reader identification. In parentheses that follow the name used, note "not his real name" or, as *Reader's Digest* does, follow the name with an asterisk, explaining at the end of the article that the "name has been changed to protect privacy." In the example above, you'll note the asterisk that appears right after the name; at the bottom of the page appeared a notation that "Carl Folks" was a composite of several people.

Question leads and *question-and-answer leads* must be short, pointed and strike right at the heart of the target reader's interest. If the question isn't answered immediately, the copy must imply that by reading on, it will be. Crisp and succinct, with just the right appeal, this lead opens a short how-to piece entitled "Double Your Pleasure" by Ann Marie Brown (page 41, November 2002, *Sunset*).

> If crisp autumn afternoons inspire you to dust off your old ten-speed, why not try a tandem bike? These bikes allow cyclists of different strengths and abilities to ride together without one of them always struggling to keep up. Because two riders share one set of wheels, wind and rolling resistance are cut in half. Tandems go farther and faster with less work, so the miles fly by.

This lead works, too.

> Want bigger strawberries? The secret is to encourage bees in your garden. A new study by researchers at Cornell University has shown that when bees are active in strawberry patches, the berries grow up to 40 percent bigger. ("Bees Make Bigger Strawberries," January-February 2001 *Organic Gardening,* page 8)

ANECDOTES GO ANYWHERE

A little nutshell story, or *anecdote,* that perfectly illustrates the subject of an article and gives the reader a sense of person or place is often chosen as the lead. The September 2002 issue of *Family Circle* ran three stories about bone marrow donors that were grouped under the heading "Uncommon Courage." The first of these, "Someone's Hero," began with an anecdote.

> Lots of people, it seems, could count on Jeff Olsen. In winter he would shovel his elderly neighbor's walks. He would always stop for stalled cars. He once even saved an injured sparrow hawk found near the lower Manhattan firehouse where he worked, spending days building a cage and feeding it, and later taking it to the vet. As with many firefighters, helping was just something he did, like breathing. So Jeff didn't think much about it when in 1999, as a probationary firefighter

at the Fire Department of New York Fire Academy, he had his blood tissue-typed and became registered as a potential bone marrow donor. He even forgot to tell his wife.

Unlike the above example, a lead that employs a *split anecdote* depends on the *end* of the article to complete it. Start the article with an anecdote—one that splits equally into two parts, each part able to stand alone—finish the first part only, and go right into the body of the story. To the reader it all seems logical: The anecdote appears to be complete; in fact, it reads like a case history. However, the remainder of your split anecdote is your ace-in-the-hole ending and a complete surprise to the reader. Shortly before concluding your article, briefly transition back to the original anecdote. Complete the second part of it in one or two paragraphs and you've ended the article on the same note you started. Use of a split anecdote is a bonus. It gives your story some extra continuity and ties it up neatly for the reader.

Because anecdotes (and case histories) give flesh and bones to a situation, they make general statements believable. They illustrate a general statement with something specific, telling the reader, "Hey. You can believe this. It really happened." You can even *craft an ending with a stand-alone anecdote* that neatly summarizes your storyline and leaves the reader with food for thought. Anecdotes and case histories are essential to many stories. They not only humanize them and build reader identity, they bring the article into sharp focus by providing specifics.

YOUR MENTAL PAINTBRUSH

Make sure that you *support all general statements with specifics.* Use a specific anecdote, for example, to lead into a general statement or use it instead to lead out of it. Use facts and statistics in the same manner. *In the use of singulars and plurals, follow the rule of specifics: Let one stand for all.* Paint a compelling graphic image with the singular rather than the plural. Let a mossy-horned steer with a flinty eye stand for a herd of steers milling around. Let one chanting, sign-waving teenager with an American-flag headband represent a crowd of anti-war protesters. Remember that the reader can only "see" images to the extent you're good with a mental paintbrush.

VERSATILE CASE HISTORIES

Case histories are specific thumbnails of people, places or situations that humanize and illustrate your main points. A single case history may be used alone within the body of the article or as a lead. However, long-time favorites such as as *Reader's Digest* and *Ladies Home Journal* know that case histories are best used as leads in multiples of uneven numbers (three, for example, rather than two). Make sure not to bullet them.

Suppose that you needed to illustrate an article on the medical disorder fibromyalgia. You'd conduct research and interviews with medical specialists, of course. But to humanize the article and pin it down as credible, you'd also speak with specific people who suffer from the disorder. One way to indicate in the article just how widespread fibromyalgia may be is to employ several case histories in the lead, using interview sources drawn from various geographic areas, age groups and both genders. Always make sure to draw your examples from a wide geographic—and if possible, depending on readership, wide demographic—sample. That way, you build *magnitude, significance and reader identification.* Remember: The reader of your target magazine has to be able to find himself or herself within the pages of the article—and quickly. What better way than up front for immediate identification? This lead from "Health: Where to Get Help in a Constantly Changing System" by Michael Lemonick on pages 29–30 in the January 28, 2002 issue of *Time* employs a two-case-history lead.

> Theresa Arnerich, 54, couldn't afford to pay for private medical insurance after her divorce, so for years she went without. Finally, in 1997, Arnerich took a part-time sales job in Los Angeles, mostly for the health coverage. "I have an EPO," she says. "I don't know what that stands for—exclusive provider something. Whatever. They tell me it is one step above an HMO." She could have chosen a PPO—she doesn't know what that means either—but it cost more. On the other hand, her trusted gynecologist isn't in the plan, so she pays his $125 fee out of her own pocket instead of finding a new one who will accept a $10 co-pay.
>
> For Mike Dickson of Columbus, Ga., choosing a medical plan for his family was a lot easier. Mike and his wife Jennifer, who worked for a financial-services company, had what he calls a "top-notch benefits department," with experts to help answer questions. Even so, Mike and Jennifer had to decide which features of the different plans they cared most about. They chose an HMO because of its comprehensive basic benefits and its maternity coverage.

The lead for "What You Need to Know About High Blood Pressure" by John Pekkanen, pp. 139–144 in the March 1995 *Reader's Digest,* employed a single case history in the lead—*but three more in the body of the story to illustrate different points.* We'll be examining a similarly constructed story in a later chapter.

"The Predator in the Classroom," a story by Tamara Jones about sex-abuse cover-ups in the schools, ran in the May 2003 issue of *Good Housekeeping.* It employed a lead of three case histories—a teacher from California, another from Ohio and an elementary school principal from Arizona who had hushed her school's scandal. The use of three—each no longer than a graf—indicates just how widespread are sexual abuse and resulting cover-ups in the elementary and secondary schools. Additional case histories ran within the body of the story. A long sidebar of quotes and background offered an intimate look at the life of a 37-year-old man whose sexual abuse by a teacher started at the age of nine.

Like anecdotes, case histories have multiple uses. Use a single case history once, as your lead, and never mention it again. Or use it once as a lead of several grafs, drop it, then use another aspect of the same case history *to conclude the story.* Remember that one or more case histories may be used *within* the article as you explore and give faces to the other dimensions of your storyline. *And certainly a multiple-case-history lead will keep your story defined and in focus if you'll use these same cases to illustrate your various main points.*

DOLE AND OTHERS

While narratives and first-person narratives typically employ a *narrative lead,* other story types can preempt it also. A revealing narrative lead about Libby Dole headlined a *Working Woman* survey article by Adele M. Stan (Nov. 1999, pp. 46–51) that talks about various political women and their gender-gap issues and supporters. The lead immediately put the reader into the picture.

> In Portsmouth, N.H., Elizabeth Hanford Dole wanders a summer fair on the Fourth of July weekend, stepping around blankets and picnic baskets, coolers and baby strollers. As she stoops to greet the daytrippers camped in front of a shorefront concert stage, a quiet buzz begins to circulate through the crowd. "Look who it is," one woman whispers to her boys. "See that lady? She could be the next president of the United States."
>
> Before long, Dole becomes a pied piper of sorts, trailed by a bevy of women in their 30s and 40s, many with young daughters in tow. They want their daughters' pictures taken with the candidate, and the Dole campaign, equipped with a Polaroid camera, is only too happy to oblige.
>
> Sheila Marchese, a trim brunette in shorts and a tank top, explains that although she's not really political, she's thrilled by the Dole candidacy. It matters to her that Dole is a woman. "I think it's awesome," she says. Her 11-year-old daughter, Lisa, stands by her side, eyes as big as saucers as she watches Dole work the crowd. "*I* want to be the first woman president," she says.

This first-person narrative, written for the January 2002 issue of *Guideposts* (pp. 421–45) by a medical doctor whose son has a learning disability, predictably employs a *narrative lead in the first person.* Because so many children suffer from ADD, or Attention Deficit Disorder, readers can identify with the "I" of a parent—and wonder about the revelations of a medical doctor.

> I shifted nervously in the stands as my seven-year-old son, Joshua, put on his swimming goggles and approached the edge of the pool. Around me the other parents chatted, but I was focused intently on my son, who was trying out for

our neighborhood Y's swim team, the Flying Dolphins. Joshua suffers from Severe Attention Deficit Disorder, and I always kept an eye on him in case he needed me.

Below is the lead for a classic *narrative-descriptive*. The story relates the experiences of a husband and wife who sailed from Bermuda to the Azores in their 38-foot ketch and the places they visited along the route.

> The GPS reads 39° 32' N, 31° 33' W. In real terms, we're 17 days east of Bermuda in the middle of the Atlantic when Flores, the westernmost of Portugal's Azores Islands, suddenly appears in the haze. Sheer green cliffs and a spray-spattered shoreline materialize eerily off our bow, as if they've been there all along. ("The Azores" by Paul Bennett, pp. 44–48, *Outside*, April 2003)

This article includes a half-page sidebar detailing how to get to the Azores and activities and available lodgings once you're there.

HOOK THE READER AT THE TOP

You're sure to hook the reader with an appropriate, tightly worded *comparison-and-contrast lead* (the way it is versus the way it was, the way it is here versus the way it is there, the way we used to think and the way we think now, the good and the bad, etc.). The first sentence of this lead from *Snow Country*'s Summer 1995 "The Lake Effect on a Family" gives the reader an immediate hint of what's coming.

> Nature once had no competition. While adults went about their business, children gathered berries and scrambled up trees, captured tadpoles and waded in streams. Today, kids are more likely to spend their leisure time with Power Rangers, Ninja Turtles and other residents of the TV wasteland, and it takes more work to connect children with the great outdoors.

Or try this from "Dahlia" by Julie Landry on page 10 in the June-July 1996 *Birds & Blooms* magazine.

> You say "to-may-to," I say "to-mah-to" . . . you say "dal-yuh," I say "doll-yuh." Both are correct pronunciations for a flower that is such an eye-catcher in summer gardens.

Another good comparison-and-contrast lead—and also a *historical reference* one—introduces this story on Vermont grapes and wine by Chris Granstrom appearing on pages 52–55 of the Autumn 2002 *Vermont Life*.

> Columbus sailed west to go east. The Wright brothers made a clumsy machine fly through the air. You have to admire those brave souls who go ahead and do

things that everyone else knows simply can't be done. And the list of marvelous human accomplishments isn't exhausted yet. Coming down to earth just a bit, here's another one: Over the last few years, Vermont farmers have planted vineyards and started making wine from the grapes.

The verb *dwarfed* sets the tone for this comparison-and-contrast lead for "Champagne Wishes," a story by the author published in the June 2004 issue of *Volusia* magazine on page 17.

They don't adorn the runways of New York, Milan and Paris, their production is small and their marketing dwarfed by the big five houses, but the quality of grower's champagne is sensational, said Tom Johnson, a sales representative for fine wine importer Stacole, a company which sells to distributors through the United States and operates its own distributorship in Florida.

For a *literary reference lead,* check out this travel profile on Sacramento, California, in the May-June 2002 issue of *Via* ("Sacramento," pp. 37–38).

"In Sacramento," wrote Mark Twain, "it is fiery summer always, and you can gather roses, and eat strawberries and ice cream and wear white-linen clothes, and pant and perspire."

And from the November-December 2002 issue of the same magazine:

"A journey of a thousand miles must begin with a single step."
                                                                        Lao-tzu
Lao-tzu was wrong.
A journey of a thousand miles begins with a question: What's the weather going to be like?

For a *figure-of-speech* or *play-on-words lead,* try this story about fiddle music from "Westfield's Fiddle Jam" by Stacey Chase on pages 12 to 15 of the 2002–2003 issue of *Vermont Life:*

On Wednesday mornings, diners at Westfield's Old Bobbin Mill Restaurant are treated to a jam that isn't on the menu.

PROSE-POETRY LEAD AND OTHER EXAMPLES

How about a *prose-poetry lead* that waxes purple in its allusion to something dear to the heart of the writer?

In later summer, when the sun turns the water into a sheet of hammered copper and there are calluses on each shoulder from humping my canoe from roof rack to river and back, the brochures begin to hatch. Slick as wet bonefish, they slide magically under the front door and flop open right to the centerfold: a soft-focus image of a naked 20-foot bass boat. ("The Bass Boat Blues" by Bill Heavey in *Field & Stream*, Nov. 2001, page 24)

Borrowed from the novelist, the prose-poetry lead sets a mood, a feeling for the story. Here's the first graf from Peter Matthiessen's novel *At Play in the Fields of the Lord* (Random House, 1965).

At four miles above sea level, Martin Quarrier, on silver wings, was pierced by a celestial light: to fall from such a height, he thought, would be like entering Heaven from *above*. The snow peaks of the Andes burst from clouds which hid the earth, sparkling in the sun like gates of Paradise, and the blue dome of the mountain sky was as pure as the Lord's pain. Where the clouds parted, it was true, dark lakes reflected wild demonic gleams, but the red roofs of the villages on the lone road traversing the sierra were signals of sane harmonies, good will to men.

Writing *dialogue leads* to recreate a situation or establish character takes more than writing skill: It takes a good ear. New Journalists peppered their stories with dialogue, believing that *how* something was said in the moment could be more important than *what* was said. (Chapter 10 discusses dialogue writing in greater depth.) The January 2002 issue of *Guideposts* carried a first-person narrative by Pamela Haskin on pages 33 through 35. While this story relies heavily on exclamations and exclamation points, and *good writing never does*, the lead on "Mom!" illustrates dialogue.

"Just look at that gorgeous fringed shirt that lady is wearing! I bet she made it. I'm going to go ask her."

"Mom!" I said. But she'd already jumped up from her seat at the restaurant where we were having lunch. With her bracelets jangling, she hurried over to talk to a complete stranger.

This dialogue lead is even better. It fronted a day-trip story for *The Daytona Beach News-Journal* in the summer of 2004 ("Bargain-Hunter's Delight" by Nancy M. Hamilton).

Sold as walnut bookends, they were twin parts of a turn-of-the-century hat block that had been split and restained.

"Twenty-five bucks," said the dealer.

I shook my head. "I can't do it."

"You can't do it? What if I'd said $60 and came down to $25? Could you do it then?"

"What if you said $25 and came down to $12?" I countered.

"I could not do that. No, ma'am."

"But you might be able to do it at $15," I offered.

"I'll split the different with you at $20."

"Hold it for me," I said. "They're heavy. I'll walk around to the other booths and come back."

"Why don't we write you up now and then you can leave it here while you walk?"

Trapped.

"I'll put them in a nice, little bag for you," he said.

I wrote out a check for $21.40. He had me.

For a story on Alzheimer's disease that focuses on the decline of a 70-year-old patient, try a *single-word lead:* "Confused." And for a story on the late NBC journalist David Bloom, who died at age 39 in 2003 of a pulmonary embolism while embedded with U.S. forces in Iraq, here's a single word that says it all: "Committed." This lead in *Money* ("A Toothless Merger" by Michael Sivy, pp. 44, 46, May 2002) offers a lead of three words in discussing the merger of Hewlett-Packard and Compaq Company.

Ambition. Intrigue. Betrayal.

How about a *teaser lead* such as this that engages readers with tight wording and graphic images?

She was afraid to tell her mother. She hoped her father wouldn't find out when he went to the basement every morning to stoke the furnace. She tried washing them out with tiny four-year-old fingers, but then the items always ended up in her same hiding place anyway, in the coal bin. Psychologists today would say she has a problem with insecurity. But 70 years ago, there weren't any child psychologists to consult. And parents, had they known of the child's problem, saw it as their own shame and dealt with it by repeated spankings. (The rest of that story deals with the failure of toilet training.)

OPTIONS FOR ENDING THE ARTICLE

Is a good conclusion essential? It is—precisely because an article *has* a conclusion. A news story does not; it just stops. The ending serves a definite purpose: It closes the storyline loop, tying up all loose ends and leaving the reader emotionally satisfied. An ending is not simply tacked on. By relating conclusion to lead and storyline, your article performs a service to both reader and magazine. Keep your conclusion short—a single graf, perhaps a maximum of two or three. Make sure to write it tightly.

As with leads, you have a range of choices for story endings. These include endings of a *single word* and perhaps with an onomatopoeic one, endings that *play on words,* stories that end with a *warning* or ask a *rhetorical question* and those that close the circle by ending with the *split anecdote* discussed earlier. And why not use a *split quote* or a *summary quote* to end the story? For a summary quote, select one from your notes that best expresses the storyline in a nutshell. It may be one sentence or more. If you like that quote but find it won't quite stand alone, then add a few of your own words to strengthen it. For a split quote, again choose one that best expresses your storyline, begin it but before you finish, interrupt it with description or a piece of action, then complete the quote solidly in one sentence.

In "History Hollywood Style" on pages 89 through 93 of the October 1996 *Readers' Digest,* writer Randy Fitzgerald says moviemakers distort and manipulate history and historical figures. The body of the article says nothing—until the end—about viewers' perceptions of these films.

> In an age when young people are gathering most of their ideas from the screen instead of the printed page, it is sobering to consider how they are being misinformed. As screenwriter Lionel Chetwynd, who wrote and directed *The Hanoi Hilton* and other historical dramas, puts it, "In too many cases the only history people get is from popular culture, and for them, films such as *JFK* are truth."

Since that final quote is too weak to stand alone—the body of the story didn't bear it out—it needed support from the two sentences preceding it. A hybrid, the ending leaves the reader with something to think about. Label it both a *quote-and-booster* and a *twist.*

The *prose-poetry (purple) ending* can fall flat if used incorrectly. Prose-poetry endings belong with stories that elicit an emotional response from the reader. Such stories aren't intended to be information-based. Make sure to keep prose-poetry endings short. And what about an *echo conclusion?* Suppose your story about the failure of toilet training kept emphasizing a phrase such as "shame of the parent." Try echoing that phrase in the final sentence—but this time give it a twist or use it in a meaningful, new way—one that surprises the reader.

The ending to Michael Ryan's *Parade* magazine story "I'm glad I didn't say No" (pp. 12–13, August 11, 1996) approximates an *echo conclusion* and *adds a twist.* Printed below is the story—the personality profile of a woman who was a stage actress when young, then a social worker in later life and finally an executive assistant to the CEO of Young & Rubicam, one of the world's largest advertising agencies. She was in her 50s when the call came to understudy Carol Burnett on Broadway and to fill Burnett's role in the play one night a week. Here is the lead.

> "'No' is an automatic reaction for a lot of people, and sometimes it's my first reaction, too," Jane Trese (pronounced TRAY-see) told me. "But I'm glad I didn't say it this time. I would have missed a wonderful experience."

And the ending:

> "I accept not knowing what's ahead," she added. "Everything has been fine so far. It is important to keep an open mind and not miss the opportunities. You have to try not to be afraid of the future. I guess that's my motto: Fear Not."

Statement endings can fool you. They are *not* a summary of the story. Short, direct and pithy, they are your words, your perspective on the situation, perhaps in a wry or ironic way. Statement endings range from one sentence to just a few. They depend for effect on your vision, your word choice, and even on your pacing. A one-pager written by a staffer in the May-June 2003 *AARP The Magazine* offers an *anecdotal lead that contains a split quote—and a twist ending.* It leaves readers with something to chew on.

> Dave Zapatka was an Arby's counter boy 30-plus years ago when one of his regular customers gave him a book that would have a profound effect on him—*The Prophet* by Khalil Gibran. One sentence in particular struck him: *It is well to give when asked, but it is better to give unasked, through understanding.* "It really opened my eyes to the importance of serving other people," says Zapatka, a hard-core capitalist and firm believer in personal responsibility. How important? "There is no higher calling than serving other people," he says.

In discussing Zapatka's work in offering free literacy education to his 700 employees, the article ends with the second part of the split quote.

> "You offer to help people," he explains. "It's up to them to take it."

"Jailhouse Talk" by Laura Fraser begins with a two-graf case history lead of a Texas convict who listens every Friday to KPFT radio-show host and former convict Ray Hill.

> Every Friday evening at nine, when the brick-red heat of an East Texas day starts to fade, Jon Buice lies on the narrow bed in his prison cell and turns on the radio. He stares at the ceiling with his headphones on, waiting for the sounds that will transport him, however briefly, beyond the walls that enclose him. Then he hears the buttermilk voice of Ray Hill, with his signature catcall: "Holler down the pipe chase and rattle them bars, 'cause we're gonna do a Prison Show."
>
> Buice, 28, has been inside Texas prisons for the past 10 years; he's doing a 45-year stretch for murder. For eight of those years he has listened to the Prison Show every week, as do many of his fellow inmates in the Wynne Unit of the sprawling prison complex in Huntsville.

The article then drops the case history. The remainder of that page and three other pages discuss the beneficial effect that Hill and his weekly Prison Show is having on convicts and ex-cons imprisoned in Texas, where the show originates, and throughout the Gulf Coast. In discussing several other case histories, Fraser's article appears to have dropped the first convict permanently. Two grafs from the conclusion, however, the man appears again for a *split case-history ending* that neatly ties up the story.

> As Hill winds up his show this evening, he takes a moment to say hello to a few inmates he knows personally. He calls out to "Jon," telling him to hang in there. "Now we've just got to figure out a way to get you out of there," he says.
>
> For that moment, listening to his friend, Buice is outside the red-brick walls of the prison. He images himself with a good job, and a family, and a place among the ex-cons who volunteer down at the station. Then he slips off his headphones and returns to reality, his 8-by-12-foot cell. But like other inmates who listen to the Prison Show each week, he is now measuring time not just in years, but in the days until next Friday night. (From *Mother Jones,* pp. 47–49, 90–91, November-December 2002)

In the coy and quietly comic story "Bargain Hunter's Delight," the dialogue lead seen earlier is matched to a *question ending with a twist.* After the author revealed that she purchased Equus, the $495 antique horse, she says this at the conclusion:

> Contrary to current home-décor magazines, Equ*mine* will have to do more than simply trot out for Christmas festivities and stand glassy-eyed by the tree. At $495, it's a great piece of folk art. Childish of me, I suppose, but for that price, shouldn't it at least rock?

Finally, not everything fits neatly into categories. A *stand-alone quote* from golfer Lee Trevino ended a *Golf Magazine* story (pp. 117–21, July 2002) that chronicled Jack Nicklaus's failure to win golf's Grand Slam at the 1972 British Open. The win went to Trevino who, as usual, uttered something memorable.

> *"God," he said after both the third and fourth rounds, "is a Mexican."*

HELPFUL EXERCISES

1. In browsing the pages of many magazines, you'll note that a story may open with several paragraphs run together as one without space break or indentation. This layout gives the illusion of a shorter read and allows more options on a single page. It also makes the story hard to digest, particularly when crammed together on a single page with photo illustrations, several smaller editorial items that are boxed or on tint blocks and various typefaces. With that precaution in mind, clip or duplicate magazine articles with the following types of leads: summary, comparison and contrast, anecdotal, split anecdote,

case history, third-person narrative, direct address, historical or literary reference, question and quote. Make sure to highlight and label each type of lead and to circle the magazine flag and issue date. Which of your leads match the body of the article? Which ones do not, and how would you improve them?

2. Highlight the endings on the articles above. Label endings that are quote, split quote, summary, rhetorical question, echo, split anecdote, prose-poetry, play-on-word, warning, single word or statement. Which of these endings refer back to lead or storyline? Which do not, and how would you improve them? Endings that don't fall into the above categories should be examined carefully to determine their purpose.

3. Now write a lead and a conclusion for your own article. Enter both on your outline.

4. Observe a crowd or some congested activity such as salmon swimming upriver to spawn, a pod of whales clearing their blowholes, tourists observing Niagara Falls, attendees at a big wedding reception, traffic during quitting time, mall shoppers attending a Saturday-morning sale, or fans milling in the stands at a sporting event. Using the singular rather than the plural and a specific moment or incident to stand for the overall event, write a short paragraph describing for the reader the activity you've witnessed. Make sure to write in the third-person objective voice.

CHAPTER NINE

STEP BY STEP

You've caught an editor and readers with your lead. Now you have to convince them to read on. You do that by building a strong, organizational framework for your story that holds up logically and makes reader navigation easy. Visualize your story *as structured by storyline, slant and focus.* In that sense, yours has a unique style or architectural design. Holding up and framing the structure are the main points on your outline and support for them—a progression of ideas linked to each other with transitions and nailed down by quotes and by illustrations such as case histories, anecdotes, statistics and other specifics. Your story will rise or fall on the strength and logic of that framework and how appropriate it is to the type of article being written.

Although the basic framework will remain the same for a particular type of story, writers follow their own vision, and each may handle the same material in a different way. Laura Fraser's "Jailhouse Talk," for example (see Chapter 8) moved from point to point by telling the story through the differing lenses of several people. Ultimately, however, the story was intentionally structured to return full circle. The story ended up where it began, with the same convict listening to the same radio talk-show host. How the writer structured that story was a personal choice. She could have approached it *cinematically.* The story then would have been a series of movie-like scenes that quick-cut from radio-show host Hill to Buice and to another ex-con without obvious transitions. Or she could have told the story in a series of full *narratives*; like two or three trains running on parallel tracks, each narrative would converge on the same destination (the station, or the storyline revisited) at the same time.

THE HOW-TO STORY

Certain story types follow a preferred structure or formula that the reader associates with them. The ever-popular how-to article is one such case. In the how-to, or self-help piece, each main point or main step carries the same weight, is structured similarly and is written in more or less the same amount of space. The difference may be in order and structure: step by step if you're giving detailed directions that must be followed in order, point by point if order doesn't matter but suggestions, or categories of information, do.

Stylistically, each point or step is repetitive: Topic sentences retain the same structure. For example, let's say you are writing an article on yoga postures. If you chose the implied "you" and an imperative structure for the first topic sentence—"Now assume the lotus posture"—the topic sentence of each successive point must begin similarly. But suppose you began the first topic sentence of instructions or advice this way: "You will find the lotus posture beneficial. After assuming that posture . . . " Or perhaps you began it with an interrogative—"Will assuming the lotus posture be sufficient?" You would then follow that structure for each topic sentence that introduces another main step or point. Remember that the first sentence of a key graf need not be the topic sentence; it may be the second or, on occasion, the third. Clarity is the decision maker here.

Since this article tells the reader how to do, be, build or improve on something or self—and promises "happy results"—reader interest is built in. The boredom of repetition is usually avoided because content—not style—is preeminent.

In the classic how-to, content must be presented in simple words and in short sentences and grafs. Directions must be simple and step by step— easy to follow and *presented in logical order*. After all, you can't tell exercisers how to use a medicine ball if you haven't told them to purchase it first, where to get it, what size to choose and the approximate cost. And will the reader need other materials as well? Time is also essential: How long will it take to do, build or improve on something or self? When can the reader expect those "happy results"? The how-to article should also include any precautions to take at each step and pitfalls to avoid. Your story may also include one or more lists; check the magazine's editorial preferences to see if lists should be bulleted.

ILLUSTRATIONS MAY BE NEEDED

And what about illustrations? If you're writing an article detailing how to build a miniature Christmas tree—and I have—photographs or diagrams may be very necessary. It may also be necessary to include photographs or diagrams *of each step*. My best advice is to put yourself in the reader's shoes—clarity makes the decision—and to check the editorial requirements of your target magazine. If photos or diagrams should be supplied by the writer, I suggest you do so. If the magazine wants to run your how-to but you're not a good photographer or can't use computer software for line illustrations or diagrams, tell that to the editor. The magazine may detail a photographer to photograph your work or have a graphic artist polish your rough illustrations.

As shown here, my black-and-white photo and rough line drawings illustrated this step-by-step how-to for an issue of *The Rangefinder*.

Hint: Watch for complacency when writing the simple how-to. Why? It's *too easy:* Like a recipe, just plug in ingredients, give the steps one by one, and the stew cooks itself. It's so easy, in fact, that the how-to story risks sounding

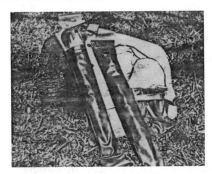

Umbrella Holsters; Two-clamp Tote

Stitch a Sporty Umbrella Case

by Nancy Hamilton

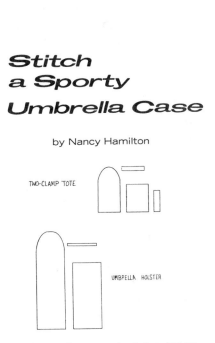

TWO-CLAMP TOTE

UMBRELLA HOLSTER

Umbrella reflectors normally come in see-through, plastic cases which tend to rip at seam edges after even limited use. For extra protection, holster your furled umbrella in an inexpensive vinyl carrying case you can make yourself in less than an hour.

For a 36" Reflectasol like mine, you'll probably need only 1¼ yards of vinyl fabric. You can find a cut remnant of material that at $1.88 per yard costs less than half the price of material still on the roll. There are several types of vinyl; I chose the cotton-backed variety. It's sturdy, pliable and not too thick for a home sewing machine to stitch easily.

With a tape measure, *loosely* encircle the widest part of your furled umbrella—I measured mine in its plastic sheath for extra body and protection—and allow half-inch seams on each side. You will be cutting a front and back section, so divide these measurements in half. Now measure the length, allowing the same seam margin at the bottom, an extra quarter-inch at the top of the front section for turning under a finished edge, and a 6½" gently tapered flap on the back section which will also be turned under a quarter-inch. Cutting measurements for each section on my 36" umbrella case were 6" by 28½", plus flap.

Next, cut two such rectangular sections from the length, rather than from the width, of the fabric to avoid stretching. On the vinyl side of the front section—the section without flap—measure 1¼" from the top, and at seam line on both sides notch or mark a ¾"-wide strip. The belt will be inserted here to fasten the flap. From the *width* of the material, cut a belt 1" wide and 6" long: Cutting from the width allows just enough stretch for a snug fit.

Now you're ready for stitching. Adjust the tension on the machine so the needle will pass easily through the folds of vinyl. Use a medium-size stitch; if you make a mistake, it is difficult to rip smaller stitches without tearing the vinyl. First, top-stitch a quarter-inch finished edge across the top of the front section—for a sportier look, choose contrasting thread—then turn under and top-stitch flap and belt. Matching the outer (vinyl) face of the front section to the inner face of the belt, stitch the two together at notched or marked area of seam lines. Now place the outer face of both top and bottom sections of fabric together and stitch both sides and bottom. With scissors, round off the squared bottom edges.

Now reverse the material, slide in umbrella and the elbow-shape light mount at one side, and examine your handiwork — a sporty holster for "shooting" that beats carrying around a cheap, plastic sheath or the cardboard box

in which your reflector was packaged. If you have two umbrella reflectors, sew a second holster from the remaining material and a matching tote for your stand clamps. Since I have two Reflectasols and often use both on the same job, I designed a two-clamp tote with a "secret" inner pouch for screws and the 6½" threaded rods which center light sources on umbrella units.

The two-clamp tote is a simple rectangle, again with flap and belt. Place both brackets side by side and measure loosely. Allowing for half-inch seams and quarter-inch top-stitched edges, each section of mine measured 9½" by 12" with a 6½" flap, 1¼" belt (the bulkiness of the clamps demanded a wider belt than the umbrellas), and 7½" by 2½" inside pouch. Follow the same cutting and stitch directions as for umbrella holster, but before stitching belt to front section, top-stitch pouch to the same section. Match the inner faces of both pouch and front, stitching them about ¾" inward of the side seam line but even at the top. After sewing on belt and stitching sides and bottom, reverse material and top-stitch lengthwise down the center of the two-clamp tote to avoid clamps rattling together. Now insert each clamp in its pocket, and screws and rods in "secret" pouch. With tote and holsters, you're a sharp shooter guaranteed to bring your gear back 'live and in good shape.

THE RANGEFINDER

34

choppy. The alternative to choppy is glib (too polished to be true), and you want something in between that reads comfortably. That's why we use transitions between thoughts, short words that paint graphic mental pictures (there's a big difference between a "piece of wood" and a "two-by-four") and sentences that vary in length (from short to shorter in the case of how-to articles). You want your article to flow—to look and sound rhythmic. In fact, *consistent rhythm* is the hallmark of the how-to story. (See Chapter 12 for a discussion of rhythm and pacing.)

In the classic how-to, your article will end on a positive note, reinforcing the promise of the lead. You want to reassure the reader of satisfaction and a strong sense of accomplishment. And remember, too, that the writer's "I" (or "we") speaks to the reader's "you" or implied "you."

LEADS VARY

Leads for how-tos and their self-help variants are flexible. For example, an article for *Lady's Circle* on how to start a farmer's market used this anecdotal lead. The happy results were presented in the fourth graf.

> A well-dressed woman carrying a shopping bag of oranges and a pint of tomatoes walked through the downtown parking lot to the back of a red-and-white pickup truck. She carefully examined the stacks of fresh turnip and mustard greens.
>
> Then she held up a large bunch of leafy turnip greens and asked, "How much are these?"
>
> Ollie Mae Robinson, who had picked the greens earlier that morning at her five-acre farm outside town, rose from her lawn chair. "They're 50 cents, but if you think that's too much to pay for them, I'll lower the price to what you think they're worth."
>
> The customer looked surprised. "Why no," she answered, "that's very reasonable."
>
> This is a typical exchange at the farmers' market in Gainesville, Florida. For little more than a year, full-time farmers with small crops and part-time farmers with backyard gardens have been offering residents fresh food at low prices. (*Lady's Circle*, July 1976, pp. 36–37, 60)

To avoid confusion, note in the above excerpt that a change in speaker is always preceded by identification; for example, *"The customer looked surprised.* 'Why no,' she answered, 'that's very reasonable.' "

"Double Your Pleasure," an article by Ann Marie Brown on page 41 of the November 2002 issue of *Sunset* (see reference in Chapter 8), speaks to the implied "you" and presents the happy results in a single-graf lead.

> If crisp autumn afternoons inspire you to dust off your old ten-speed, why not try a tandem ride? These bikes allow cyclists of different strengths and abilities

to ride together without one of them always struggling to keep up. Because two riders share one set of wheels, wind and rolling resistance are cut in half. Tandems go farther and faster with less work, so the miles fly by.

Note the rhythm of that lead. It's *suggestive:* In sentence construction, sentence length and use of simple words, the lead rolls off the tongue *like an easy and pleasant bicycle ride.* The second graf of the story contains the second happy result—cost—followed by where-to-cycle information. Detailed rental information is presented in a sidebar. Almost as an afterthought, some basic tandem cycling pointers are given in three bulleted grafs at the end. This information could have been expanded, perhaps into two or even three stories, and the abrupt, leave-the-reader-hanging ending avoided.

SOURCES CAN HELP

How many sources nail down a how-to? The simplest article will use one—enough to make the story credible. Use that source early, usually right after the lead. This presents an authority for the information that follows. In fact, *you* may be the authority. If you have the credentials to write this how-to—you're a gardener, a candle maker, a cyclist—and are writing about the topic, let the reader know that in a summary sentence following the lead.

A frequent contributor to *Southern Living,* Charlie Thigpen wrote the easy-to-follow how-to shown on page 134. It appeared on page 78 of the magazine's Spring 2003 issue. Although the one-pager lacks authority for its information, regular readers accept the magazine as a credible source and thus its contributors as well. Moreover, the title is a gardening grabber: "One Easy Iris."

Robert Blechl was a magazine-writing student at Humboldt State University when he directed his article on candle making to readers of *Careers and Colleges.* The appeal of such an article is obvious: Said Blechl in his query letter: "Such a business allows a young person [about to embark on a college career] the opportunity to earn extra money and fosters independence and discipline." His authority? Melissa Johnson, a student and successful part-time candle maker herself. Here's the lead for the story.

Have you ever thought about owning and operating a small business? If you have a flare for creating things with your hands and a few hours to spare during the week, candle making may be just what you are searching for. Not only can it rake in extra money, but such a small business can also appeal to your artistic side and provide an escape from the pace of today's hectic lifestyle. And it doesn't have to bite into that precious time you've allotted to other activities.

One Easy Iris

Japanese roof iris make an attractive ground cover, but they're really too pretty to be classified as just that. This perennial will cover the garden at a speedy rate, and its spiky foliage provides interesting texture.

These iris *(Iris tectorum)* are a cinch to grow. (They are actually grown on rooftops in Japan, hence the name.) They prefer a fertile, moist, and slightly acid soil. They'll grow in sun or shade but bloom more in a sunny site. The neatly arranged foliage works well with hostas and ferns in naturalized areas and woodland settings. Mass plantings under deciduous shrubs, such as hydrangeas or native azaleas, look great too. They can also be used in containers.

Leaves have an exotic look, rising 10 to 12 inches tall and growing in a fan or whorled arrangement. New foliage stands straight, creating a jagged look, and old foliage flops or curls.

Blooms are about 5 inches across and appear in April and May on 10- to 12-inch stems. Each stem usually produces two or more blue or white blooms. The blue flowers vary from dark to pale; the white ones are pure white with yellow centers.

Don't remove spent blooms. Seedpods will appear where flowers have bloomed and can be collected in midsummer once they've turned brown. Pods have seeds, which can be sown in the garden or containers. Bury them about ¼ inch deep in loose soil. Seedlings emerge in a few months.

If you don't care to mess with seeds, your plants will still multiply. Established plants have creeping rhizomes that spread and form clumps, which can be divided. With the ability to multiply by seed and rhizomes, these iris will naturalize in the garden.

Many flowering plants bloom and have little to offer the garden once their flowers are spent. But Japanese roof iris just keep on giving by creating a leafy mass that covers the garden's floor. CHARLIE THIGPEN

PHOTOGRAPHS: VAN CHAPLIN

The exotic-looking leaves of Japanese roof iris produce a unique ground cover in this landscape. Beautiful white or blue flowers are a delightful bonus topping these spiky plants.

JAPANESE ROOF IRIS
At a Glance

Height: 10 to 12 inches
Flowers: blue or white, 3 to 5 inches across
Location: sun to partial shade, slightly acid, well-drained soil
Range: Upper, Middle, and Lower South

SOURCES page 160

Although the lead lacks start-up costs, Blechl's interview with Johnson conveys the main how-to points of the story and provides its human voice. Here's graf two as it introduces his authority and substantiates the appeal.

> Melissa Johnson, a senior at Humboldt State University in Arcata, CA, started such a business two years ago when she was 21. With her own small business, Johnson is able to devote a few hours a week to candle-making yet still work another part-time job and attend school full-time.

The closing adds a twist—the emotional fulfillment Johnson gets from her customers when she sees the look of amazement on their faces. "A lot of times they can't believe this is something that someone can actually make."

When I co-wrote "How To Sound Younger" with J. Clarke Weaver, we used a single, informative source: Weaver himself, a Ph.D. and renowned speech expert. When should the how-to or self-help use several sources? As a rule of thumb, the longer and more complex the article, the more sources used. You're more likely to employ multiple sources in the self-help rather than in the basic how-to piece, and that can present an organizational issue: Should you back up each main point with a separate authority? Should you weave in sources randomly? Group them together? Here are my suggestions: You don't need to quote a source for every point nor even mention one. Use only the strongest sources *in* the article; use the rest as background information *for* it. Quote one, perhaps two, of those strong sources directly; summarize the information, paraphrase or indirectly quote the others.

In contrast to the how-to (do), the self-help piece—help *yourself*—focuses on the *how-to be* or *how-to self-improve.* Psychological or motivational in nature, it often employs anecdotes and case histories that illustrate the befores and afters and at the same time build reader identity. This article may be organized step by step; more often, it's main point by main point. A typical framework looks like this:

- A lead of one to three grafs that states and illustrates the problem or situation
- Some background that both fleshes out the problem or situation—usually the history and what caused it—and gives the compelling reason for adopting or modifying an outlook or behavior
- The main points and backup for each, usually grouped by category
- A conclusion that leaves the reader satisfied or issues a call to action

A CLASSIC EXAMPLE

With three sidebars—probably copy lifted from the main text—and editorial on four pages, the article "Get More Done in a Day" by Ted Tate (*Florida Realtor,* pp. 30–34, 50, June 2002) is a classic example of a well-written how-to for a business readership. Note the predominately "you" voice. No quibbling here about direction—the storyline is up front. Most sentences are short and direct, the writing style is conversational, and quotes humanize the piece. Leading off with a question, the story presents the happy results in graf four. The ending restates the lead.

"Get More Done in a Day" contains four main points and quotes from four authorities—all of them in real estate sales. Note that quotes aren't always matched to the story's main points: They don't need to be. Three sidebars pep up the article; these contain information that could otherwise distract from the main story. The last graf restates the lead.

■ ■ ■ ■ ■

GET MORE DONE IN A DAY

You don't need 30 hours in a day, you just need a better way to manage the 24 you have. Here are some solutions from fellow real estate professionals.

By Ted Tate

Why is it that some salespeople earn more, while others, who put in just as many if not more hours, are struggling to make a living? In many cases, it boils down to one thing: time management.

Roger DeLeon, a broker with Century 21 in Miami, says it's easy to become disorganized in real estate since you are juggling so many hats. "I see some [salespeople] start out with no plan for their day, doing less important tasks in the middle of what should be their prime selling time, changing priorities every time the phone rings," says DeLeon.

We interviewed real estate salespeople and brokers from around the state to find out how they manage their time.

Here are some key time management issues along with some suggestions on how to effectively deal with them:

1. DETERMINE YOUR PRIORITIES

Do you have friends or business associates who are always busy, running from one task to the next, frazzled? They have constant phone interruptions, people walking in on them asking for favors or assistance, barely able to get focused on one task before the next issue pops up and worse yet, everything feels like an emergency.

"Focus on your priorities and make sure you are working with qualified buyers," said Doug Dennison who manages the Keyes branch in Boynton Beach. "Some people dislike asking qualifying questions so they spend far too much time working in situations that really can't be sold."

"Priorities" says Dennison, "are critical to success in real estate. You simply can't go in your office to put out fires and see what the day brings."

"Successful salespeople always have their day planned in writing the night before, making sure the top priorities get done first."

These are also the people who claim that time management isn't the

Can I Delegate This? Finding Help

A key to being more effective is delegating the lesser but still important duties such as sending direct mail, keeping up mailing lists, handling paperwork, returning routine calls, etc.

Roger DeLeon, a broker with Century 21 in Miami, pointed out that salespeople who do trivial tasks such as their own direct mail could pay an assistant per hour to do these tasks. That way, the salesperson can focus that time on selling homes—which can produce an income of $100 per hour.

DeLeone [*sic*] says some salespeople who don't need a full-time assistant should consider getting together with two or three other salespeople and share one full-time assistant who divides an equal number of hours working for each.

Here are three [*sic*] work force pools often overlooked by salespeople when seeking a part-time assistant.

Retired people. People are retiring at a younger age and many are not comfortable just sitting around. Living on limited incomes, many are happy to find an opportunity where they can be useful by contributing and getting paid for it.

Stay-at-home moms and dads. Many people have working careers before marriage and children. While some never work again, others really miss it. Unfortunately, they can't work full time but they make enthusiastic part-timers.

If you focus on what you need done, you'll find people from these groups who have excellent skills and talents to do the work.

---

problem, that they are organized, they just have too much to do. They show their lists of things to do, pages upon pages of all kinds of things.

What you are witnessing is someone who treats everything with equal importance. Reading the mail is just as important as making sales calls. People coming in or calling must be addressed immediately. They fall into the trap of dealing with everything that comes their way, no matter how trivial.

Some people equate success with keeping busy. Keeping busy really means nothing unless it takes you closer to your goals. Running around helping other people do their job [*sic*] or dealing with trivial tasks all day gets you nowhere.

Good time management starts with focusing on your goals, what you really want to accomplish. It means you write these out. Without focused, written goals time management becomes very difficult, with them it becomes very simple. Our interview subjects also were very firm in setting priorities, knowing what is most important and dealing with it first.

Setting priorities is simple as ABC

"A" means something you must do, a very important task.

"B" means something you should do but if you have to, it can be postponed [*sic*]

"C" means something nice to do but not necessary.

Clarify priorities by asking yourself these questions: Why am I doing this now? How does this relate to my goals and objectives? Is this really the most

(continued)

CONTINUED

important task on my list? Is this urgent, does it have to be done right away?

Some people procrastinate doing the "A" list because those are frequently the most complex and sometimes unpleasant tasks. Only after completing the "A" list do you start on the "B" list.

Fight the urge to switch to "C" tasks. These are always the easiest and most appealing. This is where it becomes difficult and requires will power.

2. DON'T LEAVE UNFINISHED TASKS
Finish one task completely before you go to the next. When you put something aside incomplete, it still remains on your mind—additional clutter that contributes to a sense of confusion.

Then, when you pick up the partially completed project you have to rethink it and decide what steps need to be taken.

3. FOCUS ON SELLING
Obviously, your main task is to sell. Everything else you do just supports your sales effort. It is critical when you make up your list of things to do, that each day has designated blocks of times when you will do nothing but either prospect or spend time with qualified prospects.

In order to succeed in this business, actual selling time is your most valuable asset. Don't allow yourself to get trapped into doing other, less important tasks during your selling hours.

One way to focus more on selling is to hire assistants, says Angela Ocampo a salesperson with The Keyes Co. in Key Biscayne. She works in partnership with her son, and they have three assistants to focus on the non-selling work. She says that the assistants are worth every penny, since having them around frees her to focus more time on selling.

She also believes she gets more from her time by planning her day the night before and likes to start each day with her top priority and a clean desk, which she feels helps keep her focused.

Top 10 Realtor Time Wasters

Florida Realtor magazine talked to real estate professionals from around the state about what they thought were their biggest time wasters. Here's what they said:

1. Spending too much time with prospects you have not really qualified.
2. Not enough time scheduled for "A" and "B" priorities.
3. Interruptions, drop-in visitors, distractions, telephone calls.
4. Taking care of personal business during business hours.
5. Getting involved in too many detailed, routine tasks—not delegating.
6. Failing to focus on the goals. A lack of objectives, deadlines and priorities which causes confusion about what to do and when.
7. Leaving tasks partly done, jumping from one task to another task. Constantly switching priorities.
8. Procrastinating—indecision, daydreaming.
9. Lack of self discipline.
10. Too much socializing, idle conversation on the phone or in person with co-workers, relatives and friends.

Time Management Systems

You can contact any of these firms and they will send you a free catalog showing their various time management systems.

1. *Top Producer* Software—http://www.topproducer.com; (800) 444-8570
2. Day-Timers™—1 Daytimer Plaza, Allentown, PA 18195-1551; (800) 225-5384—http://www.daytimer.com
3. Franklin Covey, 2200 West Parkway Blvd. Salt Lake City, UT 84119-2331; (800) 654-1776—http://www.franklincovey.com
4. Time Design, 265 Main Street, Agawam, MA 01001; (800) 637-9942, http://www.timedesignusa.com

4. EXAMINE YOUR ROUTINES

For some people, being busy spells success. They spend all day hopping from one trivial task to another trivial task only to complain in the evening that they are further behind than when they started.

Being busy means absolutely nothing to your success unless the task takes you closer to your goals.

Emphasize results instead of activities. Think carefully about your goals and objectives. How do those trivial tasks add to your effectiveness, to your success? Remember, it's not how much you do that counts, but how much you get accomplished.

Examine your daily routine tasks and ask yourself, "What if they weren't done at all?" If the answer is "Nothing," then stop doing them. The tasks you must do, try to delegate or determine if you can do the task less frequently. For instance make bank deposits once or twice a week, not every day.

Louis Erice, with the The Keyes Co. in Sunset Kendall, stays productive by staying home several days a week from 9 A.M. to noon to do his paper work. "I can do in three hours in my quiet home what might take me six hours in the busy office with all the interruptions," says Erice.

Spending time organizing prospect lists, filing, making copies, keeping detailed records, rearranging your desk, personal business during working hours and all the other trivial tasks only keep you from having time to be a success. Learn how to focus on the activities that will give you the greatest return.

Service articles usually are organized in much the same way. They tend to be shorter than self-helps, and their main points usually bulleted. The service story may or may not quote a single authority. Usually it ends without formal conclusion, on the final point, as does the piece by Cheryl McGrath in Chapter 5 ("The Healthy Way to Donate Blood").

UNDERSTANDING *PROCESS* FIRST

You're writing a personality profile about a man who had laser surgery on his throat and lost his voice. How does a laser work? You're researching a story on Alzheimer's Disease: What does this form of dementia do to the brain? You're writing a piece on the joys of owning a grandfather clock: How does a grandfather clock work? You're writing an article on rice as a healthy dietary staple: How is rice grown? How does a firefly light up and a dishwasher work? How do you use a fly rod? As every good writer knows, in order to describe something to the reader, you have to understand *process* first.

In writing an article on the revolutionary breakthrough of bioglass, the implant material that bonds with bone, I watched oral surgeons remove some of a chimpanzee's natural teeth under anesthesia. Surgeons then inserted bioglass implants in their place—artificial teeth that looked exactly like the real thing. How did surgeons contour these "teeth" so the chimp could eat naturally?

I explained the process this way: "The implanted teeth are cut to size, then shaped to the chimp's own teeth by a pantograph, a device that works on the principle of a common key maker." In explaining the process in terms of something familiar—the key maker—I avoided two dangers: Use of a technical term that a lay reader wouldn't understand (*pantograph*) and being didactic, talking down to, a reader rather than creating an *instant mental image* to which everyone can relate. *Remember that if a reader can't see a process, the story can't unfold. Don't tell readers how something works; show them. And do it as quickly as the flick of a light switch.*

Edwin C. Coolidge, a retired college professor, wrote this short piece for my continuing education class. Although he never submitted it for publication, Coolidge—who owns a grandfather clock—learned how to explain *process* by the simple expedient of placing himself in the reader's shoes. He visualized each piece alone and in combination with others, then he used familiar images (soft drink can, a skewered hot dog) to explain how the mechanisms worked.

Edwin C. Coolidge

WHAT MAKES GRANDFATHER RUN?

By Edwin C. Coolidge

If you were living in Europe a thousand years ago, you would probably be a peasant, working for some lord in return for shelter and life's bare necessities. Your work hours: sunrise to sunset. Never would you see or need a clock. But if you were fortunate enough to be a monk or nun, you had to perform devotions at certain hours. How to know when to obey? You could check the sundial, hourglass or water clock, of course, since all were used to measure time. But all of them had serious flaws.

The answer was the pendulum clock, invented sometime in the 13th century and soon the rage of Europe. The clock became available in any size or shape, was relatively accurate and reliable, and was easily read and quickly adjusted. For more than 500 years, the pendulum clock was to rule the world of timepieces. The key to its success was a simple device that controlled how fast the clock hands moved.

A clock with moving hands is easy to design. Imagine a cylinder such as a soft drink can, but with gear teeth added to the top and bottom edges. The cylinder is pierced through its center by a rod extending from the clock's frame, as a hotdog is skewered on a spit. On the end of the rod is an hour hand which rotates with the cylinder. It rotates, as a weighted cord wrapped around the cylinder unwinds. One gear on the cylinder meshes with a much smaller gear supported by the clock frame and attached to a minute hand. As the weight sinks, the clock hands move at speeds related to their gear sizes.

But how to control the cylinder's turning speed? The answer, called an escapement mechanism, was what made the pendulum clock feasible. Visualize a bar that rocks back and forth and has a tooth at each end. One of its teeth engages the gear at one end of the cylinder, to prevent its turning. As a pendulum attached to the rocking bar swings, the bar rocks and releases the cylinder gear tooth, simultaneously engaging another tooth as the cylinder turns slightly. The cylinder and clock hands can turn no farther until the pendulum swings back to repeat the process. Each "tick" and "tock" we hear reminds us that the bar has rocked again to disengage and engage a tooth. Since a pendulum with a longer arm swings more slowly, a movable weight on the arm makes it easy to fine-tune the effective pendulum arm length and adjust the speed of the clock.

Philosophers suggest the unknown inventor of the escapement mechanism changed the course of history. Given a clock, the peasant became conscious of the passage of each hour and began to think about "saving" time. A new work ethic soon developed, based on efficiency and control of the physical world. With the Age of Enlightenment came a new phrase we still use: "Time flies." Today, we understand better just how.

USE SPECIFIC IMAGERY

Whenever you have to describe something or explain a process, make sure to follow these principles.

- Avoid using technical terms; if not possible, explain them.
- Use familiar images to describe process.
- Don't talk down to readers.
- Avoid clichéd descriptions: "skinny as a mouse," a "bark as bad as his bite," "sturdy as an oak" and a "large, milling crowd." (Aren't all crowds large? And don't they all mill?) Overused and unoriginal, clichés can sink an article "in the blink of a reader's eye" (also a cliché).

Imagery can be used successfully in other situations and in other types of articles. Statistics, for example, can be incomprehensible to most readers. What makes them meaningful? Which creates the stronger mental image— Twelve eggs or a dozen? A 360-foot-long sinkhole or a sinkhole *the size of a football field*? A bruise or a contusion? The use of such quick mental imagery adds texture, depth and perspective. From retired journalism professor Harry Griggs, here's a night-time view of Los Angeles from the San Fernando Valley hills above the city: "A jeweler's tray, the contents spilled and strewn for miles, winking and glittering in the dark." This immediately captures reader attention by providing a unique perspective on Los Angeles.

Only a disciplined, creative writer knows how to work in the medium of such mental imagery. It takes inspiration and experience to keep those images fresh, and to keep them *consistent, focused* and *appropriate* to the subject. For example, what's wrong in the following examples?

■ "Stolid as an anvil, he had a personality that corralled others to his way of thinking." (Although *stolid* personalities could not by their nature do any *corralling*, the metaphors of *anvil* and *corral* produce inconsistent mental images.)

■ "A rising tide of mediocrity steamrolled through the nation." (Focus is lost when *tides* and *steamrollers*—totally unrelated images—are used to refer to the same thing.) Or this newspaper headline: "Fighting Continues To Blossom in Iraq."

■ "He painted ideas that floated over the heads of colleagues." (Loosely speaking, *ideas* may float, but you don't *paint* them.)

See Chapter 10 for a further discussion of imagery.

HELPFUL EXERCISES

1. Choose five of the following items. Using familiar mental images, describe how they work. If necessary, explain their purpose as well. Remember that you're not writing for yourself but for a lay reader who won't be intimately familiar with these processes.

   Milking a cow by hand versus milking a cow by machine

   Manufacturing Swiss cheese

   Growing and manufacturing coffee for market

   How dolphins communicate

   Stem cells and their infusion

   Hot air balloon

   Laser surgery

Custom fitting and use of a prosthesis

Land mine

Structure of a span bridge

Bicycle or motorcycle

Fly fishing

2. Write a service article of 500 to 1,000 words that is targeted to one of the readers in your family tree. Send it with a cover letter but *without query* to one of the magazines you've matched to that reader. Make sure to check *Writer's Market* or the appropriate web site first to find out whether the magazine wants the material e-mailed or snail-mailed. (See Chapter 16 for further instructions on manuscript submission.)

CHAPTER TEN

FROM THE INSIDE OUT

What makes a person unique? Genes? Hair color? Voice? Posture? Height and weight? Occupation? Attitude? Ambition? Philosophy of life? How do you describe this uniqueness? How do you profile a person to reflect it? And why should the reader care?

Detail makes the difference. Whether you're painting a person *round*—the classic personality profile—or painting a person *in brief*, here is where your skills of observation come into play. Look. Listen. Gather. Do you use everything that your keen eye and ear note? In today's information-overloaded society, the answer has to be "no." Were you a writer in the 60s and 70s, however, when New Journalism was the reigning genre, the answer could have been "yes." Detail we discard today was for New Journalists such as Tom Wolfe a highly developed frame of reference. Here, Wolfe cinematically describes a scene in a Las Vegas casino of

> . . . old babes at the row upon row of slot machines. There they are at six o'clock in the morning no less than at three o'clock Tuesday afternoon. Some of them pack their old hummocky shanks into Capri pants, but many of them just put on the old print dress, the same one day after day, and the old hob-heeled shoes, looking like they might be going out to buy eggs in Tupelo, Mississippi. They have a Dixie Cup full of nickels or dimes in the left hand and an Iron Boy work glove on the right hand to keep the calluses from getting sore. (From "Las Vegas (What?) Las Vegas (Can't hear you! Too noisy) Las Vegas!!!")

In some ways, New Journalism was a throwback to an oral tradition—history passed from mouth to mouth, each storyteller adding embellishments. New Journalists employed four major techniques in telling a story: They constructed it scene by scene, they used dialogue without editing it, they observed and included a plethora of minute detail we'd regard today as insignificant (routine gestures, how a person keeps house, orderliness of someone's desk, etc.) and built reader identification by relating the story through the eyes of someone else, usually the story's main subject. (Truman Capote's book *In Cold Blood* is a case in point.) The results were insightful and penetrating if not always easily readable. In much smaller measure, some of these techniques—detail, in particular—continue to be used by writers today.

WHICH DETAIL TO USE?

Select only the details that highlight and support your storyline. Use them to make a person come alive and seem real to the reader. Use details to paint this person three-dimensional, in all his or her strengths and vulnerabilities. After all, that's what makes this person different from anyone else—but still a person with which your readers can identify. Don't be afraid to dip your literary paintbrush into *sensory* detail when building a profile. Smell, sight, touch, sound, even taste—the senses can yield a richness of information. Make sure to sort through it: Let material from one of those senses predominate; more would only confuse. And don't be afraid to discard a good one-fourth of the material you've gathered. Remember that too much detail will obstruct reading flow: Your story bogs down. That's why good writers today *use a little to suggest a lot,* and they work detail and imagery together.

I'll never forget this description I read somewhere of the late southern playwright Tennessee Williams: "His tongue seems coated with rum and molasses as it darts in and out of his mouth, licking at his moustache like a pink lizard." Or Clifton Daniel, former editor of the *New York Times,* describing Winston Churchill in 1945 as "an elderly cherub with a cigar almost as big as the butt end of a billiard cue." Deborah Franklin, writing in the January-February 2003 *Via,* described the late William Randolph Hearst's San Simeon Castle this way: "Fifty-six bedrooms, 61 baths, 41 fireplaces—the scale alone is embarrassing. It apparently took a village to house this man, who had the wealth of a Medici and the ego of Nero."

How you use detail is as important as *what* you gather. Your use of detail should be *suggestive,* unobvious. *Show* rather than *tell* the reader. Use analogies, for example. Use anecdotes. Compare my flat description of Churchill with Daniel's, above: "Churchill was fairly short—no taller than 5' 8"—heavy and smoked a huge cigar." My description is adjectival and leaves nothing for the reader to "see" or discover. Because they are generic and cosmetic, adjectives— "a pretty flower"—and even adverbs—"smelled sweetly"—fail to capture the *unique essence* of a person, place, object or institution. *Their use in any magazine piece should be limited:* They keep a reader from forming a mental image.

DESCRIPTIVE TECHNIQUES

A good writer employs seven descriptive strategies to gather material for a personality profile. From this material, the writer builds an image that allows readers to form a conclusion about the subject.

1. Record *what* a person says—or doesn't say. Saying nothing may indicate an aloof person, or perhaps a shy one.
2. Record *how* a person says it.

3. Record *what other people say* about the person.
4. Record *what the person does*—action or inaction. Failing to take action is also a revealing trait.
5. Record the subject's appearance and the physical description of surroundings.
6. Record the subject's mannerisms and gestures, both physical and vocal.
7. Record the subject's background. Historical information textures the profile and explains the *now* of a person or business in terms of the *how*—the past.

Take a look at the first five grafs of "Cancha King," printed in its entirety here (from the November 1975 issue of *Today's Viewpoint*). By the end of graf six, we had used material from six of the seven descriptive strategies to paint Bolivar on-court and off-court as an extremely complex and competitive individual.

■ ■ ■ ■ ■

CANCHA KING

Some men still expect to marry a virgin—really!

By Nancy M. Hamilton and Katie Bartolotti

They call him Cancha King, the 22-year-old *macho pelotari* of the Florida Jai Alai circuit who turns the toughest returns into points, and he loves it, and lets the hushed adulation of spectators outside the huge wire cage sharpen his concentration and distract his opponents. But this afternoon the rubber grin and the braggodocio [*sic*] strut were gone. Spectators in the Tampa fronton clutched their quiniela tickets and sensed it. Jose Antonio Illoro known to fans as Bolivar had a beef.

"He is nervous," confided the wife of another Basque, as we watched him sit apart from the other players on the sidelines bench, moodily strapping on the white helmet. "Always they pair him with a weak backcourt partner, and he is going to play a special *partido* with two players from Miami who are watching and he doesn't want to look bad."

The seventh team lost, and Bolivar took the front court, the center position where he dominates play like no other, and waited for the opposing team's serve. The ball slammed into the front wall and rebounded high, and his Basque temper got the best of him. He snatched the ball from the air in his hooked *cesta*, whirled and smashed it in a two-shot against the side wall, watched in frustration as his partner lunged for the ball on the second return and missed, the point going to 30-year-old veteran, Gorrono.

Bolivar shrugged and walked off the court in disgust.

"He is always like that," said the woman as we walked through the parking lot behind the Tampa fronton. "He can't stand to be under anybody else."

The player's door opened, and Bolivar exited alone in a red windbreaker, dark hair plastered against his forehead. He turned to the girl waiting for him at the door and frowned. "You go home!" he thundered. He walked to his car and drove moodily home.

"You always work harder and learn a lot when you play against men of more experience," he said later, changing from swimming trunks into shorts in the apartment near the fronton he shares with another player. Calmer now, he had joked with friends around the pool, tweaked a girl's hair.

When the Tampa season ends this year, he's going back to Spain for seven months to prove it. He'll be playing *partido*—the more strenuous, longer version of Jai Alai—testing himself against the toughest competition in the sport. Back near where he made his debut as El Chiquito de Bolivar—the wiry, smalltown kid of 15 from Bolivar, a Basque village in Northern Spain.

"In Spain," he scoffed, "people are very sexually repressed. The custom is still to go out in groups."

"When I go on vacation to Benidor this year, I plan to meet women. I have friends who have been there," he warmed up, "and they've really had a good time."

Benidor, a beach resort in southern Spain, caters to the tourist industry. In Spain, as in America, Bolivar frequents the beaches, likes to meet women in night clubs where he can dance, have a drink or two—"If the other guy pays," he laughed—and listen to music. "I have an elegant voice," he said, reaching for the harmonica to play the moody Basque folk melodies he loves.

At a wedding reception that night, he is once again moody, standing off from the crowd drinking a can of beer, waiting for his present girlfriend.

Does he go out with other girls while dating this one? "Yes," he confided, "and if she finds out," he put down his beer can, "she'd kill me." He leaned over and whispered in mock seriousness, "She wouldn't do my laundry anymore."

"I'm too young to be married," he frowned, as the groom—a fellow Jai Alai player—circulated among the guests. "Maybe in two years I'll start thinking about it. I haven't found a girl to my taste yet."

His taste is for girls who are cute, agreeable—"I don't like to be around a person who is contradictory just for the fun of it; I like a girl who has nerve and an opinion of her own but knows when and how to express herself—and attractive.

"One time I went out with this girl—she was a regular at Jai Alai, and I was really desperate," he confessed. "I told her to get off my back, that I never wanted to see her again." He laughed. "With her, it was really necessary."

"She was everything he didn't like in a girl," a friend explained later. "Fat. The kind of person who makes herself available to other players. After she went out with Bolivar once, she expected to be with him all the time. Bolivar is sometimes . . . ," she groped for words, "unreasonable. He likes to make all the advances."

Friends say his attitude toward women is one of the most old-fashioned and traditional of Basques. Family unity is stressed in Spain, and divorce infrequent. Although he has dated divorcees, "You always feel something different about a woman who is divorced." He frowned. "I could never think seriously about a woman who is divorced." He feels comfortable around a woman's children—the Basque is a family man, and Bolivar plays with them regularly in the swimming pool—but "I have no future with them," he shrugged.

Instead, he prefers not to be seen with a date and her children and entertains her alone—as he does with others he dates—comfortably in his apartment, usually for the night.

"But first," he laughed, "I like to impress her by going to a nice place for a drink. Two drinks of Scotch," he chuckled, "and I'm gone."

(continued)

CONTINUED

Friends say he is a good recanteur, a showman. "I enjoy talking to a girl, telling stories, telling jokes." He is more persistent with a girl who levels with him and is interested in Bolivar the person rather than Bolivar the superstar. "I like to go out with a girl who doesn't seem to be doing me a favor," he frowned. "If I have fun with her, and she's pleasant and easy to get along with, and if she's honest—I don't like a girl who isn't honest—it's worth going out with her again."

What if a girl doesn't want sex? "I don't like an easy girl," he made a face. "I believe in total respect." If a girl he cares for doesn't want sex, he'll find another girl for sex purposes rather than pressure her.

For marriage, he wants a virgin. "If I'm dating a girl I think could seriously be in my future, a few kisses are okay." He put down the beer can firmly. "But forget about anything else until I marry her." Of course, he laughed, "after we marry things will be different!"

Someone hurled an epithet across the noisy reception hall. Bolivar rubbed his nose in disgust. "I don't like a girl with a vulgar mouth—it lowers her category." Friends say it hurts him to hear a woman he cares for using vulgar language. He's still stung by an incident two years ago in Gainesville, where he lived while playing at the Ocala fronton 30 miles away. He invited a woman to stay with him for the weekend at the apartment complex. One night she got very drunk, broke the bedroom door, wandered drunkenly out on the second-floor balcony and shouted obscenities. He was embarrassed.

"A woman should always demand respect," Bolivar said. "I'd like to marry a girl I can take anywhere and be proud." He surveyed the long dresses and modest-length skirts worn by women at the reception. "Short skirts are tacky. Honestly," he boasted, "if a girl is with me, I don't want her showing too much to anybody else.

"I can tell her anything," he says later of the other woman, a childhood playmate from his hometown. "We share the deepest secrets. I ask for her opinion on how to treat my girl, and she asks for my suggestions." Bolivar refers to her as one of his best friends. "I can be as good a friend with a girl as with another guy."

Bolivar has little time for recreation during playing season, but in Spain he plays handball and *paletia*—a light version of Jai Alai played with a ping-pong paddle and a ball similar to a tennis ball. He follows the Basque custom of challenging his opponent for money.

He'll take a slight money loss to play *partido* in Spain this year, but he welcomes the challenge. More inexperienced at *partido* than most *pelotaris*—he began playing Jai Alai in the United States at age 16—he nevertheless feels he will be "as well as and better than" he's been playing.

The special partido at the Tampa fronton against Miami's two best players gave him heart. Teamed with his rival, Gorrono, the four men battled it out in a grueling, nighttime performance that had hometown spectators sitting on the edges of their seats. It was a two-two that won it, a dos *paredes*, Bolivar's favorite driving slam against the side wall and the front before hitting the court. He grinned and received the crowd's standing ovation. It was a personal victory for the one they call Cancha King.

Take *In Style*'s profile on actress Lisa Kudrow, a story more interview—"she said," "another said"—than it is action or background. (Hint: When the profiled individual is well known to the reader, it won't be necessary to fully flesh in the background.) Kudrow was interviewed in a setting neutral to both writer Johanna Schneller and Kudrow herself—a suite at the Beverly Hills Hotel. Now read Kudrow's reaction to that setting.

> On a linen-crisp May day, the actress swings into a suite at the Beverly Hills Hotel, blonder and tanner than she looks on TV (she has just returned from fellow *Friend* Matt LeBlanc's wedding in Hawaii), wearing a suede jacket, khakis and a fitted T the exact green of her eyes. She checks out the baby grand piano, fireplace, wraparound terrace, kitchen and wide-screen TV and says, "Oh, this would be perfect for a little family holiday!" Only after the remark is long gone do you realize it was a joke.

Now read Kudrow's comments as she and Schneller watch a DVD together, the 1948 comic drama *Mr. Blanding Builds His Dream House*. Her comments are revealing and serve to launch and define the direction of the interview.

> Over a room service lunch of avocado soup and chopped chicken salad, Kudrow watches the film closely. "What is she wearing to bed?" she asks, delightedly, about one of Loy's [actress Myrna Loy] frilly confections. She cracks up when Loy says to Grant, who has just negotiated a harrowing series of domestic obstacles, "John, dear, I do wish you'd try and make a little effort."

And later:

> Kudrow flips off the TV and sighs, a bit sadly. "Could you imagine anyone making this movie today?" she asks. "They would say it's too slow. There's no faith that just observing people's behavior is enough." Kudrow, 40, has made a career of it. (From *In Style*, July 2003, pp. 188–192)

WARNING SIGNAL

There's a danger in writing a personality profile, particularly that of a well-known person and certainly of a person well known to a particular readership: You beg the question. You assume that Hillary Rodham Clinton is driving and ambitious so you overlook the softer side of her nature. You ignore Tiger Woods' anger on the links when the distraction of whistles and catcalls destroy his focus. You assume that the conservative head of a corporation is automatically unsympathetic to people who are gay. You expect Jay Leno and Jim Carrey to have comic natures, and your readership anticipates that. So, unfortunately, may your editor. Best solution? Don't disappoint either.

Stick to your assignment, but remember that people are multifaceted. Make sure there's more to your story than a person painted flat, in one dimension only. Hint: If writing a thumbnail or brief profile such as you would find in *People* magazine, try to devote at least one-tenth of your copy to those other facets.

LOCATION OR NO LOCATION?

It's tough to re-create a setting. Johanna Schneller could have *rounded* Lisa Kudrow, had her assignment been to interview the actress on the *Friends* set and perhaps at home, with her son and husband. Time constraints and the lack of more appropriate venue meant Schneller had to resort to physical descriptions of Kudrow, to adverbs and adjectives and to lengthy blocks of Kudrow's comments—all of which *told* readers about Kudrow without being able to *show* them. Going on location for interviews is always my choice. It allows me to observe and gather detail far easier and more accurately. Schneller thus was limited to *asking* Kudrow certain details that under other circumstances she could have *observed*. Such secondhand information inevitably lacks a sense of reality, that sense of *being there* that readers so highly prize.

Being on location allows me to note how the person interacts with others. It also supplies me with a set of *prompts*. I can use items in that physical setting to supply me with additional background about the person: the condition of his desk (he's disorderly); furniture that looks vintage and doesn't match (a collector?); cast-iron cookware (gourmet cook?); small, burning candles and potpourri scents (New Ager?). Those same items supply me with questions to ask my subject. ("Oh, you're a collector?") Although I did interview shark behaviorist Beulah Davis on location—in her hotel room and at the premier Sharks and Man Conference—it wasn't the right place. You can't write *in absentia* about gill-netting in South Africa for sharks: You have to be there to observe. You have to feel the tide, feel fear as a shark is hauled on board, listen to and watch the interaction between Davis and those who work with her. I wrote the article as though I were there, *in situ*. I wasn't, and it showed. As I mentioned earlier in the book (see Introduction), the article failed to sell, although not for that reason.

THE PEOPLE'S STORY

It would be hard to profile a community without talking to and about the people it serves. That's what writer Rob Gurwitt did when he wrote "Fostering Hope"—Hope Meadows in Illinois, that is—for the March-April 2002 issue of *Mother Jones* magazine. This corn-belt subdivision is a community where foster kids and adopted-out foster kids live, kids who are loved and supported by a network of resident families, 60 of whom are retired senior citizens—"grandparents" on a fixed income. As with any good story—as with life itself—the article explores not only the positives of the community but some downsides of it as well. In speaking with supporters of the concept and its detractors, Gurwitt painted the community *round* and made it real to readers. Hint: A situation always has positives and negatives. Examine all facets, but to keep readers engaged, emphasize the positive twice as much as the negative.

It's equally difficult to profile a business without speaking to those it serves, to its employees and vendors and to those who either started the business or run it now. That's a tall order if you're only allotted a two-column "well" for your story consisting of a single page. That's what writer Paul Lukas had to work with in profiling the man and the company responsible for the manufacture of today's barber poles. *Barber poles? In the 21st century?* Forever the symbol of Main Street USA, they're still being manufactured, still being used. Ever heard of the late William Marvy? He's "the only nonbarber ever enshrined in the Barber Hall of Fame," says writer Paul Lukas. "Marvy didn't invent the barber pole . . . but [his improvements were] the last word on it." Lucas wrote a one-page business profile of the William Marvy Company for the March 2002 issue of *Fortune Small Business* (page 96). Although heavy on historical background, "Stars and Stripes Forever" does include a few statistics and a few paragraphs on the company's current sales profile and its diversified marketing efforts. The story comes alive through short sentences, a conversational style and the direct quotes of Marvy's son Bob, who runs the $3 million firm.

WHEN PEOPLE TALK

Although New Journalists weren't exactly "new"—a few magazine writers had used their four-point style at least a decade before—they were novelistically close to fiction writers, particularly in their use of dialogue and in their ability to reproduce interchange and the way a person speaks. For instance:

> "I tried."
> "What?"
> Her voice was smothered in tears. "I said I tried. What more do you want of me?" She dabbed her eyes with the corner of a pink-flowered handkerchief and looked up. "He threw a book at me."
> I sat back in shock. Our eight-year-old son had always been a behavior problem. But until now, it had only been verbal. (Exercise written by the author.)

Here's hard realism, and the dialogue works. There's no confusion about who is speaking, and the "he saids" are unnecessary in this short, deliberate interchange of "The Detective" written by James Mills for *Life* magazine. Note how the cadence of short sentence after short sentence with no interruption conveys the frustrating monotony of the process.

> A detective questions a 25-year-old A&R man arrested for attacking a passerby with a knife on 48th Street. "What's your name?" he asks.
> "Who, me?" The prisoner is a pro at countering interrogation.
> "Yeah, you. What's your name?"
> "My name?"
> "Your name. What's your name?"
> "My name's Sonny."
> "What's your last name?"
> "My last name?"
> "Look! What's your name, all of it?"
> "Sonny Davis."
> "Where do you live?"
> "Where do I live?"

A. E. Hotchner's profile of Elaine Kaufman, founder of the Second Avenue saloon in New York City that bears her name, features lengthy interviews and quotes from a variety of people, long blocks of paragraphs in which Elaine herself speaks without the "she said," and numerous anecdotes about the literati and luminaries who have gathered at her place over the years. Here's an anecdote and some telling dialogue.

> One early evening, Molly Ringwald occupied a front table with a large group that included her mother. Everyone ordered from the menu, except mother Ringwald, who ordered a cheeseburger. Elaine's does not serve burgers, cheese or otherwise, but Molly somehow managed to have one delivered from the deli across the street. Elaine hadn't arrived yet, but when she walked in, she surveyed the Ringwald table, then summoned her headwaiter.
> "What the hell is that?"
> "What the hell is what?"
> "What the hell is that goddamned cheeseburger doing on my table?"
> "That's Molly Ringwald's mother. She wanted a cheeseburger." Elaine confronted the group the way Moses coming down from Sinai faced Aaron and his infidels before the golden calf. She raked the Ringwaldian table with her choicest invective. When the mother shot back, "Do you know who I am?," Elaine told her in no uncertain terms who she was, and the entire group was escorted from the premises, along with the cheeseburger. ("Queen of the Night," *Vanity Fair,* July 2002, pp. 140–56)

In Hunter S. Thompson's scene-by-scene construction "The Kentucky Derby Is Decadent and Depraved" (*Scanlan's Monthly,* June 1970), we see a New Journalist capturing very realistically *the way* people speak. Thompson starts the scene with his arrival at the Louisville airport.

I got off the plane around midnight and no one spoke as I crossed the dark run-way to the terminal. The air was thick and hot, like wandering into a steam bath. Inside, people hugged each other and shook hands . . . big grins and a whoop here and there: "By God! You old *bastard! Good* to see you, boy! *Damn* good . . . and I *mean* it!"

In the air-conditioned lounge I met a man from Houston who said his name was something or other—"but just call me Jimbo"—and he was here to get it on. "I'm ready for *anything,* by God! Anything at all. Yeah, what are you drinkin?" I ordered a Margarita with ice, but he wouldn't hear of it: "Naw, naw . . . what the hell kind of drink is that for Kentucky Derby time? What's *wrong* with you boy?" He grinned and winked at the bartender. "Goddam, we gotta educate this boy. Get him some good *whiskey.* . . ."

"TIGER OF THE PROVINCE"

You don't have to write like a New Journalist to capture the way people speak. When I interviewed Beulah Davis, South Africa's "Tiger of the Province," I found her a very determined woman with a decisive, even dramatic, way of speaking. In writing the story, I selected anecdotes and quotes that painted her that way. I also used certain phrasing and dramatic pauses between sentences that made her tasks seem formidable—or ominous—and Davis determined to overcome them. Because her manner of speaking reveals much of her character, and simply because I wasn't on location to observe her working and interacting, I let Davis speak for herself in long blocks of comments. "Tiger of the Province," a 3,550-word article for which I accepted a kill fee from *International Wildlife* (see Introduction), is reprinted in part here. Note the story's organization. Early paragraphs set the physical stage and placed *International Wildlife* readers on the scene. These grafs are followed by some background on Davis's first encounters with the Natal Anti-Shark Measures Board and on Davis herself—enough to establish character and decisiveness. More details on her background are saved for later; premature use of too much background detail would turn readers off.

> Dawn. A Northeaster has blown hot and humid for three days toward the ruggedly beautiful Drakensberg Mountains, sweeping across the sugar estates and the popular beachside resort city of Durban, brushing south several hundred miles along the Natal, South Africa, coastline.
>
> Along the coastline, the signs are already up—*Bathing Banned*—shark attack likely.
>
> On a ridge in the North Durban suburb three-quarters of a mile away, Beulah Davis has dressed with determination in the blue uniform of the Natal Anti-Shark Measures Board. She studies the sea from her second-story bedroom window, calculating whether to launch the five-man, 15-foot ski boats for net salvage operations. Risky anytime in the shark-infested waters, the operation would be doubly so now against the rip-current, north-south inshore channel.

*Beulah Davis, former head
of the Natal, South Africa,
Anti-Shark Measures Board*

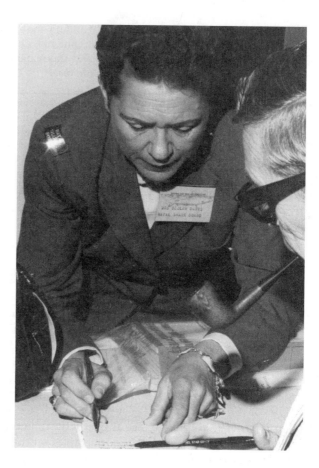

It would be a dramatic, bow-on launch into the pounding surf, so demanding of the strong-gutted crew that to speak is to bite out your tongue.

"Our coastline," she said quietly, "is one of the most terrifying in the world. I have seen steel beams—things weighing tons—twisted like pieces of straw! You will keep nothing, and I repeat nothing, in the surf zone along the Natal coast. When we haven't been able to put to sea for three consecutive days, we ban bathing automatically."

At 45 a darkly handsome woman, divorced and the mother of two daughters, Beulah Davis drives the helm of an organization unique in the world. Created by a single piece of legislation in 1964 that was prompted by at least 74 recorded shark attacks in the province, the Natal Anti-Shark Measures Board protects a multi-million-dollar tourist industry from the slashing predators.

A highly dedicated field staff of 23 whites—the majority qualified scuba divers—and more than 80 Zulus work dawn to dusk, patrolling and protectively meshing with offshore gill nets about 143 miles of Indian Ocean coastline from 39 meshing stations. The risks are high. Scuba diving deep into shark-infested waters to untangle snarled nets or hauling on board a sand tiger shark that appears dead but without warning snaps open its jaws, the men are in constant jeopardy.

To meld a force of this size and dedication and install a system of offshore gill nets that is both protective and scientific has been a ten-year struggle for the battling woman they call "The Tiger of the Province."

Beulah Davis was born in the hinterland province of Transvaal—born with the grit and determination to win inherited from staunch French Huguenot parents. She swims poorly, can't scuba dive because of a middle-ear imbalance and gets seasick on ocean liners. "Ski boats," she dismissed the craft, "don't worry me a scrap. I've never been sick on them. Never even come close to it, no matter how smelly it's been on board with rotten sharks." A former zoology professor with little interest in fish, she became the first—and at that time sole—staff member of a Board which had no concept of systematic beach protections, much less of the prime opportunities for research and data gathering on sharks.

"When I first met with the board in 1966," she related, "they asked me what sort of research program they should have. I said, 'Look—I don't know very much about this yet. But it strikes me one can use nets not just as an anti-shark system but as a biological sampling and monitoring service.' " Board members asked what equipment she would require. "Well," I said, "you've already got the Land Rover." Because—you with me now?—what they really wanted was a young man—someone who would go up and down the coast, go out to sea with the missions and liaise with the board and local authorities.

" 'Yes,' they said, 'Do you have any objections to driving it?' I said, 'Listen—I've driven Land Rovers over some of the toughest country in South Africa to collect specimens for the university.' " But, she thought a minute, " 'I do need a fairly substantial life jacket because I don't swim so well, you see.' Well," she laughed, "they nearly fell off their chairs! They said, 'But look . . . uh . . . surely you're not intending to go to sea?!' I said, 'If I can't go out to sea, in that case I don't want the job. I'm not sitting here in a beautiful laboratory with a white coat on, trying to direct operations I don't know the first thing about.' "

"Operations," she soon learned were neither systematic nor scientific. Funds parceled out willy-nilly by the Board to local authorities were sometimes funneled into macadamed roads or street lighting. Cities were arbitrarily erecting any type of beach protection device—"the most Heath Robinson sort of things," she said wryly. "Sorry—'Rube Goldberg,' I believe you call them. Tripods with steel mesh gates that were immediately spat back up on the beach."

One bright community tucked into a tiny bay stretched a single rope from concrete pillars at either end of the rocky reef promontories and dangled dog chains from it. "Every time a wave came in," she said in disgust, "the chains were spun clean over the rope." Acoustic data now show that sharks may be as much attracted to noise as they are to bright, reflective colors. Meshing for sharks was just as helter-skelter and ineffective—a case of saying to a local commercial fisherman, " 'You have a ski boat? I'm the authority. Now here are the nets, just go and drop them in.' The nets," Davis said darkly, "could have ended up in Australia. Nobody would know, nobody monitored them. They didn't even know how many they needed."

Nor did the Board believe in the effectiveness of offshore gill nets as a shark deterrent, despite the meshing success on East Australian beaches since

1937 and that of the self-contained [city of] Durban operations dating from 1952. Bathers wanted the reassurance of a solid, physical barrier—something they could see or touch.

"It's the fear of the unknown," Davis said in a hushed, ominous voice, "that strikes the heart of every individual entering the water—particularly turbid water where you can't see. Something brushes your leg—dear Lord," her voice rose, "it could be seaweed, it could be anything. But you get the *hell* frightened out of you! You jump like a lunatic and you're right on top of the water."

With something of the relentless sea coursing in her veins, she persisted, molding raw fear into respect for a system that worked, one which bathers on the beautiful, white sand beaches of Natal now accept without question. To date, 238 nets have been strung off bathing beaches—each net 350 feet long by 20 feet deep—set in two parallel rows, with the outer nets overlapping the inner row by 60 feet in either direction. As a shark passes through the net and thrashes violently to untangle itself, the mesh wraps even tighter around its body, virtually immobilizing it. Too traumatized to ventilate by forcing water over its gills and lacking an internal buoyancy chamber, the shark sinks and eventually suffocates.

The next 1,000 words of "Tiger" are packed with anecdotes and comments about Davis's experience at sea with her crews. Those pages discuss the use of gill nets as a biological sampling device for sharks. They include essential before-and-after statistics on shark attacks on the coast as well as the costs of running her organization. As Davis fights to gain respect for her operations, fights for funding, fights for her staffers, the *rounded* picture of a very human woman begins to emerge:

In earlier years, she would have conducted these operations [such as echo soundings to grid seabed topography] personally. Now she gets to sea less and less, to her irritation virtually commanding an administrative desk—or what detractors would call her "empire." But she lives by her family motto—*la main a l'oeuvre*, the hand of work—and to do less would be inconceivable. She fought first for field staff—"because there was nothing in provincial government structure to relate the posts to: we were so unique." Battled nearly five years to get her people equitable salaries: "I don't care how long it takes, I will fight for the rights of my staff. I will go on and on and on and on and on until they get so sick and tired of me they give in." Finally, for her research officer, Tim Wallet:

"I had to really fight for that," she said wearily. "They could see no reason why I should have one. I said, 'Look—I cannot process this data myself. I just have not got the time. I'm taking home work every night. I've got to train my staff to take over more and more responsibility. I have visitors in and out daily.'"

In those days, Beulah Davis was busy planning the new headquarters for the Anti-Shark Measures Board—a white, stucco complex with exhibition area, administrative offices and nearby cold room and morgue [for sharks]. Characteristically, she insisted that the architect not only design something functional but that the entire complex be built around her favorite fig tree.

"I'm a keen gardener," she said wistfully. "The only thing that does bug me a bit is that I've had to let my garden go. I was just looking at my hydrangeas—

we call them Christmas flowers. I used to grow some so big I even had birds nesting in the blooms. I was so very proud of my garden."

She is also, in her words, "a bit of a homebird," preferring house and her daughters to much social activity. "I don't think anybody can . . . Well, people can accuse me of an awful lot of things, I guess, but they can't accuse me," she frowned, "of not making time to be with my girls. We are so close it's absolutely unreal."

It may have been the early, money-lean years that knit the girls and their mother in a conspiracy of mutual support. Gaye and Rosemary were only seven and three when Davis resigned her university lectureship in Durban in a vain attempt to save her marriage. A year later she was newly divorced, out of a job and frantic for money. In desperation, she began selling Tupperware products. "I couldn't . . . Look," she said. "Ask me to sell a concept—something I really believe in. But a product? I couldn't sell an icebox," she grinned wryly, "to a guy who got lost in the Sahara Desert if it was jammed full of his favorite beer!" She applied for a position with the National Institute of Water Research. "I thought, this is it, I've got it," she said. But a stiff, formal letter from the Institute arrived shortly, informing her the post would go to a man—because "The incumbent will have to go to sea once a month to collect water samples."

"But when one door closes," she said, "another opens." Nearly in tears, she made two desperate phone calls for jobs. One, to a former professor doing bacteriological research, was busy. The other was to a friend, Dr. Anne Alexander, principal research officer with the Oceanographic Research Institute, a woman she hadn't seen in years.

"Anne," she said in a husky voice, "it's me. I'm frantic. Have you got a vacancy?" The reply was negative. But, her friend said, the Natal Anti-Shark Measures Board was looking for a liaison officer. "Hang on," she said, "I'll call you back." An interview was arranged for the following morning, and the next thing Beulah Davis knew, she was attending her first meeting of the Natal Anti-Shark Measures Board, an organization she would build from spotty protective devices to a pinnacle of research respected by scientists worldwide.

The article continues, winding up with:

Despite the insistence of former university colleagues that the title "Dr." Davis would somehow validate her position, she has never earned a Ph.D. "Quite honestly," she said softly, "I have reached the top of my tree. I've had, oh, a tremendous amount of help. I might get thrown out of my tree—I don't know. The winds of change might fling me clean . . . out of my nest. But if I am," she paused, "then let me hand it over to a younger person who's just starting on the ladder of life. Let that person get the degree. Surely," she asked, "isn't the data more important?"

SECRETS OF DIALOGUE

Think of accents, dialects, and English spoken with sloppy diction as normal distortions—shadows hiding detail within them. The ear can make distinctions among most distorted vocalizations and quickly figure out what is being said—"Are we goin' ta town fer food taday?"; the eye, unfortunately, can't make such allowances. Reading flow stops as the reader tries to figure out what's going on. Hunter S. Thompson, referred to earlier in this chapter, knew a few secrets about writing *readable* dialogue in a personality profile. Here are five of them.

1. If there are some peculiar mannerisms of speech (or physical gestures, for that matter) that serve to define the person, then use them—sparingly. Let one or two such mannerisms stand for the whole: *A little suggests a lot.*

2. Choose one or two colloquialisms or regional words and phrases to stand for the rest as in, "What's *wrong* with you *boy*?" or the Vermonter's *eh-ah*? Discard the rest. Use those one or two whenever they appear naturally in dialogue.

3. Don't abbreviate, phoneticize, apostrophize or otherwise distort normal, spoken English. Remember that most people slur their syllables and break off word endings in everyday usage. Except for standard contractions, use the full word of dialogue *without apostrophe* even though a syllable has been dropped. Save that apostrophe for those special situations where you need to *regionalize* one or two words the person uses; for example, the word "drinkin'." You may be able to acceptably write "Ah'm" for "I'm" and "ya'll" for "you all." However, remember that readers bog down quickly when trying to decipher in print most regional contractions, slurred syllables and modified vowels of the Deep South. Again, *a little suggests a lot.*

4. Since apostrophized words become confusing if used too often, try to substitute actual words or phrases when capturing something about a person; for example, instead of writing "You ol' houn' dog," try "You ol' hound dog" or even "You old hound dog."

5. The best way to indicate an accent is not to *state it*—"*said the native of Spain*"—but to *suggest it.* How? By altering standard English phrasing and sentence order, and by occasionally using a foreign term that you need not explain. Look again at the first few grafs of "Cancha King."

"He is nervous," confided the wife of another Basque. "Always they pair him with a weak backcourt partner and tonight he is going to play a special partido . . ."

It wasn't necessary to say that the woman had an accent: The structure of those few sentences indicates a nonnative speaker of English.

Amy Tan, author of several bestsellers including *The Kitchen God's Wife*, re-creates in the latter the English-speaking dialogue of her Chinese-speaking forebears.

"Tofu, how much do you pay?" asks my mother, and I can tell she's eager to outdo me with a better price, to tell me how I can save twenty or thirty cents at her store. But I can't even oblige her with a guess. "I don't know. I've never bought tofu."

"Oh." She looks disappointed. And then she brightens. "Four rolls of toilet paper, how much?"

"One sixty-nine," I answer right away.

"You see!" she says. "My place, only ninety-nine cents. Good brands, too. Next time, I buy you some. You can pay me back."

Also from the Tan book but another character in another chapter:

And then she began inspecting everything, criticizing what she saw. She poked her finger into a crumbling part of the wall. "Ai!" She pointed to another wall, where bugs were marching through a crack of sunlight. "Ai!" She stamped her feet on the floor: "Wah! Look how the dust rises up from the floor and chases my footsteps."

PAINTING THE CHARACTER ROUND

"The (Un)conventional Wisdom of Isabella Rossellini" is a perceptive, very human profile of the late Ingrid Bergman's daughter, herself an actress and model. Marilyn Johnson, writer of this sensitive portrayal on pages 40 to 45 of the May-June 2002 issue of *My Generation*, draws on many of the seven descriptive strategies to paint Rossellini round. The writer approached the story cinematically—an ingenious choice, considering the limited time allotted her with Rossellini and that actress's famous reluctance to be interviewed. "Scene 1, Acting" gives us an insider's look at Isabella Rossellini as an actress. "Scene 2, Modeling" paints in her historical background. Scene 3, in Ronkonkoma Train Station, Long Island, is the stop-off point for a brief look at Rossellini's life on the big screen, while the final scene tells the reader much more about Rossellini and her life today. Interestingly, the profile concentrates on the accomplishments of the daughter; her more famous late mother (*Casablanca*) is barely mentioned.

THE (UN)CONVENTIONAL WISDOM OF ISABELLA ROSSELLINI

By Marilyn Johnson

SCENE 1, ACTING

Perhaps you were expecting Isabella Rossellini, the chipped-tooth supermodel, the only woman to master looking beautiful and cute at the same time. The sixth most elegant woman, according to a survey of British fashion mavens, not just in the world—in history.

Instead, an almost ordinary looking person with sleepy eyes stands in the harsh light of the lecture-hall stage at Suffolk County Community College in

(continued)

CONTINUED

the middle of Long Island, New York. "Forgive me if I sit," she says, settling her loose silk clothes, and the body hidden in them, on a chair. "I have a bad back." She has created more than 35 roles, including a deposed queen, various goddesses, both virtuous and unfaithful wives, a sado-masochistic lounge singer and, recently and most impressively, a Hasidic mother in *Left Luggage*. She's been directed by such talents as David Lynch (*Blue Velvet* and *Wild at Heart*), Peter Weir (*Fearless*), Stanley Tucci (*Big Night* and *The Imposters*) and John Schlesinger (*The Innocent*). But today she is playing the role of mentor to future film crews, addressing several dozen students scattered in banked rows in front of her.

"Generally I keep by myself on a set, so as not to break my concentration. It's terrible when someone comes up and says, 'I saw *Casablanca,* I really loved your Mom,'"—quickly she switches voices— "'Thank you! Thank you!' It completely distracts you." Her words tumble over each other, varying in pitch, and ending in an earthy, almost peasant laugh. Her audience joins in the laughter; none of them will ever commit such a faux pas.

Her view of acting is as down to earth and demystifying as the short boots she has planted on the stage. Auditioning for directors is "like taking an exam." It's easier to play a dramatic scene than "to ask if someone wants a cup of coffee—how do you infuse that with emotion? So much of acting is reacting." She adds, "The fear is enormous! You just want to get on a plane and go to another continent, never to be found again." She is scrupulously considerate of the students' experience, identifying everyone she mentions. "My father was an Italian director, Roberto Rossellini, who was very important in

the Fifties," she'll say, or "Catherine Deneuve, this great French actress." Referring to her early inexperience she says, "Acting seemed a mystery to me," and tosses out, self-mockingly—"though my mother was Ingrid Bergman, I should have known what it's all about."

Her accent is charming and pronounced, even after 30 years in the United States; it would be difficult to gauge her charm without it. There are other clues that she is not a native speaker: for instance, when she apologizes to her audience in advance for cursing, then uses the word *pee*. There is a slightly puzzled shift in the room; did she mean to say *shit*?

Her voice skates from one insightful anecdote to the next, her hands with their short, uncolored nails in constant, Italian motion. Every time she rakes her fingers through her short hair, she looks different, creating the flickering effect of the working model who tilts one way, then another. Ordinarily, she confides, actors improvise together to overcome the social aversion to eye contact. But Stephen Rea, who played her husband, Bruno Richard Hauptmann, in the 1996 HBO production, *Crime of the Century,* was so shy "we could hardly talk to each other off the set." And yet, she says, her voice hushed, "When we were the characters, I felt so close to him. I could look so deep inside him—I felt I could look at his soul."

Her audience is completely still, aware that the actress who spent the morning demystifying her craft has just rekindled its mystery.

And by the way, how could she ever have appeared almost ordinary?

SCENE 2, MODELING
Isabella Rossellini drops her simple black cashmere coat on a molded chair

and it falls open to reveal a shimmering bright pink lining. She takes a seat at a veneered round table by a big plate-glass window in the faculty lounge, off-stage, as it were, in the community college where she has just demonstrated the power of acting. The outside light is wintry and filtered by fog, beautifully illuminating a natural face with faceted bones and generous lips.

For 14 years, that face papered the world. "A famous model of the Eighties; one of the first to snare a multimillion-dollar contract" she might have described herself to the students. So ubiquitous was her image for Lancôme, in fact, that in her offbeat 1997 autobiography, *Some of Me*, she confesses to identifying with Chairman Mao.

Then, in 1994, two years after she turned 40, Lancôme fired Rossellini. Rather than paste her experience into scrapbooks, she decided to put it to work. She'd front her own line of cosmetics—"a very American thing to do." She signed an agreement with the Lancaster Group, a division of Coty, became a vice president, and launched their upscale line of makeup as Isabella Rossellini's Manifesto.

She meant the name Manifesto playfully, ironically, as a comment on her belief in beauty for every woman. The products are first-rate and innovatively packaged; the foundation comes in single application pods because "carrying a bag of makeup is not modern." Manifesto's models were also fresh: a girl in braces, a white-haired woman in her 60s, and a radiant, aging Isabella Rossellini, her hooded eyes uncut by the surgeon's knife. Perhaps she started too boldly for the tradition-bound cosmetics industry; Bloomingdale's, one of Manifesto's American distributors, has recently given up on it; but Isabella is hoping to find more outlets here. She stresses that this is her first foray into her own cosmetics line. She expects to learn from her experience—and she still sees an opportunity to model for her peers the art of aging without apology.

"I don't think that looking younger is very seductive. It seems to get the biggest publicity, to look younger than you are, or thinner, but I have found it not to be a particularly successful strategy." She laughs her earthy laugh. "I think other things work better—for instance, humor."

"My sister [her twin, Ingrid] is a scholar, and she looks at the world of cosmetics and fashion as completely ridiculous. That's why it was interesting to me to intervene in that world. Women are now lawyers, executives, whatever—but the image of how we have to be seductive hasn't changed. It's old-fashioned."

There is nothing old-fashioned about Isabella. She was born to be unconventional. Ingrid Bergman and Roberto Rossellini created an international scandal when they left their families to be together; they had Isabella's brother out of wedlock, then were married long enough to produce the twins. Both parents went on to other partners, and have been dead some 20 years. Today, their daughter embraces a large and scattered family of siblings, half-siblings, nieces and nephews of mixed Mediterranean, Jewish, Scandinavian, black and Indian blood. "Growing up, this made me feel our family was very avant-garde [and] evolved," she wrote in *Some of Me*. Roberto, the child she adopted as a single mother, is another mix: a blue-eyed African-American now 9 years old.

Her love life has also been wonderfully modern, marked by her unique fusion of the sensual and the cerebral. She has been married twice, to director Martin Scorsese and model Jonathan Wiedemann, father of her daughter, Elettra, an 18-year-old college student;

(continued)

CONTINUED

and she's been involved with, among others, director David Lynch, actor/director Gary Oldman and dancer/choreographer Mikhail Baryshnikov. At 5-feet-8-inches, she towered over some. "If you've seen my husbands or lovers, you'll know I don't go for beauty," she has said.

So—she likes directors? "I have news for you," she says, laughing. "I've had many lovers, and most of them are not directors."

SCENE 3, IN RONKONKOMA
TRAIN STATION, LONG ISLAND

Isabella Rossellini ducks into a sandwich shop minutes before her train departs for New York City and orders a turkey sandwich and a bottle of water. Two women behind the counter keep looking at her and whispering to one another. Finally, one says, "Excuse me, are you an actress?"

"Yes, I am."

"My friend here thinks she saw you in something. Have you been in movies?"

"Yes." This is a businesslike dialogue, straight questions and straight answers.

"She says it was called something like *Kiss My Hand*." The woman who claims to have seen her in the movie looks eagerly at her and pantomimes kissing her own hand.

"Hmmm," says Rossellini, as if the train has not already pulled into the station. "I didn't do anything by that name. Where is your friend from?"

"Turkey."

"I wonder if that's a bad translation?"

"No, she says she saw it here. It was about a mother and a little boy."

"Perhaps *Zelly and Me?*" Rossellini wonders, though *Left Luggage,* in

which she plays the Hasidic mother of five, has recently been released on video and DVD.

The Turkish woman shrugs. Who knows? Here is something fantastic, an actress from the movies walking right into her shop. Who cares what her movie is called—*Zelly and Me, Left Luggage, Kiss My Hand . . .*

SCENE 4, GLIMPSES OF A LIFE

At New York City's Penn Station, Isabella Rossellini expertly negotiates a number of corridors to take a bench by the tracks of the uptown subway. She moved to New York from Paris, despite her father's objections, when she was 19 and has been a resident and straphanger for most of her life since. She sits stiffly on the bench in the middle of the afternoon crowd, not because she is a trained dancer or self-conscious, but because her "bad back" is, in fact, a severe case of scoliosis. Diagnosed as a young teenager, she was repeatedly stretched on a medical rack until she passed out, then encased in torso casts, until her spine was deemed straight enough for the vertebrae to be fused. She spent six months in bed, "totally dependent." Her mother took two years off to nurse her, a fact that engenders in Rossellini both gratitude and guilt. These days she controls the pain with physical therapy. "I am a woman of my generation," she says, "and I grew up with that dream of independence. I hated being dependent."

So this scarred beauty (who did not even start modeling until she was 28, or acting seriously until she was 30) is now both independent and independently wealthy.

She spends her weekends and holidays in Bellport, a seaside resort town on the south shore of Long Island. She loves Bellport because it feels like an

Italian village. "There are even Italian newspapers for sale in the stationery shop!" She can bicycle almost anywhere she needs to go, an advantage for someone who doesn't drive. She has been renovating her home there—an old barn strung with trapeze nets and ropes and ladders, much to the delight of her son and his friends. She is almost ready to leave New York City for the small town, she says, but has to wait until Roberto is finished with school. Meanwhile, on weekends and weeks off, when she isn't visiting Elettra at college in Boston, she hangs out in the local restaurants and works for Bellport's historic preservation committee. She and her friends, an artist, a professor and a local coffee-shop owner, have also started a film society. They show old movies on 16mm projectors in the community center;

they once showed *Stromboli,* and Rossellini spoke candidly about her parent's first collaboration and their tumultuous relationship.

Now, far from Bellport, she sits on her own island, deep in thought in a noisy, littered subway station. Perhaps she is revisiting her role as the passionate empress Josephine (her miniseries, *Napoleon,* will air next year on the A&E network.) Perhaps she is puzzling over the difficulties of the cosmetics business, trying to figure out how to sell eye shadow and scented soap to her liberated contemporaries. Perhaps she is remembering tooling around on a rattletrap bike in her seaside village, as she did a few weekends ago, calling out to friends and neighbors, "I'm turning 50! Don't forget my party!"

Who'd want to interrupt that?

Marilyn Johnson

Is it easy to interview celebrities? Marilyn Johnson says "no." *Emphatically.* In her own words:

I prefer writing celebrity obituaries to writing celebrity profiles—you don't have to talk to them. Celebrities are what all the magazines I write for seem to want, and it's impossible to get any kind of time with them, unless they're inexperienced or stupid. Smart celebrities like Oprah and Isabella Rossellini limit their contact and exposure. I once was sent to California by *Life* magazine to interview Kathy Griffin and Carol Burnett about being comedians. The only time they gave me was during their photo shoot and five minutes afterward; they talked quietly to each other during the shoot, and the few comments I got on tape I erased accidentally. In a panic, I did a skittery, jazzy little piece in free, indirect discourse from Burnett's point-of-view and got away by the skin of my teeth. Creativity solved the problem there, as it did with Isabella Rossellini. Desperate creativity!

Isabella Rossellini despises reporters. They ruined her family's life. So I wasn't surprised that she was a bit frosty to me. This was an interview set up by my editors. I had to get myself to some outpost in Long Island, hours from my house, at an ungodly hour, and sit in on a class she taught for a friend. Then I was to have only 45 minutes in the cafeteria afterward. She was courteous—but a bit frosty. She talked about makeup for 40 minutes, almost none of it useful to me. The very first personal question I asked her, she blew up. My editors wanted to know who she was dating, and that kind of thing, and she didn't even want to tell me her son's age.

I was shameless afterward, bumming a ride with her and her professor friend to the train station, and I promised in return that I would leave her in peace on the train. But I paid very close attention during the car ride there and while we waited for the train, and I had the great luck to run into her on the subway platform once we got to the city. I didn't tell her I was going to use every little crumb I could gather, and she didn't tell me that the distribution of her makeup line was being discontinued in the United States. It's a silly business all around.

STRUCTURING THE PROFILE

The image of a woman at war defined my structure for the "Tiger of the Province." Each section of the profile dealt with another battle overcome, and each battle gathered momentum and created suspense for the one that followed. Had I begun the article with a strict chronology, the first battle would have been to save her marriage, the second, to defy stereotype and be hired at a job that convention said was for men only. Since most readers of *International Wildlife* had never heard of the Natal Anti-Shark Measures Board, let alone Beulah Davis, the introductory grafs had to serve a different purpose—to acquaint readers with the situation and introduce them to the "tiger of the province."

These early grafs laid the foundation for building a storyline in which *sharks* became a metaphor for her tenacity and brute determination. As Davis battled the elements (weather, sharks, ocean), battled for a job, battled the ideas of an outdated board, battled for adequate funds for her operations and her staffers, battled and finally succeeded in gaining respect and international renown for her operations, the metaphor of sharks faded. When the second part of the article picked up a chronology only hinted at earlier, another metaphor emerged: The tenacious *fig tree.* Although vulnerable to being cut, this tree was left standing as the centerpiece of a newly designed headquarters. Symbolically, the fig represents the softer, more vulnerable side of Beulah Davis's nature. At this point in the story, readers are introduced to Davis the gardener, the loving mother, a woman trusting enough to reveal details of some very private hardships.

FORMULA PROFILES

In years past, the personality profile followed a more or less standard formula. Writers jumped in with an anecdotal lead and followed it with a brief graf letting readers know the direction the story would take. This was followed by quotes or factual material that provided some perspective on the person being profiled (loosely, the storyline). The article would then use quotes, anecdotes and other storyline-supporting material to cover the rest of the points in the outline (including supporters and detractors, strengths and vulnerabilities, etc.). The article came to a decisive conclusion with a telling anecdote, perhaps a split anecdote relating to the lead. (See "Cancha King" on p. 146.)

As a writer and editor, I still favor an article that builds true reader involvement. I still favor a lead that jumps into the story and character with action—or at least with an action-based anecdote in the *now*. I believe this type of lead is stronger than one preceded by brief historical background or by descriptive scene-setting as in this lead from "The Business of Being Oprah" in the April 1, 2002, issue of *Fortune* magazine.

> Somewhere en route from dirt-poor Mississippi schoolgirl to RV news anchor to talk-show empress to award-winning actress to therapist for an anxious nation, Oprah Winfrey became a businesswoman. It's a title she doesn't like much. "I don't think of myself as a businesswoman," she announces at the beginning of a four-hour sitdown—the first extensive interview she's given to a business publication. "The only time I think about being a businesswoman is now, while I'm talking to you. There's this part of me that's afraid of what will happen if I believe it all."
>
> You'd be hard pressed to find another American chief executive this disarming, this confessional. But it's oh-so-Oprah.

Given the cold economics of magazine publishing, however, some leads may prove to be a luxury. Today's magazines have allotted fewer pages to editorial. This has produced a loose, shorter setup for personality profiles, many of them single dimension in such formats as the brief catch-you-as-I-can interview (Lisa Kudrow), the question-and-answer interview and the writer's quickie—the background-only profile compiled largely from the files.

Although numerous magazines still favor the classic *round* personality profile, it's the writer's responsibility to check out editorial requirements. A case in point: The editorial requirements for *Today's Viewpoint,* a magazine about men written for female readers, mandated that "Cancha King" be focused in a single dimension—on Bolivar's relationship with women.

HELPFUL EXERCISE

1. Choose a woman you know well. Using several or all seven of the descriptive strategies, describe the woman in her kitchen by how she acts or fails to act in it, has designed or organized it, what she says or doesn't say in it, what others say about her in it, and so on. By the conclusion, readers should feel they know the woman and should have formed a conclusion about her.

CHAPTER ELEVEN

MOMENT OF TRUTH

In the mid-1950s, CBS anchorman Walter Cronkite hosted a TV series called *You Are There*. ("What sort of day was it? A day like all days, with the events that alter and illuminate our time—And you were there!") Through film clips, narration and other dramatic devices, viewers were in Tokyo as the first atom bomb exploded and seated in the Ford Theatre when President Lincoln was assassinated. The series was popular not simply because it re-created a moment in history but because *it put viewers into the picture,* carrying them along with the action as it began to evolve. For the same reason, reality TV enjoys popularity: The reader is *there*—part of the action as it unfolds. (In the September 5, 2003, issue of *Time* magazine, filmmaker Steven Spielberg called reality TV "America starring itself.")

The personal-experience narrative charges the writer with a similar responsibility: *build immediate reader identification.* How? Through fiction techniques. Fiction techniques won't alter facts and they won't change chronology, but they do make it possible to start the story somewhere in the middle—usually right before the climax—and through foreshadowing and flashback create interest and bring it all to resolution. They also make it possible for readers to find themselves in the article *immediately.* Why? Because in some way they, too, have experienced the emotions that accompany a personal tragedy, an adventure, a nostalgic trip back home, a life-threatening choice. Suspense, drama, danger, sorrow, joy, love, fear—those are very real emotions and they're being faced *now* by the main character. For example, look at this piece by William M. Hendryx in the April 2003 *Reader's Digest*, on pages 131 to 136.

> The pulsing electronic pager jolted Dan Misiaszek from his thoughts. Glancing at his wife, Kathy, he snatched the device from his belt. She was working beside him on their 30-acre ranch in the Texas Hill Country. They did most things together—remodeling a kitchen, building a horse barn, mending fences. Physical labor was an outlet from the stress of their jobs. Both were cops with the San Marcos Police Department. And both were members of a dive team that recovered drowning victims.

"Somebody's dead," Kathy said. It was a morbid assumption but one with ample precedent. In the 14 years since Dan established the volunteer San Marcos Area Recovery Team (SMART), the Misiaszeks [mee-SHAW-sheks] had never pulled a live body from the water. The two quickly grabbed their gear. . . .

This is a first-person narrative from "A Writer's Dream, a Mother's Nightmare" by Tawni O'Dell, on pages 44 to 48 in the February 2001 *Ladies' Home Journal:*

When the call came I was making dinner: beef stew, something I rarely prepare, but it was late February in Chicago—a cold, gray, endless time when even the most health-conscious seek solace in gravy. I glanced at the phone, suspicious. At this time of day, with my hands caked in beef and flour, it could only be a telemarketer.

"Get that, Mom," my daughter, Tirzah, shouted from the adjoining room where she and her five-year-old brother, Connor, were watching TV. "It might be for me."

At age eight, she already received more calls than I did and had a much more enviable social calendar.

The phone range again. A little voice in the back of my mind urged me to answer it. Then it came to me: This call could be important.

This excerpt is from "Saved by Strangers" by John Pekkanen, on pages 80 to 86 in *Reader's Digest,* October 1996:

As she drove home along Route 1604, which rings San Antonio, Air Force Captain Margaret Herring, 35, savored the beauty of the Texas countryside—the afternoon sunlight glinting off amber fields of waist-high grass lining the road.

That Thursday, May 11, 1995, Herring had just finished work at Kelly Air Force Base, where she was chief of education services, and she looked forward to being home soon with her husband, Mike, 40, and their two children, Mack, four, and Cammie, two.

Cruising at close to 45 miles per hour on a straight stretch of road, Herring took little notice of a dump truck approaching from the opposite direction. Suddenly—

As these personal-experience narratives unfold in the first person or the third, the main character will face some moment of truth, some life-altering event that will change forever the way this person views the world and his or her place in it. Having said that, I'll admit of exceptions. Personal experience stories need not be so dramatic to be interesting. For example, witness the humorous narrative by Michelle Slatalla on page 170. Some inspirational, spiritual and nostalgic pieces also qualify. The key factor is this: Does the narrative build reader identity?

BUILDING A CHRONOLOGY

Where to begin the task? First, examine your notes. Select those events that support your storyline; discard those that don't. From events remaining, build a chronology, or timeline. Start at the beginning, *Hansel and Gretel* fashion, and assign letters to the events. (A) Two little children go for a walk in the woods. (B) Afraid of getting lost, they drop little pieces of bread to leave a trail they can retrace. (C) Meanwhile, hungry birds hover overhead. . . . Now examine your completed event timeline. A bit boring when written chronologically, wouldn't you say? There's drama in the story, all right, but the drama is buried. Your task is to reach into that chronology and *bring the past forward.* Begin the story *out of sequence,* as though it were happening *now.* That's the way to grab reader interest. To build tension and invest the reader in the story, begin at a point just before the climax—just before those seconds when the protagonist finds herself hanging by her fingers on the edge of the cliff. Once the story has climaxed, there's a natural letdown in tension. If you get to that point too soon, you risk losing reader interest.

This article began earlier, with a few grafs of background. Then:

> Chad was the daredevil. As his boss and his senior by more than a decade, my role was to be the sensible one.
>
> *Not today.* I looked him right in the eye. "Hey, I thought we were gonna have some fun."
>
> Chad rose to the challenge without hesitation. "Now you're talking. Let's do it."
>
> Chad shot off and I revved up to follow. As my [snowmobile] treads bit into the snow, I felt the sled sink a few inches. That was no big deal. A sled this heavy often dug in a little before grabbing. I revved again and sank farther. *What the . . .*
>
> The engine screamed. Bluish ice walls flashed by. I let go of the handle-bars and started free falling. Then I smashed onto something rock hard.
>
> Stunned from the impact, I lay totally still. *I'm in a crevasse! I must've stopped right on top of one.* (From "A Patch of Blue Sky" by Marv Schouten, pp. 25–28, January 2002 *Guideposts*)

Having started your story at "flash forward," you now must decide how long to continue in that *now* before flashing *back* to the point when the chronology of events leading up to the climax began. Remember that your lead has already used a little background information for orientation. But when to flash back? You have a snowmobiler stuck in a crevasse, his survival hanging by a thread. Do you simply stop the narrative and leave the reader hanging with him? After building tension and drama, wouldn't that be disappointing and unfair? I'd continue with the events of the "now." When you reach that point where tension has begun to lessen (he knows rescue help is on the way), you'll find readers more relaxed and their curiosity peaking: How did the situation begin in the first place? Go back to your chronology and pick it up, describing each event in lettered sequence. When you reach the lead, transition to it with a short sentence or graf. This is the point where your story began and the reader entered the narrative. Hint: Limit your flashbacks to one per narrative: To flash back, then forward, more than once will only confuse the reader.

What about foreshadowing? It's a useful literary device that writers have adapted to nonfiction; for example, the use of such phrases as "Meanwhile, hungry birds hover overhead" (birds will eat the crumbs later on), "the afternoon sunlight glinting off" (sunlight can blind a driver) and Tawni O'Dell's mention in graf two of her eight-year-old daughter Tirzah and the girl's "enviable social calendar" (Tirzah would become critically ill after the good news of this phone call). Think of such foreshadowing as little crumbs, little clues that drop a hint. These clues tell the reader very subtly that something momentous is about to happen. They may be so subtle that only *after* the momentous event can the reader say, "Oh, yes. I *knew* this would happen." After all, you can't just pop up with an incident and expect the reader to accept it without subtle forewarning, or foreshadowing. Hint: Maintain story focus. If your lead reveals there's an unsafe driver on the road, for example, but you fail to use that driver at a key narrative point, your story will fail.

INSPIRATION

All personal-experience narratives involve a change. The lead usually foreshadows it. A paraplegic with little interest in others has an awakening experience and becomes an elementary-school teacher. A physician with an ADD child learns from a swimming coach the healing power of encouragement. An NFL quarterback who found he couldn't call all the plays when his son became paralyzed learns how to let go and accept. The Misiaszeks of SMART (San Marcos Area Recovery Team) found in their rescue of a nearly-drowned boy the satisfaction that had evaded them in 14 years of rescuing corpses from the water: the grateful cheers and applause of a victim's family and friends. Many first-person and third-person narratives are unabashedly inspirational. They're popular with readers, too, because in the changing of a person's life—the revelation—are the seeds of change, or hope, for the reader.

Here's a first-person narrative that's just plain funny. Note the overtones of a personal essay. Michelle Slatalla ("Look Who's Talking!," pp. 44–47, *Rosie* April 2002) knows how to *foreshadow* the equivalent of a punch line (the twist at story's end). Like all successful humorists, she turns the lighthearted humor on herself. Her writing is simple and not belabored.

LOOK WHO'S TALKING

By Michelle Slatalla

I once asked a woman on a street corner in Mexico for directions. Here is what I thought I said in my uncertain Spanish: "Where is the zoo?" With an astonished look, she slowly backed away, a response I found puzzling until much later when I consulted the phrase book I'd left in the hotel and reconstructed what I'd actually said: "I am a hairless dog. I must be seeing myself, please, to the right?"

I have managed to put that experience behind me and hope she has as well.

Still, it has become clear that I am not the sort of person who should venture willy-nilly into a foreign country without the benefit of a few basic language lessons. This year I'm planning my first trip to France (and my French skills, by the way, are quite a bit worse than my Spanish-speaking abilities), so I turned to the Internet for help.

Since I wanted basic, introductory lessons, I decided to skip the more in-depth online courses that cost money (and take more time). For example, www.berlitz.com offers serious immersion as well as four-to-six-month advanced business courses in French, Spanish, German and English for around $900. But the site also provides free placement tests to help you figure out just how much help you need. I decided I'd take the tests and then go elsewhere for free instruction.

I took the Spanish and the French tests, answering 50 multiple-choice questions in each language. Since I'd practically majored in Spanish in college (a fact that might surprise you, in light of the "hairless Michelle" incident), I could tell the tests were aimed at speakers who knew the difference between past and future tenses, as well as whether a sentence's subject was "you" or "I." Once I'd figured that out, I planned a careful strategy for taking the French test: I guessed the answers. A day or so later, I received my test scores via e-mail—Spanish: 76 percent, French: 10 percent (a score I earned by answering "A" to each and every single question).

No doubt, I was in dire need of some lessons before heading to the Eiffel Tower—and I decided that brushing up on my Spanish wasn't such a bad idea either. Sticking with my plan not to spend any money, I turned to www.transparent.com, where free lessons are accompanied by audio clips of a native speaker. Clicking on helpful "Word of the Day" recordings, I repeated out loud until I was sure I knew how to pronounce words like *fixe* (French for "fixed") and *cenar* (Spanish for "to dine"). I also spent a little time playing with the site's games and quizzes, which are available in six languages including Italian, German, Brazilian, Portuguese, and English for Spanish speakers.

Confident my pronunciation sounded nothing like "I am hairless," I moved on to Transparent.com's "Phrase of the Day." Things went fine with the Spanish interpretation, which prompted me to remember lessons I learned long ago. But when it came to repeating a full sentence in French ("We are interested in the fixed-price menu."), I was on shaky ground.

I would have liked to blame my imperfection on an awkward translation. But after I double-checked it at www.dictionary.com, where you can convert any word or passage of text from five languages to English or vice versa, I had to admit the translation was fine. No matter how many times I replayed the audio clip, though, I couldn't get past the tongue-tying first words: "*on s'interesse.*"

In truth, once I arrive in France, I might not even be interested in a fixed-price menu. So I decided to focus on everyday words and phrases I was definitely going to need. At www.travlang. com, a site that sells language-instruction and translation software, I found a free feature called "Foreign Language for Travelers," which teaches you how to count and ask for directions in 80 languages, including Latvian, Vietnamese and Zulu. With the help of audio recordings, I left the site feeling certain I could say "to the right" in French.

The next step was to get used to the cadence of the everyday conversation that would be going on around me.

To get a taste of the local culture, I visited www.parlo.com, where you can experience "virtual immersion" by listening to dozens of foreign radio stations featuring music or talk in Spanish, Italian, German or French. With a Parisian talk-radio station playing in the background, I took the site's free multiple-choice diagnostic test, which was similar to the Berlitz assessment test, to see whether I was making any progress.

The bad news: Parlo.com recommended I immediately enroll in one of its online French courses, at a cost ranging from $39 to $69. Apparently, it didn't do me any better to answer "C" for every question. The good news: My low score was enough to make me rethink my travel plans. Spain might be a good destination.

HUMOR AND ESSAYS

There's an ingredient in humor that's also found in the personal essay. I'll call it "universality and disarming humility." It's the difference between a shotgun, force-my-ideas-down-your-throat-and-tell-all-without-focus approach and one that follows a storyline and strikes a responsive chord with readers. Why responsive? Because both article types deal with a universal truth; they simply provide a new take or twist on it—in this case, yours. Readers should be able to see a bit of themselves in the essay or humorous story. The successful humorist knows that humor can't be forced and contrived and turns the humor on herself. Similarly, the essayist realizes that his content stems from the universal condition we all share.

Some years ago, a female civil engineer who used to work in sanitation asked me to ghost her book. Her on-the-job experiences, she said, were sometimes so funny that she knew people would enjoy reading about them. With some misgivings, I agreed to be her ghost. We signed a contract, and I accepted an advance. Within one week of working with her, my doubts were realized: What were funny incidents to her weren't "ha-ha funny" to anyone else. Her humor was labored—angry even—and her tell-all anecdotes actually made fun of people and institutions.

NARRATIVE-DESCRIPTIVES

The narrative-descriptive, another type of narrative and a favorite of several magazines, including *National Geographic,* doesn't have to be a cliffhanger to be gripping. It does have to be interesting and informative, and it should be organized much the same way as the personal-experience narrative. The story begins just before the climax, but with a difference. In the narrative-descriptive, the action will remain secondary to description and detail. This excerpt is from a sea kayak trip through the East Greenland fjords.

> Our camp sat at the base of a mountain that had torn into the clouds. Patches of moss and ground-hugging scrub wrapped its lowlands like a moth-eaten cape. Water from a snowfield draped between two cusps in the southern ridgeline, fell in ghostly white streaks across and cliff [*sic*] and vanished where it met broken rock. Flowing from the flanks of the mountain as if from a buckshot-perforated bucket, the water tripped past our tents in a dozen streams and bled into a bay dimmed by the reflection of a leaden sky.
>
> I stood astride the stream closest to the campsite and filled my water bottle. I drank until my teeth ached with cold. The tall conical kitchen tent showed a tuft of steam rising from the vent in its peak. Walking past the five chiton-shaped sleeping tents that sat in an arc around the kitchen shelter, I unzipped the door and crouched in to join the others. Baldvin, the Icelandic guide, was at the back of the tent tending to the stoves. Looking on at his right were the three Danes—Kirsten, Ole and his wife Jette—and the Welsh woman, Jackie. To Baldvin's left was an American couple, Randy and Barbara, and my tent-mate and paddling partner, Eric, a Belgian photographer.
>
> Although jet-lagged, I managed to stay awake through dinner. Afterward, Baldvin outlined the next six days and the route ahead. . . . (From "Glaciers and Ghosts" by Christopher Cunningham, *Sea Kayaker* magazine, August 2003, pp. 34–47)

Although the foregoing excerpt could be interesting, it suffers two ways: from stage directions to the reader ("to my left," "to his right") and a notable choppiness resulting from unvaried sentence structure ("I stood astride . . . ," "I drank until my teeth . . . ")

"Phantom of the Night," a narrative-descriptive by Douglas H. Chadwick that ran on pages 32 to 51 in the May 2001 *National Geographic,* is typically more descriptive than narrative. Notice how the opening graf immediately establishes atmosphere, location, time of day—perhaps even some mystery.

> A single gas lantern hissed above the camp table, orbited by beetles and moths. Shadows cast by their wings danced across the face of the hunter, Tony Rivera. "The local people believe every mountain has its jaguar," he said over the night sounds of Mexico's Yucatán Peninsula. "There is an old song that goes: 'I would like to be the jaguar of your mountains / And take you to my dark cave. / Open your chest there / And see if you have a heart.' "

Early the next morning as the darkness unraveled, Rivera joined a half dozen hounds, their handlers, and a couple of trackers to scout for fresh jaguar sign. They found paw prints leading away from the torn carcass of one of the big cats. The dogs were loosed on the scene, and the fastest men sprinted off after them. I came behind with a second party at a pace between a forced march and a jog, snagging on thorny vines and hoping none of the half-seen root shapes were snakes.

On all sides stretched the Calakmul Biosphere Reserve, its 1.8 million remote acres connected to more backcountry in the Yucatán, neighboring Belize, and Guatemala's Maya Biosphere Reserve. These areas are part of the largest swath of tropical forest left in the Americas north of the Amazon-Orinoco region. They also take in much of the former territory of the Maya civilization, whose golden age lasted from the third to tenth centuries A.D. and was marked by the building of grand pyramids and ceremonies of human sacrifice.

Chadwick, the author of this piece about jaguars, had come to that remote area of the Yucatán to learn about the animal's natural history and its chances for survival. He joined the researchers who were using the skills of former hunters to track, radio-collar and study the elusive animals. The article continues:

Finally the shouts and barking grew fixed in one place. Wiping away sweat, spiderwebs and ticks, I struggled around a palm thicket and gazed up to find a 130-pound male jaguar high in the branches of a tree. Where the sun reached through the leaves, the animal's coat glowed like gold ore and its eyes were green fire. A Kayapo Indian near the headwaters of Brazil's Xingu River once told me that jaguars are shamans, but the creature above seemed more like a seriously pumped-up leopard.

. . . A dart zinged into the male's rump. The sting spurred the cat to climb down. It reached the ground and bounded away, hounds in full cry at its heels. With an immobilizing chemical coursing through its bloodstream, we should have found the animal sprawled out within minutes. Instead, we encountered only trampled plants where it had spun to swipe at the pursing pack. The drug dose may have been too light. Tracks led on to the mouth of a deep limestone cavern.

Enter my secret cave, where I wait strung and angry. Come, you men with your modern devices, and let me see if you have a heart . . . Rivera and Javier Diaz, a lead tracker, probed the echoing darkness a short way and turned back shaking their heads. "Se lo tragó la tierra," Diaz said, "the earth swallowed him."

This article is a mother lode of information for readers interested in the threatened species and its dwindling habitats. Natural history and ecology, behavior, breeding and hunting background, statistics—readers can find it all in this story and learn that at least one jaguar could still be found in Texas in the 1940s. Although the narrative continues as the group searches for jaguar, the early pages of this article fail to carry the quotes and anecdotes that enliven the later pages. Since it's top-heavy with information, the story needs a stronger narrative line to keep reader interest. Better pacing and stronger verbs would help, too, in building the drama on which a narrative-descriptive often depends.

Also from *National Geographic* and also from Yucatán comes this excerpt from the Web in September 2003. Note the imagery used by writer Pritt J. Vesillind ("Maya Water World") as he probes a Yucatán sinkhole where human sacrifices were made.

> On the third day it was my turn to test God's vigilance, letting the metal chair plop me down into the cool pond like a piece of bait. Treading water, I adjusted my eyes to the moonlight of the cave. The cenote was shaped like an old Chianti bottle—a narrow neck leading to a wide chamber about 90 feet (30 meters) across and 120 feet (40 meters) deep. The bottle was half full, the water surface 35 feet (11 meters) below the domed ceiling. Stalactites dripped, and the roots of trees were spread on the walls in delicate dark webbing. Spanish records tell how live victims were thrown into the sacred cenote at Chichén Itzá, a major Maya city, on the premise that, as sacrifices to the gods, they would not die—even though they were never seen again. I scanned the slick limestone walls, and my heart pounded, feeling their terror.
>
> Sinking deeper into the white noise of pressure, I bottomed out at 50 feet (20 meters) and glided across piles of shattered limestone. A side cave, shaped like a sock, spun down and off to the west. Resting in the sand was a mahogany-hued skeleton, already tagged, the eye orbits of its skull bleak with expectations of eternity.

Some stories, however, don't benefit from a narrative-descriptive format. "Tahiti: A Voyage of Discovery" by Tom Wuckovich that appeared in the March-April 2002 issue of *AAA Going Places* won't make it that far with readers. A narrative-descriptive needs some excitement and imagery to hold reader interest. Instead, *words* overwhelm the "Tahiti" narrative—words that *tell* the reader but fail to *show*. As a result, the story plods. Here are the opening grafs. Note the flat description and clichéd adjectives.

> Tahiti. No other word so stirs the soul, or tugs at the spirit of adventure within us, or offers such hope of mystery and escape. Escape from worldly cares, from the mundane, even from civilization itself. It opens its arms like a beautiful woman to dreamers, artists, romantics—the quintessential haven for those seeking the true meaning of happiness.
>
> I was filled with myriad emotions that must have enveloped the early discovers of Tahiti—and others who go there today. Most arrive not by ship, but by modern, sleek jets that thunder over transluscent blue water, tranquil lagoons, and craggy peaks of mountains disgorged by the sea centuries ago and sculpted by mighty volcanic explosions.

HELPFUL EXERCISE

1. Choose a fairy tale you're familiar with and build a chronology, or timeline, of events. From this timeline, rewrite the fairy tale as a personal-experience narrative in the third person using fiction techniques discussed in this chapter.

CHAPTER TWELVE

MOVING FORWARD

If I teach you to dance, will you learn to be rhythmic? If I teach you the mechanics of writing, will you have learned the rhythm of writing so that your sentences flow? Yes and no. The rhythm of writing stems, I believe, from a distinct love of words and a definite ear for how things sound by themselves and when put together. It stems from an ability to admire the primitive rhythm of a crow as it struts and stalks. From an ability to hear *murmurs of silence* when others perceive silence only as the absence of sound. And from a keen sense of the changes within us and outside of us. Most of all, it comes from a perceptive heart—that ability to feel what others can only talk about and dismiss, that capacity to fully appreciate life in all its currents and crosscurrents.

Rhythm is natural to life itself. Pine trees retain their needles but oaks drop their leaves in the fall. Gentle rains can be soothing; storms can be noisy and violent. Daffodils and violets awaken in the spring of the year but dandelions wait for summer. And winter forgives its ordinariness and allows poinsettias to defy the calendar. Even boredom and impatience have their rhythms: the incessant drip-drip-drip of a faucet, the constant drumming of someone's finger on the desk. When hungry, babies cry. With age, hair may become thin. Nations and street gangs periodically clash at war, and anger makes us say things we're sorry we said.

A rhythmic writing style isn't easy to achieve. For instance, I rewrote the graf above this one five times; it can still use improvement. Why? Writers know that items grouped in uneven threes read more rhythmically than do items grouped evenly in pairs. In the first graf of this chapter, I used a group of five examples, beginning with the second sentence. That graf gets its rhythmic balance from repetition, from use of the words *stems* and *from* in sentences two to four and a sentence structure for each that's fairly similar. The fifth and final sentence in that graf is deliberately longer, its structure deliberately altered. In effect, it provides counterbalance for the repetitive sentence structure preceding it. By using a longer sentence—one, in this case, that uses both a comma and a dash—I have given readers the opportunity to slow down and mull it all over. In a more contemplative frame of mind that's augured by the transition word *life*, the reader should be more receptive to the graf following it.

For most of us, life is hectic when we'd like it to be serene. As a reporter and a writer, you're trained to see life as it is—punctuated with noisiness, busyness and periodic outbursts of violence. In short, life has a music of its own. At any point—often without warning—that music will change. A trotting horse breaks into a gallop. Birds fall silent before an approaching storm. Marines on routine patrol drop suddenly to the ground as a rocket-propelled missile screams overhead. Water flowing toward a river boulder has to slow its pace, swirl and eddy to get around it. Kayakers on an otherwise peaceful river may be forced to maneuver frantically as rapids appear. The water keeps flowing, the kayaks keep moving, but *action and emotion have changed.* Your writing has to orchestrate that, and that's where rhythm enters in.

Rhythm has several components and variables: cadence; pace; the length and structure of words, sentences and paragraphs and the variety you achieve among them; balance; and overall story structure. It's nearly impossible to discuss one of these without discussing them all. Chief among these components is story structure—how you arrange the various components that give a story spine: the events, case histories, anecdotes, quotes, exposition, observation, facts and the transitions among them. Each element should flow logically into the next and the next one into the one following until the whole is revealed, much as the opening of a flower's petals. A good narrative, for example, creates a certain rhythm or flow, by beginning near the climax or moment of revelation, flashing back, then again flashing forward to the "now" to tie it all up. A story ending also can create flow if it comes full circle, tying itself to the lead or storyline. A *general* statement continues story rhythm as it transitions for illustration to something or someone *specific;* for example, a statement that unemployment stands at 6.5 percent nationwide may be illustrated by the case histories of several unemployed people.

A story shouldn't be orchestrated for a fever pitch—life isn't like that. In writing narratives, profiles and even some survey articles, you might build up to the climax, the main point or the moment of truth in more or less breathless fashion, with words and sentences that read increasingly faster because they're increasingly shorter. You'd then save the longer grafs of exposition and factual matter, and the more explanatory quotes, for the winding down, when it's time to slow the story and give readers an opportunity to find out more.

Here are a few helpful rules for maintaining pace and balance.

- To speed up a story, choose short words, sentences and paragraphs; slow it down with longer ones.
- Balance short sentences with sentences that are longer.
- Vary sentence and paragraph construction to avoid choppiness and a boring sameness.
- Alternate longer paragraphs with shorter ones and short words with longer ones.

- Use examples in multiples of three.
- Contrast loud sounds with soft ones or silence, and action with periods of inaction, or calm.
- Build suspense into forward momentum by narrating a two-track story.

Most stories won't lend themselves well to parallel, two-track narration. Here's one that might: the story of PFC Jessica Lynch. Seriously wounded in the second Gulf War when her Humvee overturned and was attacked, Lynch was captured by Iraqi troops. U.S. special forces rescued her nine days later from the Iraqi hospital where she lay in fear and pain. The parallel second track? The agony of her family at home. Formally notified by the U.S. Army that Jessie was missing in action, they were frantic for news that she was still alive, fearful that she had been killed. Together with the 300 residents of tiny Palestine, W. Va., they waited, harboring a sense that television was their lifeline. This second track is narrated *at the same time* as the first. As you cut between Lynch and the military, and the family and community in Palestine, the story builds suspense and a dual momentum.

PACING AND SOUND

Speed up the story, slow it down—it's all a matter of pacing or forward momentum. For instance:

> Big Gill Ruderman normally walks with the easy slouch of a man accustomed to command. But not this afternoon. Rugby under the hot Florida sun and girls on the sidelines in halters and shorts yelling "Tear him up!" and the 31-year-old Army captain dives for a tackle, misses and is pinned and mauled by 29 sweat-grimed bodies. Gill Ruderman staggers off the field with a bruise on his forehead the size of a small grenade.
> "Where am I?" he mutters thickly. Someone hands him a beer.

Written by the author for a 1975 issue of *Today's Viewpoint,* the profile "Rugby One" *begins* with a short action sequence in the first graf, above, that put readers immediately into the picture. The first sentence is structured to sound as though the man ambles, which he does. The second sentence—short, almost staccato—is designed to make readers sit up and take notice: Something's going on. The third sentence sounds like the action we're reading about: It's a run-on sentence, the action rolls and we're dirty and we're part of it. The beginning of the second graf effectively stops the forward momentum of that run-on by balancing it with two short sentences that will lead into several grafs of background.

Is the use of a run-on sentence grammatically correct? No. But it's indeed useful at times when you need to maintain the continuity of some *continuous* action. In "Cancha King" we used a run-on in its multi-graf action lead. It's not for every type of action, however, and should be used judiciously.

Can you feel that frantic sense of helplessness in the words and pacing of the excerpt below? It's from the first-person narrative "The Day the World Cracked Open" by Abigail Thomas (pp. 159–62, 232–34, of the March 2001 edition of *O, The Oprah Magazine*). The timing is excellent—largely the function of varied sentence lengths. It achieves balance by using brief words to express fleeting, frantic thoughts and full sentences to convey action and exposition.

> "Your husband has been hit by a car," Pedro said. "113th and Riverside. Hurry."
>
> Impossible, impossible. Where were my shoes? My skirt? I was in slow motion, moving under water. I looked under the bed, found my left shoe, grabbed a sweater off the back of a chair. This couldn't be serious. I threw my clothes on and got into the elevator. Then I ran along Riverside and when I saw the people on the sidewalk ahead I began to run faster, calling his name. What kind of injury drew such a crowd?
>
> I found my husband lying in the middle of a pool of blood, his head split open. Red lights were flashing from cop cars and emergency vehicles and the EMS people were kneeling over his body. "Let them work," said a police officer, as I tried to fight my way next to him, managing to get close enough to touch his hand. They were cutting the clothes off him, his windbreaker, his flannel shirt. Somebody pulled me away. "Don't look," he said, but I needed to look, I needed to keep my eyes on him. A policeman began asking me questions. "You're his wife? What's his name? Date of birth? What's your name? Address?"

Regardless of the type, a story that stays on track and moves forward shows good pacing. Jockeys pace their mounts. Distance runners, sprinters and bicyclists pace themselves. It happened twice to American bicyclist Lance Armstrong in the 2003 Prix de France: He went off pace. Once, his handlebars caught on a spectator's bag and he fell; so did the bicyclist riding near him. Both lost their timing for precious seconds. In the other, he nearly fell over a downed rider. Armstrong caught himself and swerved onto the grass that time, but he had to dismount and carry his bicycle back onto the roadway. In both cases, continuous movement stopped, forward momentum was lost.

Try this scenario: A group of people sit in the living room chatting and drinking coffee. The windows are open. Suddenly, a shot rings out. Here's the problem: How do you get a character from a seated position in the living room to investigate that shot? Does "Frank" put down his coffee mug on the table, get up quickly from the sofa and cross over to the window where he puts his head out to check? No—there's too much unimportant action here. Try this: "Frank ran to the window. 'Nothing here,' he said. 'Are we sure it was a gunshot?' " Hint: This type of solution does two things: uses pacing to build tension and eliminates unnecessary detail that if left in would stop forward momentum of the story.

Here's a story excerpt that makes me hungry, probably because it literally rolls off the tongue when read aloud. Nothing complicated here. Pay close attention to the way it moves forward by *not wasting words.*

Take parsley out of the kitchen, and you may as well throw out the salt and pepper too. Not only does a beautiful, curly sprig of green enliven the appearance of many dishes when used as a garnish, but parsley, in all its forms, is by far the most popular culinary herb. It's useful and delicious by itself, but it also blends well with other herbs such as basil, oregano, rosemary, marjoram, savory, and thyme, resulting in tastes quite different from using these herbs alone. (From "Don't Forget the Parsley!," pp. 42–43 of the March-April 2001 *Back Home* magazine)

CADENCE

You wouldn't use cadence in the above excerpt—parsley is anything but so brittle. But you might use it for the chop-chop-chopping of the knife as it cuts the greens into small pieces. Or dices onions and celery. And you can use that cadence to set a mood or establish a setting.

She was rushing. "I don't like this."
>   *Chop.*
"There's never enough time to cook."
>   *Chop.*
"I'm sick and tired of rushing dinner." *Chop.*
She threw the onions into the pot with the floured beef cubes. "Enough. That's enough. I've had it."

Cadence: The words *Enough. That's enough. I've had it.* mimic the chop-chop-chop of the knife. Short. Quick. Single-word sentences standing for the whole. They could be used without the chopping sound and still convey mounting anger, frustration, irritation. What about the *rat-a-tat-tat* of a woodpecker's beak as the bird mistakes the tin roof of the shed for the bark of a tree? Have you ever heard someone speak like that—sharp, quick, words bitten off at the end? Or the lockstep of marching soldiers? *Left. Left. Left, Right, Left.* Monotonous. Or the sound and appearance of a Fourth of July night about 9 P.M.? *Crack. Ka-boom!* Actions speak louder than words or, in this case, the *cadence* of words may be more effective for setting tone and mood than the written representation of any sound we may hear. Even description may do the same thing if the right words are used. Which is more effective, for example? "Bang!" or, "A shot rang out." Hint: Written representation of sounds should be used judiciously.

Words, of course, have their own rhythm. By sound, appearance, meaning and a certain amount of emotional weight, words can advance your story, slow it down, change its tone. An "awful" chore, for instance, is thick—heavy with meaning and confusing, too. But suppose you simply meant a tough or time-consuming chore. The word itself—and certainly its inappropriate use—will slow up the story. So would a word whose meaning is obscure, or a word difficult to pronounce. Suppose you found a drama "stark and compelling" or "rich with meaning." In either case, these are weighty thoughts, and these phrases can be expected to slow up a story also. If you want the reader to pause and contemplate, then use them. Make sure that's what you meant to do. Select each word, each phrase in your article with care: It has to fit with the overall tone and rhythm.

BE CAUTIOUS WITH TONE

Regardless of the article you're writing, its tone should be pleasantly conversational and consistent throughout. Both of these build rhythm. A sensitivity to reader needs and interests should be your yardstick for gauging tone. I've found that a writer's *attitude* toward certain subject matter—even toward a particular readership—may dictate the tone used in the story and the writer's approach to the material itself.

A woman may have been mauled to death by a rabid dog, for example, but if you look for levity in the situation, you'll offend, and if you become too grisly in depiction, readers back off. An overly serious story or one that reads as heavy-handed or didactic, a story that ridicules readership or story personalities or one that may be flippant, sarcastic or maudlin and written for pity carries a sure and immediate loss of readership. So do stories that gallop: The pace leaves the reader no opportunity to digest the storyline and with nothing to take away. To gush and be overly effusive about someone or some situation because you're impressed can push readers aside: People should be left to make their own judgments. The greatest danger? The writer's tendency to paint a humorous or sarcastic coat on situations readers hold dear—death, funerals, surgeries, birth and birth complications, addictions, abuse of all types, poverty, joblessness, hunger, homelessness, rape, race, kidnapping, felonies and even some misdemeanors, among others. It always helps to remember your target reader. Remember that subjects such as sex or environmental pollution may be sacred to one set of readers but not so to others.

PUNCTUATION MARKS HELP

It's possible: Punctuation marks such as the dash and ellipses, the comma and period, can convey rhythm. A dash represents a pause in thought or action—something you want to add to it. A period represents a cessation of the same thought or action. A comma hooks that thought or action to something related to it with barely a pause. Take a simple sentence—"It was hot."—and end it with that period. Make the sentence a complex one using an *and*, a comma and two verbs: "It was hot, and her bangs became little tendrils of brown against her face." If you want equal impact of each thought and action with emphasis being the important factor, end each sentence with a period: "He chewed his lip. Were they watching him, he wondered? Did they know he was afraid?" If impact isn't essential but getting on with the story is, use commas: He chewed his lip and wondered if they were watching him, wondered if they knew he was afraid." Of the latter examples, which is more emphatic? Which creates some suspense? Which could be part of the buildup toward a climax?

And what about ellipses? They're used occasionally in articles to indicate a thought trailing off. They indicate some hesitation, as if they were . . . on-paper representations of mental wheel-spinning. Ellipses should not be used in magazine articles to indicate gaps in quoted material. For direct quotes, simply choose the strongest and most representative and let them stand for the whole. Place partial quotes in quotation marks; they belong as part of a sentence or paraphrase that you yourself write.

Despite their too-frequent use in magazine articles today, putting material in parentheses destroys story rhythm. Reading flow stops. Although an experienced writer might use a few words in parentheses as a stylistic device, parentheses usually result from lazy writing or from hasty story organization. Regardless of the reason, parenthetical material in a magazine article almost always says to the reader, "Oh, I forgot something. Here, I'll put it in parentheses."

Hint: Don't use exclamation points in your article or even following quotes or lines of dialogue. They're no substitute for good writing and good verb or noun choice. If you want the reader to get excited, that's your clue to build excitement or suspense *through verbs and story construction*—not through exclamation points. Words and phrases can punctuate by themselves. So can sentence construction and length. Cadence, even pauses, can punctuate. But not little black marks with dots below them. Why have to *tell* the reader to get excited? If you haven't created excitement and suspense by *showing* the reader through story construction and word choice, no amount of little black marks on paper are going to do it.

DEVELOP YOUR OWN STYLE

I read voraciously as a youngster and wrote my first three-act play in fourth grade. In college, I tried to emulate the style of such writers as Ernest Hemingway and Louisa May Alcott with little success. As an editor at *Audubon* magazine in New York City, it was even tougher: I had to shorten and edit the works of such esteemed authors as former *New York Times* columnist Hal Borland and novelist Peter Matthiessen. Sacred ground to me: I edited them poorly, I believe. Nevertheless, my exposure to the writing styles of others had a deliberate effect: It encouraged me to develop my own, and I've found my style to be very much like the way I talk. The profession cites three cardinal principles for developing your own writing style.

1. Read everything you can get your hands on.
2. Write constantly, as though your life depended on it.
3. Study the style of others—not to imitate, but to learn.

Usually, it takes years and a mature outlook on life to develop a writing style. It may also take very deliberate effort. When you read something you like, ask yourself why. Make it an exercise, a voyage to help discover your own voice. What is there about the style that speaks to you? Is it rhythm? How is that achieved? Sentence length? Repetition for effect? The sound of certain words or phrases or their simplicity? How detail is used? The use of dialogue? Is it point of view or voice? Cadence? The way images are painted? Don't be hasty, and don't limit yourself to just one writer. Read them all. Discover in various writing styles what you do like and don't, and why. Study those "why's;" if some things could be fixed, find out how. In time, you'll develop a signature style of your own and a cadre of faithful readers who'll recognize a work as yours and call for more like it.

HELPFUL EXERCISE

1. On a scale of 1 to 10 with 1 being heavy, 5 being neutral and 10 being light, rate the following words for their emotional weight:

_____ butte		_____ pursued
_____ slink		_____ surmountable
_____ opossum		_____ clouded
_____ worm		_____ vibrate
_____ grazing		_____ ethnic
_____ sand		_____ gazelle
_____ gruesome		_____ reversed
_____ farming		_____ modest
_____ gorgeous		_____ virulent
_____ trotter		

CHAPTER THIRTEEN

SECRETS THAT SELL

The current explosion of color and graphics on the printed page prepared me to dismiss titles as a waste of time. In a majority of the more popular magazine, they've become simply unreadable. Cramped for space, they fight with the other elements on the page. Too cramped, or printed too large and splashy to be instantly readable, they fail in their task to grab and hold the reader. Some magazines print their titles in dropout type, as line reverses; because they appear white—actually the color of the paper stock showing through— they fail to stand out against a darker, graphic-heavy background. (Print black ink on white stock, says the magazine bible: It's more readable.)

However, I've been pleasantly surprised. On the pages of numerous other magazines appear titles that are clean and readable—and they do their job fairly well. Graphics and title work together, both to pull in the reader. Here are some fairly current titles that I like. Embedded in these titles are some of the secrets that can sell a story.

"For Your Eyes Only" ("Keith Melton's museum contains the finest es-
pionage paraphernalia anywhere—and it's so secret we can't even tell
you where it's located," reads the article's staff-written blurb in the July
2001 issue of *Smithsonian*)

"One Easy Iris" (*Southern Living*, Spring 2003)

"Don't Be Afraid of the Goths" (August 2001 *Charisma*)

"Easy Ways To Avoid an Argument" (October 1996 *Reader's Digest*)

"Saved by Strangers" (October 1996 *Reader's Digest*)

"You Can Raise Your Child's IQ" (October 1996 *Reader's Digest*)

"It's a Jungle Out There" (article on the incoherence of daily life, October 2000 *Atlantic Monthly*)

"Flies 'R' Us" (April 2002 *Discover*)

"Quebec City at Its Finest" (April 2002 *Ocala*)

"After Halle's Oscar: Why Black Actresses Still Can't Get Any Respect
in Hollywood" (March 2003 *Ebony*)

"What Makes Grandfather Run?" (unpublished article by Edwin C. Coolidge)

"The New Range Wars" (ranchers versus wildcatters in the November-December 2002 *Mother Jones*)

"A Confederacy of Cronies" ("Ruling by corporate fiat is no way to run a democracy," says the blurb in the November-December 2002 *Mother Jones*)

"Instant Stress Relief" (August 2003 *Parents*)

"The 10% Solution" (blurb about a weight-loss plan in the January 2002 *Reader's Digest*)

"I Will Survive" (Mariel Hemingway profile in the April 2002 *more*)

"Pregnant at Fifty" (April 2002 *more*)

"Secrets of A+ Parents" (September 2002 *Reader's Digest*)

"Rules for Pools" ("What you have to know about above-ground pools—before you jump in," says the blurb in the June 2002 *Popular Mechanics*)

"Under Siege" ("Meet the new Bobby Bowden—defiant, combative and no longer the good ol' boy we thought we knew," says the blurb in the July 21, 2003 *ESPN The Magazine*)

"The Dating Dilemma: Who Should Pick Up the Check?" (March 2003 *Ebony*)

"How to Get Kids to Listen and Behave" (August 2003 *Parents*)

"55 Smart Ways to Get Set for School" (August 2003 *Parents*)

"Tahiti: A Voyage of Discovery" (March-April 2002 *AAA Going Places*)

"Viva Gloria" (profile of Gloria Estefan in April 2002 *Rosie*)

Like leads, titles are both hook and promise. Spend as much time crafting your title as you do on your opening grafs—it may be *all* an editor takes time to read. Titles may surprise you: More than once, an idea for an article has popped into my head *as a title*. Be original, but keep your titles appropriate to the content of your article. We all know what readers want and editors look for in terms of content: information that will help a person save, spend, improve, compete, be successful, be wealthy, do their job better or easier, get something for nothing; stories on the famous and the notorious; hero stories; adventure and crime stories; sports and recreation stories; stories about kids, about animals; medical success stories and surprise healings; Horatio Alger stories (*there but for me go I*); success stories in general; stories that make us feel better about ourselves; stories that help us nurture our inner selves; stories that respond to our doubts and insecurities with positive messages; stories that confirm our long-held opinions and so on.

Winning titles paint pictures and show action; the least successful titles are simply pasted-on labels that have no forward motion, hawk no special message. They won't grab an editor's interest (and you want to make that sale), and they won't interest readers either. The staff-written blurb below the title is their prop. If an editor does happen to read past a poor title and likes the contents of an article, the magazine is free to change the title as it sees fit. Usually, you'll have no control over retitling and shouldn't even ask.

That's what happened to a career story on archaeology I wrote some years ago for the teenage readers of *American Girl* magazine. Still in love with the sounds of alliteration, I titled the article "Ancient Pots and Arrow Points." Bless the editor—she bought it. But when it appeared in print, the article had been retitled. I've never forgotten the lesson of what became "Dig for Your Life." It was quite an improvement.

Although you can rely on staff abilities at reputable, well-known magazines, it does happen that an editor acts in haste or ignorance. I wrote an article for a photography magazine concerning the difficulties an American can experience when photographing in Germany. Because the way people relate to each other spatially can differ from culture group to culture group—and I didn't want to alienate anyone—I took some time and sensitivity to craft a pretty good action title. I wish the editor had taken some time, too. Apparently, she never proofed what a staffer had rewritten. On publication, the title read "Gemütlichkeit and the American Photographer in Germany." A label. A label with phrases that had little bearing on the subject and little relationship to each other. I believe I was a contributing editor for the magazine at the time of this article's publication. We parted company shortly thereafter.

INSTANT WINNERS

Some words are bell-ringers, guaranteed to capture an editor's attention. Use them in titles that are short, crisp and written simply with few or no multi-syllabic words.

secrets

free

quick (instant)

easy

fun

how-to

money

save

tips

steps

magic

healthy

happy

attractive/slimming

you or the implied you

succeed/success

win/winning/winner

Titles that play on words

Anything in multiples of ten (Sometimes you'll see five; 10 is more effective.)

Anti-anything that normally causes problems or alarm

Words of exclusivity such as *biggest, smallest, tallest, shortest, best, the only*

Titles in the first-person voice (A choice for the personal-experience narrative, such titles resonate with readers, allowing them to identify with the feelings if not with the situation. Such titles may also carry a true-confession element.)

A direct quote from the article or a paraphrase of one (Quotes are personal: They make the reader sit up and take notice: "Someone's speaking to me.")

Alliterative words (the repetition of sounds, or syllables, "Secrets that Sell" or "Stitch a Sporty Umbrella Case")

Questions that hook, provoke or speak to the interests of readership (Try taking a simple statement and turning it into a question: "Raccoons—The Camper's Pest" or "Are Raccoons Really Campsite Pests?")

Titles that shock or deal in controversy ("When Your Child Has Lice" or "The Benefits of Smoking")

If I put together some of those magic words, I come up with titles such as

"Ten Easy Steps to a Healthier Lifestyle"

"Free Car Care for a Year?"

"Be an Instant Winner"

"Quick and Easy Tips for Saving Money"

"How to Slim Down with Five Easy Exercises"

"You Can Control Aging"

"They're Anti-Education and They're Your Neighbors"

"Cents and Sensibility"

"World's Fastest Sport"

"The Stitch That Came Too Late" (from *a stitch in time saves nine*)

"I Left My Baby in the Gulag"

"Male Menopause: Do Biologically Identical Hormones Actually Help?"

Most writers begin story drafts with a working title. Somehow, it just helps us to organize our thoughts a bit better. By the time we've finished the manuscript (ms.) and revised it several times, we're likely to have revised the title as well. Sometimes only one good title comes to mind. It seems to grow out of the material, and we never have to change it; for example, "How to Sound Younger" or the title of a chapter in this book, "Get Joe."

Should sidebars be titled? Remember that sidebars are short: Titles for them should be brief. "Tacoma Takes Off" headlined a short *Sunset* magazine travel piece on that city in Washington State (April 2002). The story contained two sidebars: "Gift-Shopping for Glass" and "Tacoma Travel Planner." Both sidebar titles were run in type smaller than the main title.

Remember the cardinal rule for title writing: Make sure your title is informative and relates to the storyline. Anything less, anything you just can't resist because it's witty or cute or clichéd, will probably hoist you on your own petard.

Well-chosen titles contribute to story rhythm and continuity. Hint: Although it won't work for all articles, by using some of your title wording in the lead, the body and in the conclusion, you can bring the story full circle.

HELPFUL EXERCISE

1. Give three options for titling your own article. At least one of them should be a quote or a question. Of the three, note which title you've selected as best for the story and explain why.

■ ■ ■ ■ ■

CHAPTER FOURTEEN

THE WRITE STUFF

I was on a Delta flight bound for a journalism convention in Kansas City. Beside me sat a man reading *Fortune Small Business* magazine. A magazine editor, perhaps?

He shook his head. "I manage a small hotel in Kansas City."

I told him I was a journalism professor.

"First annual," he said.

"I beg your pardon?"

"First annual," he repeated. "You can't have an 'annual' until you've had a 'first.' Check the AP stylebook."

He was right. Like this former editor of his college newspaper, we see and hear English abused all the time. I call it the Rodney Dangerfield syndrome of the literary world. You lose immediate respect from an editor, an employer and from readership if you misuse a word, misspell it, punctuate it incorrectly, even make a typographic error because you forgot to proof what you wrote and blithely took the word of "spell checker." It can happen: I misspelled *commitment* and *tomorrow* in my first memo to a new boss. Result? He paid more attention to the misspelled words than he did to my request. And he never let me forget it. I use a good dictionary and thesaurus these days.

What do *flowers* do, I wonder, if "*Violence* Continues To *Blossom* in Iraq," as a newspaper headline stated? And if *adage* means "a wise saying seasoned with age," what are readers to think about this phrase from the lead of an alumni magazine article: "There's an *age-old* adage that says whom you marry affects what you may become"? That's redundant. And what about the outdoor signage that reads, "Think how this *effects* your children"?

And punctuation? What about those inarguable apostrophes? This one indicates possession: "The girl's book." This one does not: "*Pecan's* for sale." The plural takes an *s*—not an apostrophe—and pecans possess nothing except, perhaps, good taste. And the comma? Red flags go up when an editor reads sentences that flow poorly because they contain a plethora of commas: It immediately indicates poor sentence construction. As a rule, commas result from trying to cram too much information into a sentence. Break the sentence into two or revise it. From an article on whale watching in the Spring 2003 *Flagler Magazine* ("Whale Watching to Preserve the Species" by Jaque Estes, page 32):

"The right whales can be easily identified. They, unlike, the humpback whale, also spotted in Florida waters, do not have a dorsal fin." Try this as a rewrite: "It's easy to identify right whales. Unlike humpbacks that also ply Florida waters, right whales don't have a dorsal fin." Even better, drop the plural and use the stronger singular: "It's easy to identify a right whale. Unlike the humpback that also plies Florida waters, the right whale lacks a dorsal fin." The rewrites flow; *read them aloud.* The *Flagler Magazine* version is choppy and didactic. Each sentence seems to stop without flowing logically into the next. Here's a hint: Don't put distance between subject and its verb by inserting words between them.

In revising for story flow, check out your use of the articles *a, an* and *the.* Eliminate as many of them as possible. Take a look at the rewrites above. By directly addressing the reader, I've simultaneously eliminated that limp *the* by beginning the first sentence with an implied *you*—"It's easy [for you] to identify right whales."

Use of the word *there* as in "there is" or "there are" immediately dumps the reader from a voyage of discovery. These static verbs stop reading flow: Choose *active* ones instead. Also from the *Flagler Magazine* story: "There is a five-mile gap between the last place we can sight the whales at Jungle Hut Road to Varn Park," he said. Confusing as this sentence may be, it needs forward motion. "We run into a five-mile gap at Jungle Hut Road," he said. "We can't sight whales again until we reach Vern Park."

Commas cause confusion in other ways. Commas can be used correctly to set off parenthetical material from the main sentence—"John Ryerson, *a history teacher from Bellbrook,* ran the 1.5 K." Captured between commas, the parenthetic material could be eliminated *without altering the meaning of the main sentence:* "John Ryerson ran the 1.5 K." The name of John's wife can also be set off parenthetically without changing the meaning: "John's wife, *Rose,* also competed." But if *Rose* is not set off parenthetically by commas, it means *Rose* is essential to the meaning and that John has two or more wives. Our original sentence, then, would speak only of one wife—*Rose*—the one who ran the 1.5 K.

Hint: Although commas are used correctly to set off a dependent clause from the independent clause that follows, they don't belong *after* the independent clause. The comma—or lack of one—is correct in these two examples:

By beginning that sentence with an implied *you,* I've eliminated that limp *the.*

I've eliminated that limp *the* by beginning that sentence with an implied *you.*

SETTING THE STANDARD

And what about contractions? The use of *we've* for *we have* and *it's* for *it is?* I find that story tone, subject and magazine readership dictate their use. Even in an article with a casual or light tone, I would only use contractions occasionally: They are friendly, but they also weaken your point. However, you'll only confront a contractions problem when your sentences have resorted to inert, state-of-being verbs that don't move the story forward—verbs such as *is, are, were, have, had, has.*

Remember that you're the writer, the arbiter of good English. You set the standard for a reading public. Anything less than correct grammar, spelling and punctuation erodes your credibility because these errors alter meaning. Look at the confusion between these pairs:

> *The wind blew off you're hat.*
> *The wind blew off your hat.*
>
> *It's my turn.*
> *Its my turn.*
>
> *Who's got a hat?*
> *Whose hat is it?*
>
> *Theirs is not to do or die.*
> *There's a lot to do.*

Now double-check my use of the word *between*. Should I have chosen the word *among* to lead into the eight sentences above? It's a common error, so I looked it up. The rule: Use *between* when speaking of two items, two people or two groups; save *among* for three or more. But to complicate the matter, if the items, people or groups have a definite relationship, always use *between* regardless of the number involved.

And when is it appropriate to *contrast* rather than to *compare*?

> "Elmendorf contrasted the watches being sold by this antique dealer with those he'd seen in town earlier." (Okay if you're looking for differences.)

> "Elmendorf compared the watches being sold by this antique dealer with those he'd seen in town earlier." (Also okay if you're looking for both similarities and differences.)

A minor point, perhaps, but it does change the meaning of the sentence. *Compared to* and *compared with* also cause confusion. When you compare items in a statistical or exact manner, use *compared with*; when likening one thing to another in a nonliteral or metaphorical sense, use *compared to* ("He compared the faces of the jury to a barren landscape devoid of vegetation").

And what about *pair, family, group, jury* and similar words? Each poses similar problems. They can be treated collectively, or as individuals. Is *pair* singular (the pair *was*) or is it plural (the pair *were*)? *Was* the family sitting down to dinner? Or *were* they? Does it even matter? It does. If you're referring to *the group* itself, use a singular verb; when talking about the *individual members* comprising a group, use the plural. Thus, use *was* or *is*—singular state-of-being verbs—when referring to a married couple as the *pair* or the *couple*. When speaking of the jury, the family or the pair as a collection of individuals, use the plural verb *were* or similar.

PILFERED PRONOUNS

Misused pronouns and confusion about pronoun antecedents—the nouns that serve as reference points for the pronouns that follow—are so flagrant in speech and broadcasting that the abuse has crept into the printed word almost without notice. Witness this help-wanted ad on a well-known web site: "A small, but growing, food manufacturer is looking for an experienced project manager within *their* bakery division." Readers naturally expect that the singular subject of that sentence—a food *manufacturer*—would take a singular pronoun, *its*. It should. Instead, the reader is misled by use of the plural possessive pronoun *their*. Hint: A company, school, organization or similar entity enjoys neither heart nor soul: Inanimate objects and singular as well, they should be referred to as *it*. But what about this exchange?

> "Who's there?"
> "It's me. Joey."

A singular, state-of-being verb, the *is* in the *it is* contraction must take a singular pronoun referent *in the same voice. Me* is a direct object—"Give it to me"—*I* is the first person singular. Thus, it's grammatically correct to say "It's I. Joey." Do most of us speak that way? I don't think so. We say, "It's me. Joey." The rule? *Usage dictates form.* Check usage in the latest dictionary and the latest edition of your stylebook. If you still can't decide, read the sentence aloud. If it sounds awkward—not as we normally speak—you probably need to rewrite it.

Here's a good rule of grammar: *Pronouns must agree in person and number with their antecedents.* Such agreement avoids reader confusion. Thus, "Each client has *their* own agenda" is incorrect. Why? The antecedent *client* is singular; the pronoun referent *their* is plural. You could make it clear and grammatically correct this way: "Each has *its* own agenda" or even "Each client has *his or her* own agenda" (if the client is indeed an individual rather than a corporation). How do you avoid these awkward *his/her/its* traps? Reword the sentence in the plural: "Clients have their own agendas."

Verbal phrases ending in *-ing* can be troubling when they're participles modifying nouns. *"Tracking the source of the disease,* the CDC investigated recent immigrants from three Southeast Asian countries." Because it lacks both subject and predicate, a participle phrase can't stand alone; it has to be placed close to the noun it modifies in order to avoid confusion. Although you do want to vary sentence structure, participle phrases make weak substitutes for those action verbs that propel a story. Many of them are meaningless—awkward, throwaway phrases used by a writer who can't think of any other way to get into a sentence. From *Flagler Magazine,* this sentence is not only weak—it's just plain wrong: "Driving up A1A, it is not uncommon to see. . . ." Who's driving? Who sees? The subject of the sentence is *it,* but the inanimate *it* cannot drive. The solution? Reword the sentence: "When driving up A1A, you'll probably see. . . ." Better and stronger, place the prepositional phrase at the end of the sentence: "You'll probably see . . . when driving up A1A." And why drive at all in order to see anything along A1A? Scrutinize your copy. Whenever you see an *-ing* word, red flag the sentence for possible revision.

Also flag and revise what I call *backward writing,* when the end or the middle of a sentence becomes its beginning and the verb and its subject or direct object are reversed: "Hushed in the shadows, took he a machete. . . ." Sentence construction like this usually results when a writer gropes for a style. However stylistic, it's not readable and doesn't belong in a magazine. You will find it in poetry, in drama, in the Bible and as a style favored by the occasionally poetic, skilled writer of longer pieces.

OTHER TIPS

You'll avoid reader confusion if you keep similar thoughts together in a sentence. This one is confusing: "The floppy disks sat in a plastic container on his desk, and his feet kept tapping while we spoke." Also try to format your sentence to keep subject and verb together. The construction of this one dilutes impact: "The floppy disks [subject] *that he had ordered from the discount supplier but had to return when they had defects* sat in a plastic container on his desk [verb]."

The right quotes vitalize and personalize an article. They weaken your points when they merely contain factual matter and duplicate what you've just said yourself. Again from *Flagler Magazine:* " 'Humpback whales also swim in Florida waters, and they do have a small dorsal fin,' Gromling recently told a group." *Didn't we say that?*

WORDINESS

Magazine articles should be experiences, a treat for tongue as well as the eye. As a logical progression of thoughts and commentary from which readers learn something that interests them, articles need to flow smoothly. Read aloud what you've written. If you have to breathe at inappropriate places, you've *over-written*. You can tighten your manuscript and reduce wordiness by systematically rooting out most of those prepositions. I'm always amazed that people who speak simply and directly in conversation, in print will pander to words such as *with, under, over, by, in, on, to, at, about* and similar prepositions: "*On* top *of* old Smokey. . . ." Followed by a noun or pronoun, used as adverbs or adjectives, prepositional phrases show relationship to the rest of the sentence. They're overused—an excuse for cramming too much information in a sentence. They're also used incorrectly, as in this redundancy—"off *of*." Pepper your sentences with prepositions, and an editor flags you as a novice writer.

Here's an example: "Buffet Style Pizza is one *of* America's fastest-growing pizza companies that has *over* 3,300 locations *in* 20 states *since* 1990." That sentence contains four prepositions and too many elements. What to do? Shorten it: "One of the nation's fastest-growing pizza companies, the Buffet Style Pizza chain, operates 3,300 outlets in 20 states. Founded in 1990 . . ."

A further hint: *Over* is where an umbrella goes—over your head. *Under* is where you might store it when not in use—under the desk or table. *Under* and *over*—words that indicate spatial relationships—are *not* interchangeable with *less than* and *more than*—phrases that refer to *quantity*; for example, *more than* 300 locations, *less than* 300 locations.

Another cure for over-writing? *The period*. Simple sentences are hooked with a conjunction to become complex—"He thought he would go and then he decided not to." Each of those is an independent clause, complete in itself; each has a subject and a verb. When you start adding a third independent clause, modifying each one and tacking on dependent clauses as well, your sentence is in trouble. Stop the ramble with a period: The sentence contains too many thoughts.

WORD WASTE

To write concisely, you have to think that way also. Some of us by nature are hedge-betters. Rather than write directly, we qualify our statements this way: "*Basically*, Smith was *pretty sure* the costs were *rather* higher than anticipated and *on that basis*, he decided to stay home." Words such as *pretty sure, rather,* and *basically*, along with *likely, quite certain, the reason that* (for *because*), *in the event of* (for *if*) and *is not in favor of* (for *opposes*) waste space and dilute your storyline. So do redundancies such as "*close* proximity," "*dead* body," "*killed dead*," "*captured alive*," "*lifeless* corpse," "*fully* clothed," "*mutual* cooperation," "*ultimate* outcome," "*end* result," "*100 percent* complete," "*experienced a* decline," "*exact* same," "at this *point in* time" and "vantage *point*." Avoid them, along with clichés such as *like the plague* and *sweats like a pig* (pigs don't sweat) and euphemisms such as *fragging, in country, deselected* (British for "voted out of office"), *servicing the target* (bombing) and *soft targets* (people).

Over-used adverbs and nouns floral with adjectives add to word waste. They're no substitute for precise verbs and nouns and both should be used sparingly. For example:

He *hustled.*

He walked quickly.

He slightly hit the truck ahead of him.

He *rear-ended* the truck ahead.

She smiled slightly.

She shook his hand and smiled. "I'm very pleased to meet you," she said.

Tall and pretty, her black hair long but straight, her eyes a deep brown, Leonora Macapagal. . . . (Note the *lack of a dominant impression.* And why not say how tall she is by contrasting her height with that of a known object?)

Her hair lay in coal-black tendrils against her neck. She brushed them aside as I looked up at her.

READERS GET CONFUSED

Jaru, an 18-year-old rapper from the Bronx, is known only by the one name. If you refer to Jaru the first time as *the rapper,* stick with that identifying tag throughout the profile. It confuses readers if you subsequently tag him as, *the Bronx teenager.* Edwin Coolidge, author of the grandfather clock piece seen earlier in this book, is a retired professor from a midsize Florida town. Choose an appropriate tag for him—*Coolidge,* perhaps—and stick with it. Avoid confusing the reader with such additional labels as *the professor, the unpublished writer, the Florida resident.*

Confusing in another way is this lead from "Good Neighbors" on page 98 of the June 2003 *Country Living.* It illustrates how easy it is to sacrifice clarity and simplicity when you're trying hard to be cute.

There's more to pet stewardship than the primary bond between you and your pet. Recently I was embarrassed to learn that some of my dearest neighbors found canine cacophony in what I merely took to be my dogs' self-expression. Their polite telephone call and fair requests prompted me to establish a strict schedule for my dogs' outdoor pronouncements, and we are still friends.

FLESCH AND OTHERS

Turn your manuscript upside down and look at it page by page. Don't try to read the words. Look at the length and variety of your paragraphs. Do they look alike? Are most of them the same length? For balance, you need a variety of short and longer paragraphs. Readers, for their part, need white space. A page too grey with type invites boredom. But one with frequent paragraph indentations and the white space that's normal between grafs gives the page eye ease.

Now turn the manuscript right-side up and examine the structure of each graf. Do they all begin the same way? With a simple or complex declarative sentence? Try for variety. Start a sentence with a question. Begin it with a dependant clause. If appropriate, start the sentence with a conjunction. And sometimes—but just sometimes—you might begin it with a single word: *No.* Like the occasional one-sentence graf, it grabs the reader's attention.

For many decades, writers and teachers of writing had been manually measuring readability with a variety of mathematical formulae. Today, computer software does it for you, totaling the number of words (and syllables in each word), and the number of sentences and paragraphs in a manuscript, dividing, multiplying and coming up with a measure of reading ease. Unfortunately, these formulae can't tell us if readers understand what they read or if it's suited to their interests. Other items have to be factored into the readability equation as well: type size and font, for instance, page layout and the amount of white space. However, you might find the Flesch Reading Ease Scale useful in gauging the pattern of your own writing. Developed by linguist Rudolf Flesch in the 1940s, it's the easiest mathematical formula to use. If you don't have "smart" software, do it manually.

Simply calculate your average number of words per sentence (AWS) from a representative sample, then figure out the average number of syllables per word (ASW). Multiply the ASW by 84.6, then subtract that total from the AWS that's been multiplied by 1.015. Now subtract your answer from 206.835 to get your score. The higher you score when rated on a scale of 100, the more readable your manuscript should be. An average score of 65, which equates with "plain English"—is suitable for most popular writing.

HELPFUL EXERCISES

1. Keep watch on these words. It's easy to misuse and misspell them and risky to rely for accuracy on a computer's tools. With a current edition of both dictionary and thesaurus by your side, write a sentence using each word in the groupings below. Make sure sentence and word use are grammatically correct: Don't second-guess yourself.

affect/effect

principle/principal

perspective/prospective

portion/part

less/fewer

compared to/compared with

preventive/preventative

lay/lie

that/which

they're/their/there

further/farther

antenna/antennae

alumna/alumnus/alumnae

pointed out/called attention to

raised/reared

2. These words are often misspelled and can reflect negatively on the writer. Check to see which of each pair is correct.

all right/alright

alot/a lot

3. These wordy phrases and sentences contain inappropriate imagery, incorrect punctuation, faulty pronouns, vague words, redundancies and euphemisms. Rewrite and tighten the awkward construction, making each sentence or word grouping readable, correct and specific.

Seasoned pro

Is in favor of

Is not known

On the precipice of the cliff

On behalf of

Is leaning toward

Is domiciled in

Executed the function of

It is not known whether or not the committee will decide to forego a variance on the issue of building permits.

Has announced the roster of new members

By the turn of the century, racial antagonisms disrupted the relations between the black soldiers at Fort Bliss and the local El Paso population.

Time passed, and the United States stumbled through a slaving period terminating with the Civil War.

A potentially dangerous situation that could prove fatal if the plan we have is not brought to completion

She derived pleasure from her vacation at the beach.

Although apparently sympathetic, the city council was not in favor of

Has decided on the terms of financing the conditions for improvements

Experienced severe dizziness

He was obsessive over the

The doctor expressed concern that she could die at 71 years of age.

Our accommodations were very satisfactory.

Defensive fire decimated one-third of the 105th battalion.

The city engineer submitted a proposal that would finalize completion of the project.

A substantial proportion of the medical research is directed toward amelioration of the disease.

Michael Jackson put in an appearance at

There was a meeting of the President's Club on Wednesday.

There was conclusive evidence in the Schram murder case, according to the prosecutor.

As a consequence of bad weather, the meeting is cancelled.

All the lawns were being mowed by the same man.

It is believed by the Pentagon that not all the prisoners are dead.

Smith said that the data has proved to be reliable.

The American Red Cross instituted their blood drive early in the 20th century.

The raucous years of the 70s and 80s

A Coloradoan and World War I veteran, Jonas Garth, migrated to France as the first in a wave of American émigrés.

The banker played a major hardship in the downfall of the Riley Company.

In doing so, he blazed a path that authored in large-scale public investigations of corporate excesses.

■ ■ ■ ■ ■

CHAPTER FIFTEEN

WHAT TO DO WITH
WHAT YOU HAVE

My editor at *Flagler Outlook* magazine e-mailed me in haste. She was preparing to put out the bimonthly issue and had a shopping list of articles to be done. Could I please investigate story possibilities? And quickly?

Periodicals such as *Flagler Outlook,* one of many owned by *The Daytona Beach News-Journal* and included loose with the newspaper on a Saturday or Sunday, are four-color magazines that work on a short turnaround time editorially. Since they're designed without excuse to attract advertising dollars but do appeal nevertheless to the interests of readership, an editor may not know until the last minute how much ad space was sold and how much space remains for articles.

The articles my editor suggested? A story on hunting and hunt clubs centering around people from the country town of Bunnell. A story on a musical group, also focused on Bunnell. A story on surfing at Florida's Flagler Beach to the east, focus to be my choice. A profile on someone who lives year-round on a houseboat at the Palm Coast marina, also on Florida's east coast.

Although I drove an hour north to investigate, I wasn't interested in doing a hunting story and told my editor. That left a musical group. I heard of a high school jazz combo; unfortunately, school was out for the summer and no one was hiring musicians in the heat. I stopped at the Flagler County Chamber of Commerce; no leads there. I had more success at Flagler Beach, interviewing several lifeguards about the free surfing lessons and the sales clerks at the only surf shop in the small beach community. How did I decide whom to interview? I wasn't a surfer: Did I even know which questions to ask? I inquired first at Z Wave Surf Shop. Sales clerks there briefly oriented me, and I was directed to the lifeguard station on the pier. At the station, I found only two lifeguards: The rest were off or on duty in the towers. Even the lifeguard captain was off duty that day. Fortunately, neither of the two lifeguards was reticent and both were helpful.

I returned to my office, transcribed my notes and realized that the information was too secondhand. I had to amplify it with on-site lifeguard instruction at a live, Saturday-morning surfing lesson. The following Saturday,

I took my first lesson, joining 50 or more people of all ages, some of whom had driven more than an hour to get there.

I wrote the story the following day (see p. 208), making sure to first transcribe my interview notes from those two days at Flagler Beach. "Surfing 1-2-3" appeared in the August 2004 issue of *Flagler Outlook.* So did the enterprise story I wrote on the female harbormaster at the Palm Coast marina to the north. A story on retired houseboat dwellers there appeared later in the year.

Appearing here is the word-for-word transcription of my notes from the "Surfing 1-2-3" interviews, complete with the typos, misspellings and abbreviations that resulted from my fast typing and a fast-approaching deadline. Transcribing word-for-word is optional, of course. I simply feel more comfortable that way. Notice that I will boldface or underline any comments or statements that I think I might use in the article. I've highlighted those sections in the notes that I eventually did use. I decided to forego comments from Katy, the young lifeguard supervisor, since they were redundant and would inject too many people into a short article. However, I highlighted her information on riding the line. Jenel Buxman made a similar statement when she took me out to the breaking waves. When a question precedes a paragraph in my notes, the question asked is mine. My notes to you appear to the right.

■ ■ ■ ■ ■ ▬▬▬▬▬▬▬▬▬▬▬▬▬▬▬▬▬▬▬▬▬▬▬▬▬▬▬▬▬▬▬

SURFING 1-2-3

10 A.M. and heat rises off the Flagler Beach sand like hot butter turned brown on the griddle.

Squinting against the sun

10 A.M. and already the day was hot and humid. Carsnose to nose, themselves hot lined. . . . . . Under a slightly overcast sky,,,requiring one to squint, young (name) Brian Willits, face slathered in white sunscreen, came into the first aid station to. . . .   **false starts**

Surfing, some say, is a little bit like sailing and a bit like heading into a wake in reverse. You aling your body with the incoming wave at an angle of about 35 degrees????

"Ever Saturday morning, starting at 9:30 we over free surfing lessons. You could be young, old it doesn't matter anybody. They teach technique and normally— know how to surf. Technique and how to stand up on the board—we help them out. We have long boards that are foam. They're easier to get up on and it doesn't hurt. Normally they're made out of fiberglass.

Any age person at all. As long as the parents want their young kids to come out, then they're allowed to. They don't need to sign anything. They just show up. The only thing they have to sitg for is Junior Guards, which we offer Tuesday and Thursday. We'll teach the Junior Guards medical, we'll teach them surf entry skills we'll teach them surfing. Everythng we do, we teach them.

(continued)

CONTINUED

Lannigan: They get a lot of lifeguard interaction. From the upper lifeguards.

Other: We use all of our lifeguards, not just certain ones. We use new people that came out after we train them. Me and him have been here over five years; he's been here like about 8. Everyone . . . we use everbody. They all give their knowledge to the young kids and. . . .

Were you attracted to this because you're surfers?
Lannigan: I've been doing this since I was 15. I just. . . .i love the ocean/ . . it's a good job and you get paid for helping people. It's a great job. You're always outdoors, you're moving around, you get to meet new people.

Interjection: And you learn how to surf. You get to work out, it's a good job.

Lannigan: Right.

Other: I like surfing. Yeah. I'm not as good as some of the other guys, but yeah. We have some guys that are awesome. we have one working for us, he's second in the nation on body boarding. We had ne—Will Tant—he was actually a professional surfer. He used to work for us.

Me: Are there profl. Surfers out here on Flagler Beach that come just to surf?
"Sometimes yeah. Freida Zamba—she's what 7-time world champion."
The Freida Zamba pool over near Buddy Taylor, the middle school., is named for her. "She comes out and surfs. Maybe not near the peir, but there's really some nice spots down the beach all around.:

How far out?
"It depends. We have a break normally that's about 600 feet offshore is a outside break, but our normal break is anywhere from 30 to 100 feet is our normal break.:Break: The way the waves start breaking so you can ride them."

How does a newcomer have to dress to come to do this?
"Whatever they want to get wet they can wear." We don't/ If they want to wear blue jeans—we advise against it, but. . . ."**We don't have a dress code.**

A wet suit?
Depends on how warm the water temp. is. If the water drops below. . . . I've never seen anyone around hear wear them."you won't see those down here.

Shoes? "probably out where the water's cold, like the Pacific Northwest.

Freida Zamba—1984, 85, 86 ad 88—WCT world champion

Me: When you start newcomers out, what is the first thing you do?
"We lay the boartds down, On the north side, near the first tower, where everybody meets in the morning. We're be there at 9:30, and we'll lay all the boards down and each person will line up behind the boards. Then we'll have a lifeguard in front of the boards. One person, as our speaker, will say, 'Okay, guys, we're just going to have you lay down on the boards and give them an example. 'This is how you paddle. And when we get out there, we're going to say, One, two three, and you're going to stand up. "And we show them how. **We show them where to put their feet, how to stand, where to look-before we even leave the land.**

NAMES: WILLIAM DRESSEL and SCOTT LANNIGAN.

That's another thing Junior Guards can learn. When we get the boats ready, we're goint to teach them sailing. About Jr. Guards: until school starts again. It's completely free, same as the surf lessons we give on Saturday morning. It's 9:30 to 11:30; you do have to sign up for those. And that's for ages 4 to 15.

What can a Jr. Guard do when they're done. Well, we'
Ll give them medals at the end. **It's just to get them used to being in the water, make them safer. . . .Let's say you're a parent and you're worried about them. We get them used to going in the water, swimming, what to do when there's a runout, how to spot a runout. . . .**

Me: What's a runout?
"A riptide, where the sandbar is lower at one point and that's where all the water comes up.

Teaching them all of that so they're more comfortable and safer at the beach.

40 lifeguards. The captain is Walter Forehand, sisterinlaw is Zoee Forehand.

For surfing, you don't wear sunglasses unless yu have chaps and you want to risk losing them. Sunblock, yes. A lo of surfers don't wear **sunblock** because their skin's so tempered by the sun.

Lannigan: "Some of them wear **rashguards** which is like a Spandex-type T skirt. It prevents rashes from the surfboard.

Other: You'll get, he snorts, horrible rashes wherever any part of your body hits the board.

Me: How much do you stand up?
Other (and the major talker): **"Most of it's is waiting. You wait for a wave, and you're waiting for a wave. You're not laying down at that point, you're astride on the board, so you're looking at the water.. You're out there looking at the waves and waiting for a set to come in, which is coming about 3 to 5 waves. A set will come in every now and then and those are the bigger wavecs. That's why you wait for them.**

And then you turn towards the way the wave's going towards land, and you start paddling. What you want to do is build up your speed to match that of the wave so you won't go over it but drop down into it and you can start. You want to turn into the wave—whichever way it's not breaking. Let's say it's breaking behind you and you want go go away from it so you have a longer ride. And you ride it all the way down.

Young fellow
He is getting one of the foam boards. "He's here all the time. Local"
He lives on 14th St. Anthony Anthony Furia. A 7th grader. (something about 8th.)\
He's taken junior lifeguard training twice.
Why do you like it (surfing)?

"Bnecause it's a really fun sport. Just to catch waves and stuff, paddling out, catching like a big wave."

(continued)

CONTINUED

Are you good?
"Yeah."
Have ambitions?
"be like a pro surfer. Or a pro dirt biker. "
He is getting a dirt bike.
"But I love surfing."
Comes out here every day during summer. "Every time I get off school, if the waves are really good."
Friends?

His surfboard just broke so he's getting a new one today. Buy surfboards at Z Waves, 22d St.,..
It's the same one, owned by the same people. One's a clothes shop, the other's a board shop.

Cost of boards:
Boy" Can range from $200 to like $500. "I'm getting one that's a year old today. $150./

Boy was checking out a body board.
Other ((not lannigan): "We have the second in the nation body boarder working for us. It only uses the top half of your body. It's smaller.
Me: what is difference between body boarding and surfing?
Boy: "Body board you lay down, surfing you stand up."
Other: You can get on your knees. One knee, one foot.
(But the boy likes surfing and tht's what he's getting.)

Are surfboards sizes to a person's height?
Boy: " Yes. If you can touch it to your nose." Depends. On whether you want to be a long boarder or a short board.er Short boards are bette4r for tricks. Long boards are good for catching waves that surfboards can't catch really.

Today-=boy was getting a short board.

Other: We use all long boards. We have shorter boards we can use with younger kids or certain lifeguards prefer the shorter board. The majority are 9'8". 7'5, 9s, 10s, (also have. The foam boards you teach on are all the big boards. If we have kids who want the shorter, we'll use the smaller 7'5s. Street—1427 South Daytona (a street in Flagler).

Lannigan: I haven't been here for three years. I just finished up at Yale. Summer gig? I was a lifeguard here wsince 96, then I left for 3 years and came back.
Other: Most of our lifeguards do this during the summer and attend school the rest of the year. I attend UF during the year and come here and work.

Lannigan—use one N to spell it.

I just finished (Yale) with a master's in biology.
Other: mine's aerospace engineering. I'm getting my bachelor's. I'm taking time off from school. I'm definitely going to do this until I find a good occupation for may major. **BUT THIS IS DEFINITEY MY FAVORITE JOB THAT I COULD POSSIBLY HAVE RIGHT NOW.**

Why do people surf? (me):
Other: They get the exhileration of dropping into a wave, the speed, the fact that you can be better than other peole—the fact that everyone will watch you.
Lannigan: **"It feels like you're standing up on water." Like walking on water, yep."**

Me: a persom comes to surf. How long, how many days/wek, how many weeks. I guess that it's free. We normallyl . . . they come wheneve3r they feel like it, and sometimes people who are really interested in learning and don't want to do the lessons on Saturday mornings will talk to certain lifeguards and they can set up private lessons on days when that lifeguard's working.

"will show up and just for 5–10 minutes and we'll have them paddling and we' 11 tell them how to do a 1-2-3 pop-up and then how to stand and everything like that. We're with every single person who's on those boards. So what we say is so we can time them standing up properly so they can catch the wave: We'll say 'One-two-three standup."

That's what we tell them before they go out into the water so they know and then they canm practice and they can practice the pop up because they're laying flat. What they want to do (he illustrates) they want to be able to pop up withut putting their knees do or anything. It's real fast. We practice that. We just tell them "one, two, three stand up"and send them to the back of the line and they go to the back of the line as soon as they do it right. If they don't, we keep making them do it. And then once they go thrpugh the line once or twice, I say 'alright, pick up the boards, and we're going in the water.' In the water, and we do probably about 3 rides each—it depends on hosw many peole we have—

We do it for two hours—9:30 to 11:30 on Saturday only. That's when we have most of our guards working.

At least 100 peole come out each Saturday. We get a bunch.

How long does it take a motivated person to do this (learn)?
Oh=—I don't think anybody. Our boards are real thick, rteal floaty. They're virtually rafts. The 10 foot foam ones; we have a little smaller but they're still real easy to learn on. I don't think we've ever had someone who came her on a Saturdgy and left without standing up and riding the waves. They normally get it within. . . ..I generally myself don't like to send a person in and have someone else come out until my target individual (the man) stands up. Even if it takes more than three tries, we normally might still go or at least we'll get him the next time. I hardly think anybody has ever left without standing up at least once. **So you learn the day you come, basically.**

Do peopole get scared"?
Occasionally"

Sharks?
Of course we have sharks. Sharks are everywhere. That's where they live, you know. We haven't had a shark attack at Flagler Beach for years and years. That's generally New Smyrna and up nortyh. For whatever reason, our area hasn't seen one in a long time. Even though it's the same coastline, "it's harder for Flagler. . . ." Flagler generally doesn't get hit by hurricanes because it is more shallow out around Flagler and they normally steer off in either direction. That may (exploain sharks, too).

(continued)

CONTINUED

Do you see sharks?
Oh, yeah, we see sharks. Sitting up in the lifeguard tower—that doesn't normally happen. Occas. We'll see one swimming shallow enough. But we normally never see them. But they do catch them off the pier—like they'll hook them.

Surfinbg clubs? No idea.
I heard someone was tring to start one up. He went to high school here, at Flagler Palm Coast. He lives in Palm Coast. Lanigan lives in Paolm Coast, also. Captain lives in palm Coast, in the C section.

The regulars surfing here> "There is no how old. They stay out young. We get kids his age, a little yunger, they try to be out here all day. We have a lot of high schoolers coming out here and then we have the ones who have already graduated. They just stay here and you know them. I've seen them come, like high school graduates and they're still here. **He is 19.**

Are t6here peole in their 60s and 760s who live here who come out?
"Oh., yeah. All the time. Locals.

What investment, other than board price, does one need?
Clothing: a leash and a rash guard. Leash attaches to leg and end of board—prob. $18. A rash guard is about $30. Tiny shirt. Tight. That's the point so it doesn't rub. It really helps prevent rashes. I used to get them bad—they'll hurt and sting, and then they'll get scabby. Women wear rash guards.

No everyone wears rash guards. Some peole don't have a problem. Maybe they can keep their chest up as they paddle.

Shorts?
Bathing suit, I mean they can . . . some surfers wear the board shorts over what they normally would wear. They're longer. Mostly longer what the lifeguards wear. There's a lot of brands. You can pay $50 to $60 or pay $20. Depends on if they're on sale, oif they're new, what style. It's just something to wear to surf. Just what people prefer."

Katy (CHECK spelling): She is supervisor Mcnitt. She lives in fagler Beach. Been at this job 'about two years." I make sure they're doing their job. That's my job. She supervises 40 lifeguards. She was not a lifeguard before being this. "I used to be a Junior Lifeguard." "I started as administrative assistant, actually.

Board wax isn't expensive. We don't need them for our boards. The shorter long boards, like the 75s, some people wax those because they're a little more slippery. They're smaller and not as flottable. You wax it on top so you can stand on it. It's real sticky. You rub it on and it's real sticky. You rub it on. It's fiberglass (board). We have a couple fiberglass there. It's realy slippery.If you slide and fall on your knees on it, youc an break the board., If you're on it, yu can drop; into the wave and turn off into it and start doing tridcks, you need to be able to move thta board and turn it.And all you're touching (?) is your feet. That's wht the wax does-=-traction.

How do you pop up that quick?
You get used to it . It's not that hard. You just got to get used to it , I guess. As long
as you can move your arms like that ,m you just throw your feeet under. A lot of
people want to sit there and they crawl up like this . . . your balance is thrown
cojpletely right at the beginning so you'll just fall right over.

What's the attraction of Flagler for surfing?
Katy, want to answer that??
"it's just depends on what the swells are like."
Swells bigger here?
"iIt all depends on the sandbars, usually. Sandbars are what cause the waves and
such to kick up. I don'yt know. It can be good in St. Augustine one day and be flat
down here the next day. "

How does a person find out the condition of the waves before coming to surF?
The Z Wave surg Shop across the street has a surf report. And when they're not
there, they have an answer machine with a surf report on it at all times."

Me: Suppose I'm in Orlando.
"We have peole who call here. This is our mobile phone here: It's 439-7867 (386).
There are peole who call and ask what the water conditions are like, what are the
rip currents like, from Orlando. They call us or they can also call Z Waves, and
they always have the tides and stuff, too.

Z Wave Surf Shop, Zoee B. Forehand, owner. 386-439-WAVE (9283), Located 400 S.
Oceanshore Blvd., (South 4th St/. and A1A), P.O. Box 2029, Flagler Beach, FL
32136

Me; What are ideal conditions?
(she asks Billy)

Billy (as before): **You don't want it real rough and choppy, meaning a lot of wind,
crosswind whatever, the waves are not smooth, they're just real choppy. Ideal
conditions are real smooth—a rain will smooth it out, make it glassy—if you can
get that and big waves, perfect.**

**During hurricane system,—dangerous, said Katy—but that's when the waves
are good.**

Captain—is the Beach Services Director, Walter Forehand. Monday is his day off.

If one were a newcomer to surfing, what else should one know?

Who takes the surging lessons?
Katy: "We have kids that come out that are four years old, all the way up to
grandparents." We have families that come and we actually have families that
come down on vacation. I guess they call the city and they give them our
number and they will call in and schedule an appointment with us for lessons,
and we can set them up with instructors as long as we know the days and
times and everything."(Mostly occurs in the summertime, because the water
is warm.

(continued)

CONTINUED

Lessons: 9:30–11:30.
I know that Freida Zamba does surf lessons, too. They're pretty expensive, tho. She and her husband just started making surgboards. They're not making them, they're shaping them..Freida Zamba boards. They sell them at surf boards. I'm pretty sure she has a Web site. There's a factory down in Cocoa that makes them.

Shaping: "All difrfrent boards are shaped differently. Boards that are rounded on the end are either a long board or a fun shape. That's what I have.
It's just a longer board. My board is 6 10, and it's not pointy. A short board is a pointy board. Those boards will cut you real easy.

And then some boards, on the tail at the end of the board, it's cvalled a fishtail.
All boards have 3 fins on a board. (on most boards.)
They can be real heavy depending on length, size. Short boards are pretty light.

You ca't have a board that's too short. Your board should be level with the top of your head. Or the nose will go down in the water.

There are body boards and then there's a drop knee. And they pull themselves up with one of their knees on the board. There's drop knee and then there's just body boarding. Drop knee is more like cvompetetive. Drop knee, you don't stand up at all—you're on your knee.

Me: The idea way to catch a wave is? You don't head into it, do you?
Katy, cont." "Well, you do. Waves come in and you have to paddle—the wax helps you with your grip so you don't slip off—and then you push up on your board really fast, and the wave catches you from behind. It's called **riding the line.** The wave goes every way. Some peole go right and other peole go left. It just depends on whatever way you think the wave is going to push you farther. The line is like the whitewash. If I were sailing, or the wake, I would go into. And some people, if they're not as experienced, you just go straight. When you/re riding the line, it's easier to go up and do tricks. If you just go straight, it's going to push you straight—you ca't go up and do tricks. And by riding the line, you can go up and hit the top of the wave and do tricks.

For example, a roundhouse. (trick, a figure 8),

We don't teach trick lessons. We just teach how to get up on the wave. Most of the kids here, they just go straight.

Today: the waves were very flat.

Notes from interview at Z Wave Surf Shop

How long has Z Wave been here? 15 years?? One next door—just opened.
Boogy boards: They're all foam. Some of them have a hard back. Boogy boards don't need fins. "A lot of the people wear the wearable fins, instead of a fin in the board which help them go faster.

How much are boogy boards? $34.95 to $199. Price varies because of length, height, width—it'll float you better if it's bigger—and manufacturer.

Some boogy boards aren't pointed—they're not boogy boards but **skim boards.** You throw it down on the beach sand and you jump on it and you slide.

Cost of fins: from 39.95 to 69.95.

The long boards and the shorter of the long boards: cost
Long Boards: (350–375) They Range in thickness, in length and width. A lot buy according to your height. Whatever height you are, buy 6–8 inches taller than you are for a fiberglass board. (shrter). For long boards, that's personal preference. The shorter boards are pointed: $399, $425 . . .

If it's cold weather, we suits:
They run between (some are on consignment) $85 for a kid's suit, new adult suit $205.

Me: Basically one can do all this for considerably under a thousand bucks. "Oh sure."

Used boards? They have. Those range between $175 and $300 depending on c

You can buy tip covers. If tips are dinged. Or buy ding repair.

Wax—theyt have chickey bumps for girls. and sticky bumps (?)—kids like them. $1.25 Personal preference.Mrs. Palmer's and sex?? Wax. And there's also wax for warm weather and we put out our cold wax if it's colder. Because you if it's warmer you want something a little thicker to stay on your board.

There may still be a surfing TEAM at the school.

On loction: **Saturday A.M. Lesson**

"One, two three, up." (no knees)
Fathers and sons and mothers and sons and daughters were out.
Jenel ? Toes at the foot of the board.
Mother and 3 children from Apopka. Sheilah O'Donnell?They drove an hour and a half to do this. First time here. Eric,three sons. Whose idea to come here? Boys? You?
She laughs. "A little of each." "One of them's on it. Alright," she watches in the distance. "That's my son," she says proudly. Her 19=-year-old son Eric is standing up and coming in.
When is she going to take instruction, I ask? "I don't know. Then, a second later and happier, "I should!"

Billy: "It's just exhilarating. The speed from just being on the board. " I'm invited to a luau at 6:30. Bonfire. Tuesday and Thursday from 9:30 to 11:30. Jr. Lifeguards. Basically, we're making them safer at the beach. If they enjoy it, we're always setting ourselves up to have better lifeguards in the future. Because we teach them about how to avoid runoffs—a riptide. There's a sandbar that's out there. And all the water is coming over the sandbar and that's why the waves are like that. But t's got to go out somewere. It follows the path of least resistance which would be a little hole. And you might not be in it (the riptidee) but the current will take you into it.

WRITING THE ARTICLE

The article, I decided, would focus on surfing as family fun rather than focus on the lifeguards or on a star surfboarder. Although the temptation to focus on the lifeguards remained viable, the appeal of the story wouldn't be as broad. The first few paragraphs would provide atmosphere and set the scene for readers. Since I had taken a surfing lesson, been tossed by the waves and actually ridden one of them to the beach on a funboard, I faced a second temptation: to include myself as participant–observer. Again, the appeal to readership would be too narrow. (In the resulting article, however, I was the "older woman" who couldn't pop up quickly enough and rode the wave in on her knees.)

The noise of the surf made it difficult to record instructions and comments the day I took my lesson. I ended up using the earlier instructions I'd received from lifeguard Billy Dressel, the "other" speaker in my notes, who had acted out a surfing lesson for me in the lifeguard office earlier in the week. Jenel Buxman, the main trainer for that Saturday morning lesson, used the same words in her instructions to me.

WRITING THE SIDEBAR

It was time-consuming to wade through my notes, selecting information for a sidebar. The option—to include both facts and narrative in a single article—would have diluted the impact of the story and buried information that a reader needs. Since I had some questions while I was writing the sidebar, I called the sales staff at Z Wave Surf Shop—a "get-back-to-you" option I always leave open when writing a story. I was glad I did: Some of my information on prices and board sizes was incorrect.

The final article and sidebar submitted to my editor at *Flagler Outlook* appear here.

SURFING 1-2-3

By Nancy M. Hamilton

Nine A.M., and the heat rises off Flagler Beach like hot butter sizzling brown on the griddle. It's already a sun-squinting day. In the distance, 25 surfers of various ages and shades of tan float listlessly on their surfboards, looking over their shoulders out to sea, waiting. The sea, at the moment, is flat.

On the beach near the north lifeguard tower, surfboards have been placed next to each other in the sand, their colorful noses perpendicular to the breakwater. Behind them, fathers and mothers and sons and daughters from four-year-olds to ages 60 or 70 have started to line up. They'll be learning on these 10-foot funboards, the size intermediate to the long and the short surfboards, because they're boards with a difference. These are foam. "They're virtual rafts," explained lifeguard William "Billy" Dressel, a Flagler Beach resident and one of 40 lifeguards captained by Water Forehand. "They're thick, really floaty. Easier to get up on, and you won't get hurt."

Other lifeguards begin to assemble at water's edge, one per board. They'll be giving individual instruction and taking the new surfers out.

"I don't think we've ever had someone who came here on a Saturday and left without standing up and riding the waves at least once," said Dressel. "Basically, you learn the day you come." The idea of the free instruction, he said, is to make surfboarders a little safer at the beach.

Each Saturday, they come by the 50s or hundreds, spending Saturday morning from 9:30 to 11:30 to learn for the first time or to polish their basic skill. Surfing lessons are free. Most who come are Flagler Beach residents; some, like Sheila O'Donnell of Apopka who brought her three sons, come to learn for the first time. She drove one-and-one-half hours. At first, she just watches.

The newcomers catch on quickly to the dry-land drill. The first wannabe's are already belly to a board when lifeguard Jenel Bruxton calls out the first instructions.

"Okay, guys, we're just going to have you lie down on the boards. Put your toes at the end of the board. That's right. Cup your hands like this. This is how you paddle." She demonstrates. The first-wave students dig in the sand like dogs burying a bone. "Now I'm going to say, 'one, two, three, standup,' and you're going to pop up," Bruxton continues. "One-two-three without using your knees. Feet apart. And

you're going to stand sideways—either direction—arms out. Keep your knees bent."

"Okay, start paddling. That's it. Now!" she commands. "One, two, three, standup!"

The first wave of students pops to its feet immediately and others take their place. Each does the drill three times if necessary. Meanwhile, the swells are building offshore, and students meet crashing waves as they follow the lifeguards into the surf. Jenel Bruxton steadies the board as an older woman climbs on for her first ride. "Don't try to ride the line," she cautions, referring to the more experienced surfer's tendency to ride the wave longer by riding it's whitewash at the crest and doing tricks. "Stand up sideways, keep your knees bent and go straight into the beach."

Buxton watches over her shoulder as a wave starts breaking behind them. "Paddle!" she calls. "One, two, three, standup!" The older woman is in trouble. "My knees are too stiff. I can't get to my feet!" she yells. "That's okay," Buxton reassures her. "Ride in on your knees." She follows the board as the surfer rides the wave successfully into the beach. "Good job," she pats her back. The woman beams, even though she knew better. To crawl up from your knees is to risk losing balance and falling off the board. With practice, she'll eventually be able to pop to her feet. "You just get used to it, I guess," said Dressler.

On the sand, Sheila O'Donnell from Apopka shades her eyes and searches for her sons in the busy surf of instruction. "One of them's on it!" she says. "That's my son," she points proudly as 19-year-old Eric, standing up and sideways to the cresting wave, rides the swell onto the beach. "All right!" she says, dragging out the "riiiight." Is she going to take instruction? "I should,"

(continued)

CONTINUED

she hesitates. "I will," she decides and heads to the car to change.

Meanwhile, the 25 surfers offshore are now alert and astride their boards. They've paddled 100 feet out, the limit of a normal break at Flagler Beach, and are watching the waves, waiting for a set of three to five that will lift them higher and farther as they ride the line. "Most of surfing," comments Dressler as he watches the group offshore, "is waiting." A set starts to build. The surfers turn into the first wave and paddle opposite from the way it's breaking, trying to build up speed to match that of the wave. Then they're up and dropping into it.

Why do people surf? "It's the speed and the exhilaration you get from dropping into a wave," said Dressler. "The fact that you can be better than other people. The fact that everyone will watch you."

Flagler Beach 7th grader Anthony Furia, who's taken Junior Lifeguard training twice, loves surfing. He surfs every day during the summer and after school if the waves are good. "Paddling out, catching a big wave—it's a really fun sport," he said.

Lifeguard Scott Lanigan from Palm Coast, who's been surfing since he was 15, puts it another way. "Surfing feels like you're walking on water."

Surfing at Flagler Beach

Instruction:
Free each Saturday from 9:30 to 11:30
Private instruction at other times, also free, by prearrangement with a lifeguard

To check the condition of the surf or to contact lifeguard trainers:
386-439-7867 (mobile)
386-439-WAVE (surf report only from Z Wave Surf Shop)

Equipment and gear:
Students and novices are free to use and check out foam funboards at the lifeguard station on the Flagler Beach pier.

Boards
If you have graduated to fiberglass boards, or prefer other types of boards, you have a range of choices, say sales personnel at Z Wave Surf Shop across the street from the Flagler Beach pier. Surfboards are shaped differently. Those that are rounded on the end are either long boards or fun shapes. Better for catching waves, *long boards* ($350 to $375) range in thickness, length and width. Length is a personal preference, although most people buy long boards sized to their height. *Short boards* ($399 to $425) have pointed tips that can easily cut the surfer. Since the nose of a board that's too short will go down in the water, make sure to purchase a short board six to eight inches longer than your height at the top of your head.

Most boards have three fins, or rudders, underneath, near the tail section, and some boards end in a fishtail shape. The all-foam *boogie boards* ($34.95 to $199), some of them equipped with a hard back, lack fins. To compensate for the lack of fins, boogie boarders often wear rubber fins ($39.95 to $69.95) to give them greater board speed. Boogie boards that aren't pointed are actually *skim boards* which surfers throw on the sand, jump on and slide.

Body boards differ from standard surfboards. Smaller, they use only the top half of the body, with body boarders either lying down or using a drop knee form to be competitive.

Wax
Don't use a fiberglass board without purchasing and applying *wax* ($1.25). Applied to the top surface of the board, the wax supplies traction so you won't fall off. Buy wax according to seasonal temperatures.

Leash
Low-cost (about $18), a *leash* attaches to one leg and the end of your board, preventing loss.

Clothing
Many surfers wear a *rash guard* (approximately $30), a special knit shirt, to prevent the rubbing and board burns that often result from lying, then abruptly rising, from a surfboard. A rash guard should fit tightly against the skin.

Some surfers wear *body shorts* over what they normally would wear for swimming. Longer than standard shorts, they range from $20 to $60. Use common sense to dictate the clothing that would protect you and at the same time be water-suitable.

Sun block of at least SPF 15 is definitely recommended. Easily lost in the swells, sunglasses are not recommended.

BUT SOMETIMES THE MATERIAL IS OVERWHELMING

In 2004, I interviewed by telephone former television actor Fess Parker of Davy Crockett and Daniel Boone fame. I tape-recorded the 50-minute session through a small device I purchased for the telephone. Fifty minutes on the telephone? That's right, and I ended up with a stack of quotes, witticisms and information almost too overwhelming to digest.

The 80-year-old Parker was delightful. Humble, humorous, disarming—"Just call me Fess, Nancy"—he told me everything I asked and more—almost all of it accompanied by a pithy statement, a bit of humor or an anecdote. How to use all of that delightful material and restrict the story to an assigned 500 to 700 words was a conundrum. Obviously, some of it had to be deleted. Since Fess Parker wines were to be featured at the Daytona Beach wine festival—the purpose of the article—everything that didn't concern the Fess Parker Winery and Vineyard could be thrown out. I did, but apparently not ruthlessly enough. When the story ran in the June 2004 issue of *Volusia* magazine, several interesting anecdotes I thought necessary were edited out for space reasons. Still, the story remained cohesive. By deliberately incorporating Parkerisms in the comparison-and-contrast lead I crafted, I made sure that those, at least, wouldn't be cut. The lead to "King of the Wine Frontier" that ran on pages 18 and 19 of the June 2004 issue of *Volusia* magazine appears here. The title, by the way, is priceless. I didn't write it; my editor did. Mine missed the obvious mark by a lot.

> You'd expect him to be quietly humorous.
> "Life is like a bumper car, you know. You go down the road, you bump and then you change directions and then you bump again."
> You'd expect him to be humble.
> "I hate to admit this, but it's very seldom that I've indulged in analyzing something. I just see a thing and recognize it as what I should do. Sometimes I don't know how I'm going to do it. I just do it."
> But few would expect the man who made Davy Crockett a household name in the 1950s and Daniel Boone one in the 1960s to be a savvy businessman with hotels and other properties and a winery producing some of the best riesling, syrah, chardonnay and pinot noir in the country.

■ ■ ■ ■ ■ ▬▬▬▬▬▬▬▬▬▬▬▬▬▬▬▬▬▬▬▬

CHAPTER SIXTEEN

THE FIVE Rs

PRUNE FOR SUCCESS

Some of us revise extensively as we write the first draft. We expend the greatest amount of creative energy early, editing every word, comma, sentence, transition and paragraph as we write them. Other writers find their work polished and publishable only after a second or third rewrite. Said Rik Kirkland of his staff writers in talking with journalism professor Gerald Grow: "The really good writers finish early, take a break, then come back and edit themselves—before turning in that first draft." Kirkland is *Fortune* magazine's managing editor. "No one ever sees their real first drafts. They edit themselves before anyone else does."

Whether you revise as you go along—and I suggest a certain amount of revision should be done at that time—or do it substantively later, *self-editing in this craft is a must*. In fact, professionals will tell you that 90 percent of writing is rewriting. By the time you've reached second-draft stage, you shouldn't have to make major revisions to your story. Why? That would involve story line, form and organization—and you already worked out those sticking-point possibilities by the time you reached outline stage. Still, revising and rewriting is usually *more* than a matter of fixing "paint spills"—of cleaning up sentence structure, spelling, grammar and style. It usually involves an overall tightening of the story, a revision and perhaps a rethinking of lead and ending, and a movement of elements already in the story from one location to another to improve meaning and story flow.

For example, I originally began this chapter with the Rik Kirkland quote. That was followed by a phrase that now appears in the second graf: *self-editing in this craft is a must*. But as I took a few minutes to mentally reread my sentences and play around with them, I realized that the Kirkland quote was weak. It wasn't strong enough to begin the chapter and be lead-in to the general statement about revising extensively. I decided to reverse the order, beginning first with a general statement, then using the quote to illustrate it. The self-editing phrase could have gone into either chapter. But it's clearly more useful where I put it eventually—in graf two, as lead-in to a more detailed discussion of editing, revising and rewriting. In fact, I rewrote the last three sentences of the paragraph you're now reading *three times* to improve flow and rhythm.

After finishing the first draft of your article, I suggest putting it aside for a week. It can take at least that long to cancel out writer's bias. After a week, read the article aloud, putting yourself mentally in the shoes of an objective, outside "other."

1. Listen first for overall rhythm, then for rhythm appropriate to dramatic moments. Do you stumble over certain words? Choose others. Do active verbs move the story along and help to build tension where necessary? If most of your verbs are passive or state of being, you'll need to revise the wording of each sentence. Check your pacing: Have you varied the length of sentences and paragraphs to speed up the story when necessary, slow it down when not?

2. Is voice consistent throughout? If you've switched voices ("I" to "you," for example), is the change an acceptable fit for a particular story formula?

3. Do your pronouns match their antecedents? Recheck pronoun usage: poor grammar says a lot about you to an editor.

4. Have you used your strongest quotes? Can they stand alone? If not, they have to be supported with your own statements. That usually means the quotes are weak; perhaps they should be paraphrased. But do your own statements *duplicate* the words in direct quotes? If so, rethink the best way to say it. You can choose one or the other but not both. Have you quoted sources accurately?

5. Are your facts correct? Your sources the most authoritative on the issue?

6. Does your lead grow out of the story material? Does it hook the reader? Do subsequent grafs support the lead in terms of tone, focus and storyline? Does your lead transition smoothly and logically into the graf following it? If your lead doesn't work at this point, go back through your material: You'll find a better one buried there.

7. Do paragraphs transition logically from one thought to another? Are your transitions appropriate?

8. Is the ending tied to your storyline?

9. Recheck story organization against your outline. Have elements belonging in one place somehow found themselves in another? This isn't the time to rethink your storyline and blueprint: Stick to the game plan. Keep similar elements together, supporting the same main point. (The lead and ending are possible exceptions.)

10. Does everything in the story relate to the *storyline*? If elements relate to the *subject* but not to the actual storyline, edit them out.

11. Does the article have balance and provide eye ease? Remember that too many quotes in a visual area not only dilute your point but defeat reading ease. Also remember that long paragraphs of exposition are often too boring to read.

12. Do you have too much information in the story? Should some of it go in a sidebar?

13. Are slant and viewpoint appropriate to readership?

14. Is your punctuation correct? Your spelling and grammar? *Don't take the word of the grammar and spelling functions of your computer software.* Refer to the AP stylebook, to a good dictionary, and to a book such as *When Words Collide* for grammar and punctuation.

15. Does the article contain what the query letter promised?

16. Do your words create mental pictures?

17. Repeat your anecdotes to someone else *the way you wrote them.* Are they clear? Do your words have the desired effect?

18. Check your sentences: Are they all tightly worded? Make sure to fix run-on and awkwardly worded sentences.

19. Have you pruned your manuscript of adverbs and substituted precise, active verbs wherever possible?

20. You may be convinced but others may not: Is there logic to what you've written and not just assumptions? Do your subpoints, facts and supporting quotes support your main points?

21. Do specific examples support your general statements?

22. Does everything in the story follow a consistent order? Your lead and its supporting grafs will create an expectation; the body of the story must follow it. If you've talked about three discoveries, for example, each one leading to the next, the body of the story must stick to that order. If a how-to story speaks of "first," "second" and "third," make sure to follow that order in discussing each.

23. Does the chronology in your article match the actual sequence of events? Have you flashed back, then forward more than once? That's confusing. Are you too deep into "whodunit" dramatic technique, foreshadowing so obviously every turn in the story? A thorough check of verb tense should give you the answers.

24. Does your title have punch? Does it relate to the storyline?

25. After reading the manuscript to yourself, then revising and rewriting it, check your final word total. Does the manuscript fit the length specified by your target magazine?

A word from wise writers: Although revision and rewriting are difficult and often emotionally painful, neither will destroy your creative spark or the particular charisma of your article. Putting in such time and effort indicates professionalism and can pay off in a sale.

SYMBOLS

Knowing how to use basic copyediting and proofreading symbols will help you at some point in the manuscript stage or at some point in your career.

Universally recognized, they're a shorthand method for correcting mistakes on the manuscript printout or making changes on the "proof" copy prior to printing. Although the bulk of today's editing is done on the computer, "our process here still requires a know-how of copyediting and proofing," says Jimmy Stewart, *Charisma*'s managing editor. Stewart sometimes sends an edited version back to the writer to okay it. "That happens pretty often although not all the time. It depends on how heavily edited the piece is," he says, "and how picky the writer is about changes to the work." Although proofreading and copyediting symbols differ slightly from each other, and proof corrections are noted in the margin rather than in the body of the story, you'll be ahead of the game by knowing the basics shown here. You can also find the symbols printed in various stylebooks.

Pipa Blau, seven of Lynn, N.H., wearing a long blonde	insert letter, abbreviate, spell out, delete
pigtail, white ankle socks and a blue and white flowered	transpose letters, add hyphens
dress, is in process of becoming Princess	add word, delete letter
moonbeam. She has not yet memorized her lines and so	upper case, insert comma, delete
she reads from a script. She and her 6 classmates, aged	lower case, spell out, correct
six to nine sit in a Acting for Children class pondering	abbreviate figures, insert letter, delete and close up
their scripts in Northern stages Educational Center	upper case, insert apostrophe, insert period
Education Dir. Heidi Fagan, who has an MFA	new paragraph, spell out, correct, delete and close up
in directing from Northern Ill. University, has directed	spell out, retain word
some of the many northern Stages professional	delete and close up, upper case, insert apostrophe
productions. Right now, she however, is directing Pippa	transpose, delete comma
Blau and company in a playlette set in Korea. "You all	insert space, delete, retain word
remembered your scripts? I'm about to have a heart attack!	insert quotation marks
Heidi tells her cast cheerfully. (Excerpt from	no paragraph

"Regionally Yours: Professional Theater Blossoms in Vermont"

by Joyce Rogers Wolkomir, Winter 2001 issue of *Vermont Life*.

The excerpt has been deliberately mistyped, then corrected

with copyediting symbols.)

Additional symbols:

blond]	flush right	blond ⊏	boldface and center blond
[blond	flush left	blond ⊢⊣	dash

NIL DESPERANDUM

If you're satisfied with the manuscript, if it reads and sounds as though a professional wrote it, then it's ready to be mailed. (In some cases, e-mailed; check the editorial guidelines.) You may have a hard time letting go of your "baby," however. I do. For a month or more, I may have worked on the story seven or eight hours a day, perhaps more in the evening. The write-and-revise pattern seems to go on and on. I worry: Will I ever get it right? The story, in fact, has become an extension of my *self*. I dream about it. I get up in the middle of the night to revise something in it. I carry a notebook with me in case a more appropriate word or phrase than the one I've written suddenly occurs to me. To relinquish my story now is almost like . . . well, if it's not like birth, it's almost like losing a part of me. Most writers feel the same way. It helps to remember that a birth produces positive results. For you, that means acceptance and publication of your story. The anxiety of relinquishing it and a brief depression that might result right after you've submitted it, may, in the long run, produce what you hope for—a sale. *Nil desperandum.* (In Latin, "don't despair.")

PROFESSIONAL APPEARANCE

Give yourself the professional's edge by following these guidelines for submission.

Type the manuscript double-spaced in a legible font such as Times New Roman and use one-and-one-half inch margins on all sides. From an ink-jet, desk-jet or laser-jet printer, print out *two copies* of the manuscript on 20- to 24-pound, 8-½"-×-11" white printer paper that has a brightness of 90 or less. (It's hard to comfortably read anything brighter.) Make sure to keep the second copy of the manuscript for yourself.

Single-spaced, in the upper right corner of page one, indicate the rights you are offering on one line and the total word count on the second. Some magazines pay per word, so a precise word count is necessary. Most computers will count words and characters for you. However, an editor has yet another concern: Will the size of the manuscript fit the well for the story? Make sure your computer has not counted your title and possible subtitle in the total word count. Those elements will be run several sizes larger and in another font. For fairly short articles you could manually count the number of words on a typical page and multiply that by the total number of pages to arrive at the final word count. (There are approximately 250 words on a double-spaced page of type.)

In the upper left corner of page one, also single-spaced, type your name on the first line, followed by a two- or three-line address, a line for your telephone number and one for your e-mail address. (The latter two may be combined on the same line.) Although you may not need your snail-mail address for an e-mailed manuscript, you will eventually, and I suggest you include it.

Below that, about one-third to one-half of the way down the same page, type your title in uppercase letters and center it. Double-space after that and type the word *by* in lowercase letters, centered. Double-space once more and type your name in caps and lowercase letters, centered. Double-space twice and you're ready to begin typing your manuscript. Make sure to indent all paragraphs.

"Slug" subsequent pages with your surname, followed by a dash and the page number; for example, *Hamilton—page 10*. Run the slug line at page left or page right, but be consistent. End the manuscript the way profession-als do with a *-30* or ### run close to the bottom margin but at the least, several double spaces below the final sentence.

SUBMITTING THE MANUSCRIPT

Never staple the pages of your manuscript; paper-clip them. Make sure to submit the manuscript with a cover letter referring to your earlier correspon-dence with the editor. Remember that despite a "yes, send it" response, your manuscript is being submitted on spec, and an editor has no obligation to re-turn it to you: Always put your manuscript on disk and keep a hard copy for yourself. If a magazine requests both disk and hard copy, keep a copy of the disk for your files.

A snail-mailed manuscript goes in a manila envelope large enough to hold both manuscript and a second, self-addressed envelope should the arti-cle need to be returned. As a courtesy, paper-clip first-class postage to the second envelope. Short articles four-to-five pages long can be mailed in a legal-size envelope; it's not necessary to query the editor first unless the mag-azine requires it. If you're including slides (transparencies), photographic prints or other illustrations with your submission, make sure to back them with cardboard for support in transit.

Transparencies should be stamped with your name, unpublished copyright notice (for example, © *Nancy M. Hamilton 2005*), e-mail and snail-mail address. Identify the subject matter briefly on one side of the cardboard or plastic frame. Transparencies should then be inserted into divided plas-tic sleeves for safekeeping and safe mailing. Photographic prints should be rubber-stamped *on the back* with your name, copyright notice and contact in-formation; a photo caption or cutline also goes on the back, but on a typed adhesive label. (You can also use a black felt pen, but don't press hard.) If you submit several photos or transparencies, try numbering and keying them to captions and cutlines typed on a separate sheet of paper. What about digital photo submissions? It isn't a universal requirement yet, but some magazines encourage them. Make sure your shots are at least 300 dpi (dots per inch).

If the people in your prints or transparencies are recognizable, you need their signed permission on a model release. (A parent or legal guardian signs for a juvenile under 18.) Photo stores usually sell these releases; buy one and duplicate the rest. The model release gives the photographer permission to use the photograph for advertising and editorial purposes or for a specific purpose that you state in print; copies of these signed releases must be submitted with the prints or transparencies.

Here's what the monthly *Family Motor Coaching* says about its photo requirements: "State availability with submission. [We] prefer North American serial rights but will consider one-time rights on photos only. [We] offer no additional payment for b&w contact sheets, 35mm 2¼ × 2¼ color transparencies or high-resolution electronic images (300 dpi and at least 4 x 5 in size). Captions, model releases, photo credits required." *Family Motor Coaching,* which is 80 percent freelance written and almost all travel-related in content, is the official publication of the Family Motor Coach Association. By comparison, the travel-related *Frontier Magazine* ("submit clips with all queries") will negotiate a separate payment for photos. Heed this magazine's warning and apply it to all your photo submissions: *Submit duplicates of your transparencies only.* If an original is lost or damaged, you've lost the shot. Can photographic prints be submitted electronically? Study the listings in *Writer's Market:* You'll note that some publications will review JPEG and GIF files.

RIGHTS AND RATES

When you agree to sell your manuscript to a magazine, you're also assigning the publisher certain rights you own in it. The more rights you sign away, the less flexibility you have to use that material in the future. Payment, unfortunately, isn't reflected in the rights you sell. Some magazines buy all rights; most buy one-time rights or firsts rights; the magazine that bought all rights may actually pay *less* for your manuscript. An editor whose magazine offers 10 cents a word will rarely negotiate that fee with a newcomer. Even seasoned writers usually have a hard time negotiating it upward. That's why writers may employ literary agents. *The Saturday Evening Post,* for example, offers a low base pay—$150 minimum for a story—but its *maximum* payment is negotiable. Check magazine specifications in *Writer's Market* to determine whether a magazine pays on a per-word basis or a blanket fee for an article of a certain length.

Once you're well known on the writing circuit and have numerous credits to your name, you may want to hire an agent and can expect to earn higher fees. Marilyn Johnson, author of the *My Generation* article on Isabella Rossellini discussed in Chapter 10, reports that she "earned as much from that one piece—about $2,500—as I did from three book-review columns in which I had to read nearly 30 books."

Although a kill fee may signal miscommunication between editor and writer, it also may be a writer's security blanket. *National Wildlife* magazine, for example, will pay 25 percent of the total fee for an *assigned* article found unsuitable. Since *National Wildlife* stories range from 750 to 2,500 words and carry payment of $800 to $3,000, the kill fee could be as much as $625. *Smithsonian* magazine's pay rate is higher for a commissioned story, but its kill fee of one-third means a 2,000-word manuscript carrying payment of $1,500 would provide a kill fee of slightly less than $500.

Your basic protection, however, is unpublished copyright. Unless you've signed it away, it extends to anything you write, protecting it for your lifetime plus 70 years. The same is true of photographic negatives, prints and transparencies. Until it's published, your creative work is protected automatically. However, copyright protection won't extend to the facts in your story, nor will it protect your ideas or even your title. (It's rarely necessary to register a story with the U.S. Copyright Office for greater legal protection. For more information, contact the copyright office at http://lcweb.loc.gov/copyright. Also helpful is the unofficial Copyright web site at http://www.benedict.com.) Since most magazines copyright each issue *as a collective unit*, the contents are protected, including your article. In general, the purpose of *not copyrighting* a magazine is to encourage free use of its material. *Beware of losing your rights: Articles published in a magazine not protected by copyright fall into the public domain; anyone can use them.* (This is still a grey area, and opinions may differ.) Experienced writers often generate additional income by executing works-for-hire. These written materials are governed by contractual agreements that give copyright ownership *to employers.*

If you're an experienced writer with extensive plans for the story, or if the story is excerpted from a published book or book about be published, magazine editors will cooperate in running your separate copyright notice on the piece, provided it was registered first with the U.S. Copyright Office by you or your book publisher. Most magazines buy only one-time rights to photographs.

Here are the basic rights you could be selling to your manuscript.

- *First serial rights* (or first North American serial rights, those with a geographic limitation)—This right to use your material first allows you to keep the other rights.
- *One-time rights*—This covers simultaneous submissions. A magazine buys nonexclusive rights to publish your story once; this allows you to sell it to another magazine *at the same time.*
- *Reprint rights*—Also known as second serial rights. A magazine buys the right to use your story after it has been published elsewhere.
- *All rights*—You lose all rights in your manuscript because the publisher now owns it. Avoid doing business on this basis.

- *Electronic rights*—Is the magazine buying the rights to run your story in its print *and* its online version? Will it be run *only* online? Does the publisher plan to include the story in a CD anthology? Make sure the publisher specifies *how* your material will be used: *Never sell blanket electronic rights.* To be safe, carefully check editorial specifications *before* you submit a story. Theoretically, a publisher planning to use your material in both its print and its online version should pay you more; that isn't always the case, unfortunately. You may find that magazines purchasing all rights will often play fast and loose with your manuscript when it comes to electronic use. Pay attention to the wording of the contract; read the fine print. And never do business by a handshake and a gentleman's agreement: Be a businessperson.

In the matter of photographs, most magazines buy only one-time rights. However, it's well worth your while to check out the policy of each magazine you do business with.

BUT IS IT ETHICAL?

Allow for contingencies and develop alternate game plans in marketing your material to publishers. For example: You're hired to write a tribute to a living legend in the music industry; he suddenly dies, and your story can't be used as written. And another example: Amtrak had an agreement with a custom publisher some years ago to publish *Sunbound* magazine for Amtrak's passengers. This arrangement is similar to that used by airline inflights. The *Sunbound* publishers purchased first North American serial rights to the survey article I co-wrote on jai alai and bought one-time rights to the transparencies I shot as illustration. The purchase stipulated "payment on publication" rather than "payment on acceptance"—not necessarily a red flag, but an arrangement that requires some caution.

A few months had gone by when the editor of my hometown newspaper ran a short news item about a story he had read in *Sunbound* while riding the train from Washington, D.C., to Sanford, Fla. He enjoyed the story, he wrote, and found it all the more interesting because *I* was the co-author. I wish he had kept that magazine when he debarked the train. Why? I never saw it. I never saw my story in print. Neither my co-writer on the jai alai story nor I ever received a tearsheet of it—a courtesy most magazines extend to their writers. In fact, neither of us received payment for the story at all—nor did I for the transparencies that accompanied it. Amtrak officials were steamed. The unthinkable had happened, they wrote. Deeply in debt, the publishing company had simply closed down operations overnight. To avoid court action, the principals had fled the country. Amtrak and its other creditors were left holding the bag—and so were the magazine's freelancers who never saw a dime. I probably was one of the more fortunate contributors: At my request, the publishers had returned my transparencies early. I still have them. But to this day and despite repeated queries, I've never been able to locate that issue of *Sunbound* in which my co-authored story on jai alai appeared.

Writer-editor agreements are almost always contractual. Never take them lightly. Use caution, particularly in the matter of electronic rights: This is still a volatile issue. Although your electronic rights are automatically protected under basic copyright law, publishers will continue to pressure writers to sign away electronic rights without extra compensation, warns the National Writer's Union (http://:www.nwu.org) in its newsletter *HearSay*. "Publishers don't automatically have the right to put your work on *their own* web site," says the Writer's Union, citing a U.S. Supreme Court decision in 2001. The court also ruled that newspapers and magazines can't automatically put a freelancer's printed article into an *electronic database* such as Lexis-Nexis or on a CD-ROM anthology without first negotiating special permission from the freelance writer. However, advises the Writer's Union, "if you can't retain the electronic rights and you can't get the editor to provide extra compensation explicitly tied to database use, argue for a higher print fee since the article is now worth more to the publisher."

The American Society of Journalists and Authors (ASJA) Inc. (www.asja.org) recommends you red-flag the traps you can find in a contract. They're listed in the Additional Resources section in the back of this book together with detailed copyright information from ASJA. You can access the organization's Code of Ethics and Fair practices by logging on to its web site. Note that neither the ASJA code nor its statement of fair practices is legally binding.

YOUR RESPONSIBILITY: ARE *YOU* ETHICAL?

Along with the rest of the journalism community, magazine writers enjoy freedom of expression. But that Constitutionally guaranteed freedom carries with it certain ethical responsibilities. Some would call those responsibilities *standards of good behavior*. As a magazine editor, I find that definition too loose. So, eventually, did that paragon of worldwide journalism, the *New York Times*, when it discovered in 2003 that reporter Jayson Blair had plagiarized, fabricated and otherwise written inaccurately in at least 36 of his 73 articles for the *Times*. In the fallout and the paper's loss of credibility, Blair resigned, the executive editor resigned and so did the managing editor. Another *Times* reporter was suspended within that time frame—Pulitzer-Prize winner Rick Bragg, whose bylined story reportedly was written largely by a freelancer. (Bragg is a collaborator on the Jessica Lynch story published by Alfred A. Knopf. Lynch, a former Army private, was a prisoner of war in Iraq before being rescued by American troops.)

Despite our use of the word *story* when we mean magazine article and the phrase "*creative* nonfiction" for the way we may write it, our concern at base is that journalistic writing remain truthful, factual, accurate and unembellished with fiction. People aren't fabricated (blind or composite use must be so noted), and facts aren't invented. Situations may be fiction*alized*, but they're never fiction*al*. Quotes are used exactly as said (cleaning up bad grammar may be an exception), and assumptions are never made that it's "okay to use this information as a quote because the source would have said it if I'd asked." *Never.* The rules are clear: No faking, no misleading, no lying, no cheating, no fabricating, no plagiarizing—a Jayson Blair arrogance doesn't suit this profession.

To the lexicon of ethical behavior should be added nine more:

1. Don't take favors from sources—expenses, lunch, free travel—lest they influence what you're writing. (Travel writers often do, and their markets usually allow it.)

2. Don't promise what you know you can't deliver—free advertising, a particular page placement in the magazine, the opportunity for a source *to edit* what you've written. If you're feeling shaky about a technical or complex topic, offer to either *check* your written material with the source or have the source *read it—in your presence*—for clarity and accuracy and then initial it.

3. Don't misrepresent yourself. Saying you're a writer for *GQ, Maxim* or the *Ladies Home Journal* when you're simply writing an article you *hope to pitch* to one of these magazines constitutes a breach of ethics; results can come back to bite you.

4. Don't make up a source, and make sure you identify a source in print that's a composite. For example, Janet Cooke, a reporter for *The Washington Post,* won a Pulitzer Prize for her story on drug addiction among young people. The story began with a case history of an eight-year-old addict. The child was fabricated and not identified as a composite. The result? Cooke lost her job at the paper and had to return her Pulitzer.

5. If asked, be able to support the accuracy of what you've written by careful keeping of your notes and tapes.

6. Some writers do, I suggest you don't, include in your story something liable to cause a source ridicule or embarrassment. I was in England, reporting on the last High Court of the Assizes to be held in British colonial dress and the trappings of the time. Sitting high up in the press box with other reporter-photographers, I looked down on the small dock in the center of the hall where three unemployed youths were on trial for breaking into an elderly woman's home, binding and gagging her and stealing her loose change and food. Arguments were heard, the three were adjudged guilty, and the bewigged judges remanded them to reform school.

The crowd broke, and we descended the concrete steps of the courthouse. I was across the street by the time I turned back for a look and noticed the slight English countrywoman in poor and tattered dress standing alone on a courthouse step. I picked up my camera and focused on her. In one hand she clutched an old cardboard suitcase; in the other, a handkerchief that wiped away her tears. A matron came outside with a chair and seated the woman in it. What a good shot, I thought—the pathos of a woman crying for her son. Although I must have been 15 yards away, I could hear the mother clearly: "But I brought his little suitcase," she sobbed, "so he could change his clothes before he came home." The matron patted her shoulder. A sympathetic gesture—one woman to another, one mother to another. I rechecked my focus, put my finger on the shutter—and stopped. I couldn't do it. I simply couldn't expose that poor woman's private sorrow to the eyes of a nation. I found other ways to illustrate the situation. You may feel similarly. In all such situations, ask yourself first: *Is it necessary?*

6. Don't lift quotes out of context. Don't move them arbitrarily from one place in the manuscript to another. Resist the temptation even if you're sure that what a source said about one situation could apply equally well to another. To quote out of context calls your credibility into question and dries up your source for the future.

7. Don't secretly tape-record an interview. It's not illegal to tape without consent, but why risk your credibility? Ask permission first.

8. Don't ignore opinions that may run contrary to the main points of your story: Those opinions deserve some space to be heard, if only to round out the issue.

9. Inform the editor of any conflict of interest before accepting an assignment.

HELPFUL EXERCISES

1. Did the author of this book breech ethics by positioning the Beulah Davis interview as though it had taken place in her bedroom overlooking the Durban coastline? How do you regard the author's use of fiction techniques to recreate the atmosphere and environment in which she functioned as a Durban householder and head of the Natal Anti-Shark Measures Board?

2. Go to http://www.journalism.indiana.edu/ethics and note the many articles reprinted there by permission of *FineLine,* a publication of Billy Goat Strut Publishing. Choose an article that bears on one of the situations discussed in this book. Explain the ramifications of the situation in terms of the article you selected.

ADDITIONAL RESOURCES

COMPANION READING: A PERSONAL BIBLIOGRAPHY

Magazines

American Heritage	*Inc.*
The Atlantic Monthly	*Mother Jones*
Birds & Blooms	*National Geographic*
Discover	*The New Yorker*
DoubleTake	*Smithsonian*
Esquire	*Vanity Fair*
Florida International	*Vermont Life*
Fortune	*Via (AAA)*
Fortune Small Business	*Vogue*
GQ	*The Writer*
Harper's Magazine	*Writer's Digest*

Books

The Associated Press Stylebook and Libel Manual (Christopher W. French, Ed., Harper Collins, 2002)

At Play in the Fields of the Lord (Peter Matthiessen, Random House, 1965)

Best American Essays 2002 (Stephen Jay Gould, Ed., and Robert Atwood, Series Ed., Houghton Mifflin)

The Best and the Brightest (David Halberstam, Random House, 1972; *The Powers That Be*, 2000, University of Illinois Press; and others)

Choose the Right Word: A Contemporary Guide To Selecting the Precise Word for Every Situation (S. I. Hayakawa and Eugene H. Ehrlich, Harper Perennial, 1994)

Choose the Right Word: A Modern Guide to Synonyms (S. I. Hayakawa, Perennial Library, 1987)

The Complete Guide to Magazine Article Writing (John M. Wilson, Writer's Digest Books, 1993)

Elements of Article Writing Series (Writer's Digest Books, individual authors and titles)

The Elements of Style (William Strunk and E. B. White, fourth edition, Allyn & Bacon, 1999)

225

The Fourth Genre: Contemporary Writers of/on Creative Non-Fiction (Robert L. Root, Jr., and Michael Steinberg, Allyn & Bacon, 1999)

The Good Earth (Pearl S. Buck, Washington Square, 1994, and others such as *Peony,* John Day, 1948. Buck also wrote *The Townsman* under the pen name John Sedges, John Day, 1945.)

Guide To Writing Magazine Nonfiction (Michael J. Bugeja, Allyn & Bacon, 1998)

Hard Times: An Oral History of the Depression (Studs Terkel, 1970, and others, such as *Working,* 1974, and *The Good War,* 1984, all for Pantheon. Terkel's current book is *Will the Circle Be Unbroken?: Reflections on Death, Rebirth, and Hunger for a Faith,* W. W. Norton, 2001)

How To Become a Full-Time Freelance Writer (Michael A. Banks, The Writer Books, 2002)

In Cold Blood (Truman Capote, Random House, 1965)

The Inside of the Cup (Winston Churchill, 1927, and others such as *Coniston,* 1935, both Macmillan)

The Internet Research Handbook (Niall O'Dochartaigh, Sage, 2002)

The Kitchen God's Wife (Amy Tan, 1991; also *The Joy Luck Club,* 1989; *The Hundred Secret Senses,* 1995; *The Bonesetter's Daughter,* 2001; *The Opposite of Fate: A Book of Musings,* 2003; all G. P. Putnam's Sons)

Le Petit Prince (*The Little Prince,* Antoine de St. Exupery, Harcourt, 2000)

Magazine Writing that Sells (Don McKinney, Writer's Digest Books, 1994)

The New Journalism (Tom Wolfe, Harper & Row, 1973)

No Uncertain Terms (William Safire, Simon & Schuster, 2003)

Other Voices: The New Journalism in America (Everette E. Dennis and William L. Rivers, Harper & Row, 1974)

Photographer's Market (Melissa Milar and William Brohaugh, Writer's Digest Books, for current year)

The Reporter as Artist: A Look at the New Journalism Controversy (Ronald Weber, Ed., Hastings House, 1974)

Roget's 21st Century Thesaurus (Thomas Nelson, 1992)

Slouching Towards Bethlehem (Joan Didion, 1996, 1998, Farrar, Straus and Giroux)

To Destroy You Is No Loss: The Odyssey of a Cambodian Family (Joan D. Criddle, 1998; *Bamboos & Butterflies: From Refugee to Citizen,* 1992; both East/West Bridge, Dixon, Calif.)

Walking on Water: Reflections on Faith and Art (and others, Madelyn L'Engle, Bantam Books, 1980, and North Point Press, 1995)

When Words Collide: A Media Writer's Guide to Grammar and Style (Lauren Kessler and Duncan McDonald, Wadsworth, 2003)

A Writer's Guide to Nonfiction (Elizabeth Lyon, Perigee, 2003)

The Writer's Handbook (Eudia G. Olsen, The Writer, for the current year)

Writer's Market (Writer's Digest Books, for the current year; see also *Writer's Market Online* at www.writersmarket.com)

Writing for Story (Jon Franklin, Plume, 1994)

Writing the Modern Magazine Article (Max Gunther, out of print)

Writers

James Agee	Garrison Keillor
Louisa May Alcott	Maxine Hong Kingston
Robert Ardrey	Madelyn L'Engle
Jimmy Breslin	Peter Matthiessen
Pearl S. Buck	James Michener
Joan Didion	John Steinbeck
Annie Dillard	Amy Tan
John Gregory Dunne	Studs Terkel
Nora Ephron	Paul Theroux
Louise Erdrich	Lewis Thomas
Joe Eszterhas	Pierre Tristam
David Halberstam	Mark Van Dorn
Pete Hamill	Gore Vidal
Molly Ivans	

RED FLAGS FOR UNWARY WRITERS: THE RIGHTS GAME

The American Society of Journalists and Authors (ASJA) Inc. rightly warns that "publisher's contracts for periodical articles may contain traps for the unwary." The following are some pitfalls the society recommends you heed.

- **". . . First North American serial rights, which includes also . . ."** No. FNA is FNA. It does not include other rights. Don't read just the contract's title. Read the whole thing.
- **". . . the right to publish, distribute and license others to publish and distribute the article *in all its forms [or in any media]* . . ."** These words do not spell it out, but they mean you transfer electronic rights along with print rights.
- **". . . only as part of the issue in which it appears . . ."** Sometimes added to electronic-rights clauses in an attempt to make the deal sound like simple archiving of an entire publication, for which the author should claim no further income. But whether your article stands with or without other material from the issue in which it first appears, the publisher will earn perpetual royalties from its continued use, generally payable according to how many times computer users "buy" your particular article. So should you.
- **". . . for educational or research purposes only . . ."** Same problem: Publishers can make a lot of money peddling your article for educational or research purposes. It's your property; so should you.

- **"... the nonexclusive right ..."** This may *sound* OK, but it isn't. The editor of an Australian magazine who loves your piece is going to call the U.S. publisher, who will make the deal; you'll never know. And if you approach the Australian editor yourself, he may well ask for a month's exclusivity in Australia; you won't be able to provide it. Because your publisher in the U.S. may be selling it to the Australian's competitor, you lose the sale. In market terms, "nonexclusive" wipes you out. Exclusive or nonexclusive, if the publisher wants the right, you ought to have separate compensation for that license.
- **"... you will be paid at our then standard rate ..."** Would you give someone an option to buy your car at an indefinite future date and let the buyer set the price at that time?
- **"... use the article and your name, biography and likeness for promotion and advertising of the publication ..."** Brief excerpts of the article, maybe. The whole article? No. Advertising copywriters are paid for their work. If your work is put to this additional use, you should be paid too. No serious professional photographer would say, "Sure, you can use my photo in the magazine and also put it in your ads, in your direct-mail pieces and on promotional electronic services."

Making contracts more equitable can mean adding as well as deleting. For example, two smart additions to the rights clause:

- Make it "First North American PRINT serial rights. . . ."
- "All rights not expressly transferred herein are reserved by the author."

- **"... if the publisher, in its sole discretion, rejects the article ..."** Could be that your editor changes her mind; a new editor (or the advertising department) changes the direction of the magazine; the competition beats you to the punch; or your interview subject dies. In any of those cases, a piece may be killed through no fault of yours, and you see only a kill fee of perhaps 25 cents on the dollar. Too much of the risk is on your part. You should offer to revise a piece if the editor explains what's wrong and how to fix it. But the kill fee should not kick in unless your article falls short of what was agreed upon in your proposal and the editor's assignment letter. If your work is professionally competent and suitable for publication, you should be paid the full fee promised.
- **"... publisher may revise, edit, augment, condense or otherwise alter the work ..."** Careful with "augment"; you don't want to be responsible for what someone else writes. And always make sure editing is done with your approval or, at least, consultation. Publisher should agree to provide galleys sufficiently in advance of publication to permit correction of any errors. If editing changes result in an unsolvable dispute, you should have the right to withhold your byline. It's your name.

- **"... you warrant that the work is original, never before published; that you are the sole owner of the work; that the work is not libelous, obscene or otherwise in contravention of law and does not violate the proprietary right, privacy or any other right of any third party ..."** No problem with the first two sections (through "sole owner of the work"); you should be able to stand behind your work's originality and your ownership of it. But can you honestly and fully warrant the rest—that your article won't violate any laws anywhere? It should be a publisher's responsibility, not yours, to have a lawyer check for libel. Obscenity laws are based on community standards; are you acquainted with local standards in every community in the nation? The last section can only be warranted "to the best of your knowledge."
- **"... you will indemnify and hold harmless the publisher against any and all claims or actions based on a breach or alleged breach of the above warranties ..."** No author ought to assume a giant financial risk that properly belongs to the publisher. Certainly, you should not agree to cover the publisher for a mere *claim* or an action based on an *alleged* breach. If you are to be held liable at all, it should be only for a proven breach, "by judgment alone sustained," so that you don't wind up paying the bill for your publisher's settlement of a baseless nuisance suit. Neither should you agree to pay half the defense costs if you are proven innocent. If you do nothing provably wrong, the risks of publishing should belong to the publisher. You're a writer. If you wanted to take on the risks of publishing, you'd be a publisher.
- **"... any action alleging a breach of this agreement must be brought in the state or federal courts of [publisher's home turf] ..."** If you get stiffed for your fee, kill fee or expenses and want to take the publisher to small claims court, you'll have to travel to the publisher's state. Will the court award you travel expenses and payment for the extra time required? Good luck.

[ASJA's Contracts Committee serves as a clearing house of information on terms being offered and contract changes being accepted by many periodicals. It offers this information to members and nonmembers alike, in the belief that better-informed negotiators help us all.]

COPYRIGHT REGISTRATION: WHERE AND HOW TO REGISTER YOUR ARTICLES

Prepared by the ASJA Contracts Committee:

First Things First: The One-Paragraph Copyright Primer

As a freelance writer, unless you've signed a work-made-for-hire agreement or otherwise transferred copyright, what you write belongs to you. You need not put a little "c" in a circle on it. You need not register it with the Copyright Office. The work need not even be published for your copyright to take effect. The copyright is yours immediately. If your work appears in a periodical, the publisher owns the copyright in the entire issue *as a collective work,* but not in your individual work. The publisher may print a little © with its company name and file the issue with the Copyright Office, but its protection covers the issue *as an issue,* not the articles within. The copyright in your writing is *yours* unless and until, induced by cash or cowed by threats, you sign it away.

Why Register?

Under the law, if your copyright is infringed, you can't sue unless the work has been registered with the U.S. Copyright Office. You can, of course, wait until there's a problem before you bother filing a registration application. But there's a good reason to file as a matter of routine.

In copyright infringement cases, courts may assess two distinct kinds of damages.

Statutory damages—up to $100,000 if the infringement is judged to be willful—are available only if the work was registered no later than three months after first publication or, where the work was registered later than that, if the infringement begins after registration. ("Publication" means public availability, which may be earlier than the cover date.) In cases where statutory damages apply, the court may also award attorneys' fees.

Actual damages are monetary losses suffered by the infringed party— losses that are likely to be small as well as time-consuming and difficult to prove. What's more, courts are not free to award attorneys' fees in conjunction with actual damages.

So for infringement of articles not registered in time, it is rarely cost-effective to hire a lawyer and sue in federal court. (A suit in small claims court, based on contract rather than copyright, may make sense in such cases.) If you've registered your copyright in time, you're in a better position to inflict pain in a real lawsuit; thus, you have far greater clout.

In short: As a defensive move against infringement—such as unauthorized electronic use of an article—it can be wise to register each magazine and newspaper article you write.

Isn't Registration an Expensive Pain?

Actually, it's neither as costly nor as onerous as you may think. Registration costs $30, but you can gang articles on a single application to save on fees and drudgery. If you're a prolific article writer, the cost per story is quite low. To meet the within-three-months requirement, you need to file four times a year, each time listing your previous three months' published work; thus, four filings and $120 give you maximum protection on a year's output.

How To Do It

To group register, you need two official U.S. Copyright Office forms:

Form TX for nondramatic literary works (the streamlined **Short Form TX** may usually be used for a single work);

Form GR/CP for grouping published works on a single application.

You can obtain the forms directly from the Copyright Office by phoning (202) 707-9100 (available 24 hours a day). Leave a message; wait two to three weeks for the forms to arrive. If you have a computer with Adobe Acrobat Reader, you can download forms from the Copyright Office's Website; see address below. Photocopy them at will, but use a good grade of 8"-x-11" white paper, use both sides of the sheet, and match the layout of the originals. Type or print in black ink.

On Form TX, question 1, if you are registering two or more articles at the same time, enter "See GR/CP, attached." In question 2, under "Nature of Authorship," you should typically enter "Entire Text" or "Co-Author of Entire Text," whichever applies. If you're group-registering: in 3a, use the latest applicable date; in 3b, enter "See GR/CP, attached." In question 4, "Copyright Claimant" is ordinarily the same as the author: you. In question 5, under "Previous Registration," check "No" (remember that registration of the entire issue by the publisher does *not* constitute specific registration of your work). For most magazine or newspaper articles, ignore question 6.

On Form GR/CP, list articles chronologically, from earliest to latest, numbering the lines consecutively; no more than 12 months may separate the first from the last.

The Copyright Office's separate instruction sheets say that you must include the entire magazine or newspaper section in which each submitted article appeared—but that needn't actually be done. The Office advises that you may instead submit simple tearsheets or even photocopies. Just be sure to include with your application a letter asking that the Office "please accept the enclosed tearsheets [or photocopies] as part of ongoing special relief from the deposit requirement"; the request is routinely granted.

Enclose a check for $30, payable to Register of Copyrights. Mail your application to Register of Copyrights, Library of Congress, Washington, DC 20559-6000. Certified mail, return receipt requested, isn't a bad idea.

Four Frequently Asked Questions

How long will it take? Perhaps as long as 16 weeks. If you haven't heard by then, call the number below.

When does registration take effect? As soon as the application and supporting materials are received by the Copyright Office.

What do you do if an article appears in more than one periodical? Submit any published version, the earlier the better; if different published versions reflect only minor changes, you need *not* register each version.

What about unpublished works? You may also submit the manuscript version(s), but you may *not* use form GR/CP, *nor* may you mix published and unpublished works. Unpublished works may be grouped using form TX alone; simply use a descriptive title for the group, such as "unpublished writings, Jan-Mar 1996."

For More Information

Contact the U.S. Copyright office:

Phone: (202) 707-3000, 8:30–5 Eastern time, Monday–Friday

World Wide Web: http://lcweb.loc.gov/copyright

INDEX

CREDITS